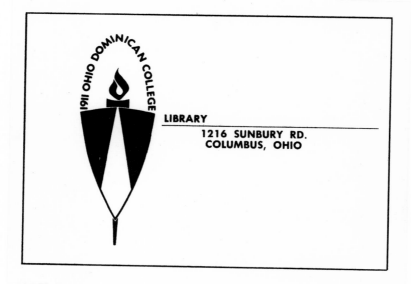

KARL SHAPIRO

THE POETRY WRECK

RANDOM HOUSE   *NEW YORK*

THE POETRY WRECK

Selected Essays: 1950-1970

KARL SHAPIRO

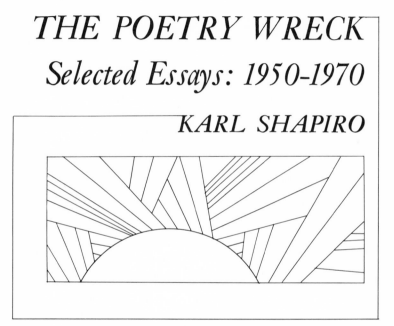

LIBRARY OF CONGRESS CATALOGING IN PUBLICATION DATA

*Shapiro, Karl Jay, 1913–
The poetry wreck.*

1.   *American poetry—20th century—Addresses,
essays, lectures.   2.   English poetry—20th century—Addresses, essays, lectures.   I.   Title.*
PS323.5.S5   1975   821'.9'109   74-22205
ISBN 0-394-49373-7

Manufactured in the United States of America

987654321

FIRST EDITION

Grateful acknowledgment is made to the following for permission to
reprint previously published material:

Beacon Press and Jonathan Cape Ltd.: For an excerpt from *I Wanted
to Write a Poem* by William Carlos Williams. Copyright © 1958 by
William Carlos Williams.

Doubleday and Company, Inc.: For an excerpt from the biographical
notes, page 408 of *The Poetry of the Negro 1746–1970*, edited by Langston
Hughes and Arna Bontemps. Copyright © 1970 by Arna Bontemps and
George Houston Bass, Executors of the Estate of Langston Hughes, and
Arna Bontemps. Copyright 1949 by Langston Hughes and Arna Bontemps.

95720

ACKNOWLEDGMENTS

In their original form the following essays appeared in *In Defense of Ignorance* (Random House, Inc.): T. S. Eliot; Ezra Pound; W. B. Yeats; W. H. Auden; W. C. Williams; Dylan Thomas; Walt Whitman; Henry Miller; Poets and Psychologists. The following appeared in *To Abolish Children* (Quadrangle/The New York Times Book Company): The Decolonization of American Literature; Is Poetry an American Art?; The Death of Randall Jarrell. The Career of the Poem appeared in *A Primer for Poets* (University of Nebraska Press). The Poetry Wreck was first published in the *Library Journal*, Febuary, 1970. I wish to thank my wife and Mr. Layton Damiano for their help in preparing the manuscript.

To Teri

Contents

xiii

FOREWORD

As OUR CENTURY approaches its long-wished-for *fin de siècle*, the poets come home to roost. The hypercritical superconscious twentieth century awaits its own last judgment. It is a time of breathless anticipation, final solutions, Infernos, Purgatories, Paradises and Guinness Record Books. It is, one might add, the busiest time of literary criticism in history, for the poetry is almost all criticism. One poet called us the age of criticism, and did not live long enough to see us turn into the age of self-regard. Our trajectory has been millennial, a hysterical recapitulation of the centuries, ending in dissolution and the hungry death-wish. It is not an inviting panorama.

If poetry, as many think, is a cultural index, then our century has much to answer for. The political simple-mindedness and viciousness of the great trio of Pound, Eliot and Yeats incriminate the Academy and the literary establishment which have made them the touchstones of our age. Such poets were bent upon creating a kind of Objective Revolution in which the artist could operate freely as the arbiter of value, the higher ruler of society. Never mind their fascism, with or without the large F; the poetics of Objectivity would cover up all that. The real triumph of these famous old poets was of course never in the world of politics but in the Academy. They defined an attitude toward literature and gave it an intellectual sanction. Sophisticated schools of criticism sprang up to defend their aesthetic—the aesthetic of anti-humanism. In the Western world, long gone democratic, it seemed an anachronism; yet Eliot and Yeats were awarded the Nobel Prize, and Pound the first Bolligen Prize, for whom apparently it was invented. One can without stretching the point accuse the Trio of politicalizing poetry for our time. The abreaction to that eventuated in a poetry that was nothing but political, a poetry of the subjective revolution, of ego, of self-pity and of self-regard.

In its final and most deliquescent stages this poetry has turned on itself and developed an aesthetic of destruction. For the first time we see poetry as big business, poetry as show biz, poetry to subvert the Academy and society itself. The Academy, always attentive to romantic innovation, indulges this brand of writing and hires teachers to profess it. The poetry of semi-literates and rock singers is equated with Shakespeare and Homer; a jail record is accorded the social status of a Ph.D. Obscenity is considered as metaphor, environmental deprivation as a sign of holiness. The subjective revolution, or maybe it is just an adversary aesthetic, occupies poetry and the Academy, aided and abetted by "adversary" law, sociology, political science and social psychology. Not paradoxically, this subjectivism, this solipsistic collapse of intellect, draws heavily on the Trio because of their stylistic ventures into violence. Violence is the last resort of the exhausted sensibility.

These essays do not follow a chronology but describe roughly the military evolutions of modern poetry, the bastions of the Trio, assaults upon the towers and their occupation, the comings and going of the ambassador Auden, Dylan Thomas (the troubadour in the kitchen), the burning of Whitman at the stake, the Tom O'Bedlam antics of Henry Miller, the heroics of Williams, down through the witchcraft of the psychologists and the rise of the rabble poets. There are no conclusions, only praises and laments.

A professor once introduced me before a lecture as the man who had turned the tide against T. S. Eliot. One would like to accept the compliment, but that is not the point. "The Age" invented its Eliots and Pounds and its various Dylans, its Ginsbergs and its rabble bards. It needed something for its empty shelf. It got what is called Modern Poetry, bits and pieces of broken images and crumbling towers occupied by anachronistic eccentrics and a numberless mob of imposters and mountebanks. Our anthologies are fat and blowzy, their pages strewn with suicides, treasons and psychic breakdowns. We judge poets not by their poetry but by what the social scientists vulgarly call their life style. Instead of poetry as the essence and culmination of the poet, we look at poetry as a by-product or excrescence of his behavior. From this angle of vision the poetry of adolescents, amateurs and psychotics seems equal to the poetry of masters. Anyone can *be* a poet, and in the contemporary pedagogy, everyone is.

Strip away from twentieth-century poetry all the sociology and all the politics, and see what is left. Precious little, perhaps, but yet something to conjure with and something our descendants will remember us by.

THE POETRY WRECK

The Death of Literary Judgment

THERE IS NO passable essay on Eliot at this time and little chance of there being one. As far as the literary situation goes, nothing could be more useful today, but the literary situation has seen to it that this essay does not exist. The very idea of a summary of Eliot's writings seems a kind of blasphemy, or an act of unpardonable rudeness. For the Literary Situation (whatever that ecclesiastical expression is supposed to mean) is largely Eliot's invention, and for that reason it is all but impossible to discuss. Eliot is untouchable; he is Modern Literature incarnate and an institution unto himself. One is permitted to disagree with him on a point here or a doctrine there, but no more. The enemy at Eliot's gate—practically everybody—searches his citadel for an opening and cannot find one. Eliot has long since anticipated every move; he and his men can prevent ingress or exit. Eliot resembles one of those mighty castles in Bavaria which are remarkably visible, famed for their unsightliness, and too expensive to tear down. Life goes on at the bottom; but *it* is always up there.

The question of Eliot as the chief obstacle to poetry today may not be a real question; it may be precisely the kind of imaginary question which Eliot himself brings up in his writing. Insofar as one tries to deal with it, he is simply playing Eliot's game, with all the odds against him. I do not myself consider the question real, but I know of no way to discuss the ultimate value of Eliot's work without first discussing the exploits of his straw men. Eliot's reputation and the antagonism to it may both be false. I propose in this essay to show both the reputation and the opposition to it in another light. That there is something of value in Eliot's poetry and Eliot's criticism is quite possible, even from my pessimistic point of view; though the valuable portion is minuscule and is much different from what has been supposed.

Eliot is both the hero and the victim of a historical predicament. And he himself is as much the author of that predicament as "history" itself. Eliot created a literary situation deliberately; he and his "situation" are fabrications, and very plausible fabrications at that. In other words, Eliot invented a Modern World which exists only in his version of it; this world is populated by Eliot's followers and is not a reality. The Eliot population consists of a handful of critics and professors and a few writers of Eliot's generation, though one would think, reading modern criticism and teaching from modern literary textbooks, that there really is a kingdom of Modern Poetry in which T. S.

Eliot is the absolute monarch and Archbishop of Canterbury in one.

You will be thinking that I am using metaphorical language and am attempting to work up a nice critical discussion, the subject of which is the overestimation of T. S. Eliot. I am saying something quite different, namely, that Eliot exists only on paper, only in the minds of a few critics. No poet with so great a name has ever had less influence on poetry. At no point in the career of Eliot has there been the slightest indication of a literary following. For example, W. H. Auden, for a decade or so, set patterns for poetry which were followed by thousands of new poets all over the world. Dylan Thomas did the same, as did Wallace Stevens. Neither Eliot nor Pound ever had any such effect on their readers or on young writers. Eliot's "influence" is confined purely to criticism. Insofar as Eliot has enjoyed a *poetic* influence, it lies outside literature entirely and is what can only be called a "spiritual" influence. This spiritual influence is itself calculated and synthetic; and insofar as it fails as a true influence, it removes Eliot's one and only claim to literary power. But here he does not entirely fail.

To deal with Eliot outside the literary situation which he has invented, means to deal with his poetry head-on. It means passing judgment upon it as good or bad poetry or, in some cases, as not poetry at all. But how is one to look at Eliot, if not from his own viewpoint? There is the rub. Eliot has arranged matters in such a way that criticism of his own poetry is impossible.

Eliot has written a small body of poetry which is sacrosanct; he has written his most favorable criticism about poetry which is like his (namely Pound's); and has surrounded both with a full-scale esthetic-social doctrine.

What I would like to do is to draw attention to Eliot's poetry—for that is the heart of the matter. For those who do not instinctively and spontaneously reject this poetry, I suppose some form of argument is required. Perhaps this essay will be of some assistance to them. I have in mind students primarily, those who are given Modern Poetry as gospel; I also have the young critic in mind, and also teachers and scholars. Poets do not need these remarks. I have met hundreds of poets in my life but not more than one or two who entertained the reverence for Eliot which they find in the textbooks. As most poets are not intellectuals and are the opposite, they are always stunned by the intellectual pretensions of Eliot and are at a loss to deal with them.

Eliot's preparation of the historical ground upon which he would found his position was the territory of all literature—excluding the Chinese, which was the preserve of Pound. He did not, evidently, intend a personal seizure of intellectual power; Eliot's famous humility testifies to his uneasiness in the face of overwhelming success. His irrational and subservient association with Pound also points to a genuine desire to refuse intellectual leadership, or at least to share it with others.

There was, it appears, a need for an Eliot about 1910. Eliot arrived on the literary scene at the point of vacuum; and he filled this vacuum which literary Nature abhors. Such at least is the accepted view. What is probably nearer the truth is that Eliot appeared at a time when the vitality of the audience was low; and when this is the case, criticism pours into the void. It is the critic in the guise of poet that we have to deal with, not a new kind of poet. For it is criticism which is the twentieth-century substitute for poetry.

The Historical Situation which Eliot exploits under the banner of Tradition was in the beginning the Educational Situation. It was local and Anglo-American, a defense of the Gentleman's Education. I put it vulgarly because that is the way it was. Too many writers have commented on Eliot's fears of being taken for a provincial for me to add my comment. These fears, however, are part of the New England heritage—the worst part—which leads the New Englander to become the Old Englander. Eliot's early life and work follow an almost hypnotic pattern; one might call him that pseudo-American, the type which finally won New England from the immigrant and gave it back to "history." The cultural dryness of New England was a by-product of this attitude which Eliot exemplifies even better than Henry James: that of relating America to New England, New England to England. Eliot was simply retracing the path back to Europe, exactly as Pound did, and as so many of our nineteenth-century writers tended to do, all but those specifically American.

The criticism of Eliot and Pound has blighted enormous literary areas, as far as we can tell.

The critics who helped establish Eliot were no less instrumental than Eliot himself in opening the frontiers of the cultural territory. Eliot with his palaver about the Tradition could gather in the entire Indo-European world, leaving North Asia and Africa to his senior. I do not want to go into the story of Eliot's critical rise to fame, but to illustrate what I mean I want to point to two literary critics who from every indication should have become his strongest foes; instead of becoming foes they were easily engaged to take his part in the high venture of Modern Poetic Culture. They are Edmund Wilson and F. O. Matthiessen.

Edmund Wilson may be fairly described as a critic in

every way the natural opposite of Eliot. In his early esti-
mate of Eliot in *Axel's Castle*, probably the first work to
install Eliot in a high position in the literary mind, he
pointed out almost every serious defect of the poet: his
"fear of vulgarity," his intention to "depersonalize" literature, his overintellectuality, his obsessive imitativeness, and
so forth. Wilson described Eliot as the Puritan-turned-artist
and expressed the fear that the extravagant praise of Eliot
on all sides would perhaps unbalance literary judgment,
as of course it did. What then attracted Wilson to Eliot? *It
was Eliot's influence on literary criticism.* Wilson walked
straight into the trap which Eliot had baited for all humanists and run-of-the-mill men of letters. Eliot had written so
high-mindedly about the literary past and so dolefully
about the present that Wilson was taken in. He even began
to praise Eliot's prose style—probably the worst prose style
in the history of the English essay, as well as the most
personal. What attracted the budding critic Wilson was, of
course, the keenness of intelligence, the range of ideas, the
feel of authority, and the sense of History. Also, a hopeful
critic like Wilson was on the search for a poet to praise,
and Wilson thought he had found him. Meanwhile Wilson
was popped into the Eliot oven to be turned into a nice
little, right little gingerbread man. Fortunately, he escaped,
but that chapter does not belong to our chronicle.

F. O. Matthiessen's relationship to Eliot is even more
extraordinary than that of the humanist critic who gazes in
fascination at the Puritan-turned-artist. Matthiessen, I
think, felt the same attraction for New England that Eliot
did, the one coming from the West Coast, the other from
the Midwest. To the critical and historical mind of Matthiessen, Eliot must have seemed an incarnation of Ameri-

can history. But Matthiessen had some adjusting to do in his own thinking in order to place Eliot in the same high position that Wilson had. He acknowledged his indebtedness to Wilson and also to I. A. Richards, the man who tried, and almost succeeded, in driving the poetic mind into the test tube. Matthiessen could not agree with Eliot's philosophy, his religion, or his politics, and yet he felt he must adulate Eliot! The result was his book on Eliot in which Matthiessen disdains the kind of criticism that deals with the poet's "ideas" and praises the kind of criticism that deals with the "forms." This book, *The Achievement of T. S. Eliot*, was published during the height of the Depression and at a time when Marxism was strong in the United States. Matthiessen was perhaps the most intensely engaged political mind among the English professors of his day, and a leftist; *yet he chose to cut himself off from the politics of Eliot's poetry and criticism to talk about the "forms."* This was a split that Eliot had invented for himself and which Eliot evidently kept from being fatal in his own life by various makeshifts of criticism. The false dualisms set up by Eliot between art and social action are symptomatic of the insanity of much modern criticism. In any case, it was Eliot's attractive formulation of these dualisms that neutralized so many critics and led Criticism itself into a squirrel cage where it still performs so brilliantly for its own amusement. Even Eliot's most favorable critics have never been able to resolve his major contradictions, which are central and irreducible conflicts rising from a false view of art as a function of history and culture, and a twisted attitude toward human nature.

Eliot's criticism is not "one thing" and his poetry another. They are one and the same. Herein lies the only unity of his work and of his "sensibility." This unity has been achieved coldly and ruthlessly, on paper. It has only as much relation to life as books can have: experience in Eliot is always and necessarily literary experience. All other experience is vulgar, with the possible exception of the religious experience, which is Eliot's escape hatch. His poems are therefore illustrations of the various stages of his "position," just as Pound's poems are illustrations of Pound's politick. Pound is not interested in poetry as poetry but in demonstrating what poetry is for. Eliot is above pedagogy, being closer to philosophy than to history. But the unifying element in Eliot is theology: and it is not inaccurate to describe Eliot as a theologian gone astray. The difference between Eliot's respectability and Pound's notoriety lies here as well. The frequent violence of Eliot's feelings is overlooked because of the "religious" context. Both his verse and his prose are held together by the main strength of certain theological abstractions. Eliot shows a positive hatred for originality and in fact condemns it in every manifestation; originality is irresponsible freedom to him. It is for this reason that he consigns Blake to limbo while hanging on to Pascal for dear life. Blake, says Eliot, is homemade religion. Eliot stays within the shadow of his theological law, which shelters his politics, his religion, and his esthetics.

How then is one to deal with his poetry without bringing in such terms as "mythic form," the "objective correlative," the "auditory imagination," the "dissociation of sensibility," the "Tradition," and fifty or sixty other concepts which are supposed to explain his poetry to us? The answer is by dealing with the poetry as poetry, as if Eliot had never published a single line of critical theory or laid down a single law or set up a single guidepost to "correct" taste.

Ignore the criticism, if possible. Eliot's criticism, like all literary criticism, has a place in the seminar room in the philosophy department; let's keep it there. How it ever got out is a biographical question which we will leave to anyone daring enough to violate Eliot's fiat against biography. I take it that Eliot is mainly responsible for the modern taboo against literary biography, one of his less publicized fields of propaganda.

In another section of these notes I have made a distinction between criticism and judgment. The strategic purpose of Eliot's criticism was to prevent judgment; that is the purpose of the criticism which he gave birth to (called the New Criticism), to replace judgment by theory. Eliot's own judgment is seldom shown, governed as it is by precept. His intellectualization of feeling and taste led him to such twisted judgments as the praise of Kipling and the execration of Whitman, the approval of Donne and the disparagement of Milton, and to pronouncements such as "the novel died" on such and such a date. One of Eliot's followers, taking a suggestion from the master, writes a long, seemingly "objective" account of the weaknesses of the poetry of D. H Lawrence. Lawrence had committed the horrible sin of expressing his own feelings in poetry. Instead of following "the discipline of a rationally constructed imagination," Lawrence *expresses*. If only, this critic complains, Lawrence had learned to use "controlled hysteria" like Eliot. And so forth. ("Controlled hysteria" strikes me as an accurate description of Eliot's poetry from an amateur psychology point of view, but the critic in question, R. P. Blackmur, egregiously takes Eliot's tightly buttoned-up pathology to be the normal state of affairs for poetry.)

To Eliot and Pound, with their provincial and educated

11

horror of the unlettered and the spontaneous, the idea of a large or mixed audience was unspeakable. Throughout the criticism of these two leaders of modern taste the audience is constantly defined as a danger to the *status quo*. Pound, for example, in making up his booklist for converts to his criticism is even suspicious of the ballad. He cannot explain to himself that the ballad may be and probably is the product of the "unliterary" mind; he distrusts Shakespeare for the same reason. Eliot's own plays, of course, are addressed to a good sound upper-middle-class audience, British preferably, even though a couple of his dramatic works have a popular appeal. Eliot must have gotten quite a chuckle out of that.

In discussing Eliot's or Pound's idea of the audience (or what they would call the *function* of literature, in their strangely mechanistic language) one runs into the old danger of bogging down in points of doctrine and definition. It is no exaggeration to say that Eliot's criticism contains a definite plan of action, leading from a theory of poetics to political philosophy and covering all the intermediate stages. I will come back to this matter in my remarks on Yeats and Pound and their part in the religion of modern poetry. As far as the audience is concerned it is enough to say Eliot and Pound have not really had one—Eliot not until a few years ago, Pound never. The public has consistently rejected almost all of their poetry from the beginning and has ignored both the poetry and its scales of values. In the voluntary withdrawal of the audience, the critics have created an academic audience, that is, a captive audience. The true audience, when it is allowed to grow, may of course reach all levels of appreciation from the lowest to the highest; it is ever the job of the poet to address himself to the present *condition* of the audience and to the language of that audience. Eliot and Pound have both attempted to find the language of their time: both have failed miserably and have succeeded only in constructing parodistic copies of the language. (This is the cogent argument of William Carlos Williams against both poets.) Eliot's style of deliberate plagiarism is the first symptom of failure to locate the language—in his case a lifelong admission of defeat. Modern poetry is macaronic because, in fact, it is not linguistically modern at all. It is high time we related the Pound-Eliot antiquarianism in ideas to the antiquarianism of their styles. Pound uses more archaisms than the Poet Laureate of Florida.

I am going to deal with only a sample of the most typical and celebrated poems of Eliot's, from "Prufrock" through the *Quartets*, trying to *judge* these poems as if Eliot had never written any criticism. I judge them from the point of view of writing, on the assumption, which is to me a certainty, that all English-speaking people can appraise their worth as English poetry. This is the way poetry has always been read—without criticism or in spite of it. I disregard, as far as possible, Eliot's talk about the form of this and the form of that. I am confident that my judgments of these poems as poetry, not as sociology or esthetics, is extremely close to the judgments of nearly all readers of modern poetry who have not been conditioned by the criticism.

"The Love Song of J. Alfred Prufrock"—this is probably Eliot's best poem and is a little masterpiece of its kind. It is highly unoriginal in content and in style, based as it is on the rhythms, the attitudes, and sometimes the very lines of minor Symbolist poets like Corbière and Laforgue. Rhythmically it is the most successful of Eliot's poems, possibly because it was conceived as a dramatic unit. The meter is varied within the conventional English line, and the rhyming is superb. There is every indication that at the time of composition (age twenty-three) Eliot still took seriously the customs of English prosody and was trying in earnest (i.e., without irony) to develop this technical side of our poetry. The general tone of the poem is that of polite sophisticated ennui, an essay in self-mockery. The literary allusions in the poem, not counting the epigraph, are of the most obvious nature. This poem does not offend on the side of Culture. The epigraph from Dante purportedly throws a special light on the meaning of the poem; it is the epigraph which critics talk about most and which teachers teach. This quotation is gratuitous, a meaningless decoration; later it becomes the actual method of the Eliot poem. The difficulties of the poem, which are intentional, are not insurmountable, say, to a reader quite conversant with poetry tending toward the baroque or self-conscious. "Prufrock" is a poem *about* self-consciousness. The split personality of Prufrock creates the chief obstacle to a first understanding of the poem. The other primary difficulty is imagistic, but this is also the main virtue of the poem. The famous opening image of the evening prostrate "like a patient etherized upon a table" is one of the most brilliant examples of the poetry of exhaustion; very possibly it is a variation of Baudelaire's statement that the sexual act is like a surgical operation. Eliot's poem, however, is humorous rather than vicious and develops a kindly pathos to the very end. The imagery of the poem is all related to suggestion, a watering-down of the extreme suggestiveness of "effect" of poets like Mallarmé and Poe, and is, in fact, a retreat from official Symbolism. (Eliot would already be conscious of all the "historical" possibilities of his "position.") "Prufrock" is a materpiece of a "period," the high point of Eliot's poetry. It is a true poem and also an experiment in criticism. It is a true poem by virtue of a personal content, which we can only guess at, for Eliot is always more sensitive about the autobiographical than any other writer I know of. But many things in the poem point to the so-called objectification of experience; even after Eliot airs to the public his problem of the personal and the impersonal, Life versus Art. The figure of Hamlet in "Prufrock" he finds particularly expressive of his own dilemma, even though Prufrock disclaims a true identity with the Prince. But Hamlet is the figure who makes an art of indecision. Indecision leads to thinking things over, soliloquizing, becoming an intellectual. Eliot's poetry all turns to talk. As it goes on through the years it becomes nothing but talk, and talk about the kind of poetry that comes closer and closer to talk. Technically, the poem prefigures all the criticism, with its debates about the personal and the impersonal, the more and more "objective," the great struggle toward "unified sensibility" and what not.

Eliot's failure as a poet is his success as a critic. Prufrock as a character is of no intrinsic interest but he is of high *literary* interest to all. In this poem Eliot has remained close enough to a human footing to make poetry out of a personal complex of crises, private, social, and intellectual. Had he written nothing else he would be remembered for this masterly little poem.

The "Portrait of a Lady" is also a young poem, written apparently at the time of "Prufrock." The "Portrait," however, is not a textbook piece; it is too much of a love poem. It is not as good a poem as "Prufrock," actually, because it has the tone of adolescence rather than the tone of a pre-figured worldliness, as in "Prufrock." In the "Portrait" the woman is made fun of; she is wiser but inferior to the young Eliot; the poem leaves the reader nothing much to dwell upon except its excellence of execution. It appears to be one of Eliot's many exercises in tone. The epigraph in this case is a falsification. Eliot takes three lines from Marlowe's *The Jew of Malta*, the meaning of which he distorts for his own purpose. The lines are these:

> Thou hast committed—
> Fornication: but that was in another country,
> And besides, the wench is dead.

These three lines are actually part of a long involved dialogue; two people are speaking, not one. Eliot does not mean to convey that only one person is speaking, but he must for convenience gloze over the sense of the play. Eliot exegetes can retrace the quotation and explain that a friar is accusing the traitorous Jew, Barabas, of a series of crimes and that the Jew is evading answering; in the same way the Eliot in the poem is evading answering the questions of the woman. Psychologically this kind of thing can become so involved that everything reverts back to the meaning of the *quotation.* This is the crux of the Eliot poem, as we all know: how does the quotation fit the poem? Very shortly the matter is reversed and the question becomes: how does the poem fit the *quotation*? The beauty of the "Portrait" testifies to Eliot's residual interest in the poem, not in its possible intellectual overtones; the quotation (virtually a misquotation) also indicates the poet's concern about what he writes rather than what he quotes. But the quote is also a loophole for the meaning of the poem, permitting Eliot to evade his meaning or permitting critics to elaborate it.

In both of these poems Eliot displays a mastery of sound and rhythm which marks the poet of genius. The rhyming is dazzling, a mixture of shock (the use of near-comic pairs such as Pole-soul) and the much more subtle effect of non-rhyme, such as we find in "Lycidas." It is almost, but not quite, apparent that Eliot at the beginning of his career is playing the weary virtuoso. But this is not sufficient, either for Eliot or for the literary scene. There is not much to be gained by becoming another Anglo-American Laforgue.

The remaining poems of this early style are even more "French" than the longer ones, but more satisfying evidently to Eliot. "Preludes" introduces the typical sordid furniture of the Eliot world, a Baudelairean rather than Laforguean world. The poem is a series of images evoking despair and disgust. The popularity of the poem comes from its seriousness, the transference from youthful, well-educated ennui to a genuine, if not very thoughtful, revulsion for all those people "raising dingy shades in a thousand furnished rooms." Eliot here imports the clichés of nineteenth-century French poetry about the wickedness (i.e., mediocrity) of the modern city. "Rhapsody on a Windy Night," a much more convincing poem, dramatizes and symbolizes the horror of the city. Eliot has already found the Culture of the modern city; by simply recording its images (a broken spring in a factory yard, a morsel of rancid butter, the toothbrush hanging on the wall) he evokes a cultured response—the response of the *avant-garde* reader to society. It is assumed, without having to say so, that the modern city is a degeneration of the Past. *Now he knows what to say:* the housemaids have "damp" souls; people await the evening paper for want of something better, the

17

old order changeth and Cousin Nancy has taken to smoking; the poet is quietly rejecting both the present and the immediate past—the American past.

The first really literary poem comes in this phase also. (I use the term "literary" opprobriously.) "Mr. Apollinax" marks the new Eliot; the Greek epigraph becomes an integral part of the poem, an explanation of it; and there is no attempt to provide links from the reader's experience to the cultural cues. The meter begins to break and the rhymes are now artfully coarsened (afternoon-macaroon). Mr. Apollinax is something of a pagan oracle to Eliot and a Priapic figure, but not to the Boston professors who entertain him. The poem is inferior to the "Rhapsody" in every way; it is already a culture poem and an exercise in footnoting.

Eliot's reputation to a large extent is based upon the poems of this early period, and rightly so. "Prufrock," "Portrait of a Lady," "Preludes," and the "Rhapsody" are among his best works. Of these "Prufrock" is head and shoulders above the rest and is sufficient to justify Eliot's claim as one of the most gifted twentieth-century poets. At the same time it is extremely close to *vers de société*, as the first reviewers were aware (and first impressions are generally valuable in literary criticism), while the other poems mentioned are almost mannerist in their attention to theory and precedent. These are true weaknesses and Eliot is evidently conscious of their defects, the proof being that he deserts these forms for new ones.

In the next phase we find the majority of the poems in pedantic and ironic quatrains. There is one attempt at a "major" form, as the critics say, in the poem "Gerontion," and there are several poems in French, which certainly cannot be judged as English poems. The quatrain poems introduce Sweeney and various minor characters in Eliot's pantheon. In this group there is also the extraordinarily crude antichurch poem named "The Hippopotamus," one of those surprising lapses of Eliot's which almost equal his good poems in number. Equally crude is the embarrassing anti-Jewish poem "Burbank with a Baedeker," a typical utterance of the modern "classical" school. Eliot's anti-Semitism, which I am not going to discuss, is connected with his view of American commercial wealth: Bleistein is "Chicago Semite Viennese" and he is described in disgusting physical detail. It is interesting to note that as Eliot's feelings become more violent and shocking the epigraphic matter becomes more talky and deranged. The quotation affixed to this poem is a hodgepodge of a French poem, a Latin motto, something from Henry James, something from Shakespeare, something from Browning, and something from Marston. It is as obscure as the quatrains are clear. The Chicago Shylock and the British baronet with a Jewish name have taken back Venice, according to this culture lyric. Stylistically and otherwise there is little virtue in the piece.

Stylistically there is little or nothing of value in all the quatrain poems, "Sweeney Erect," "A Cooking Egg," "Whispers of Immortality," "Mr. Eliot's Sunday Morning Service," and the famous "Sweeney Among the Nightingales." In these poems Eliot is exploring the possibilities of character symbols; most turn out to be mere caricatures and do not appear again. Sweeney survives as a representation of Eliot's dim view of modern man. Eliot tries humor in the poems, if humor is the proper word (a highly polysyllabic bumbling kind of pseudo-British joking); and this he alter-

19

nates with scenes of horror and disorder made ironical by the propriety of the meters. The close of the "Nightingale" poem is said by critics to mark a high point of nobility, why I am not sure, unless it is that Eliot leaves off "Rachel *née* Rabinovitch" and switches to Agamemnon and the Convent of the Sacred Heart. These closing lines, if indeed they are serious, are cheap rather than noble and so poorly articulated that they can barely be pronounced. These poems show a drastic falling-off from the poet's earlier work. (I have said nothing of the complexities of cultural allusion in these poems; most people know them and accept them as part of the rocky road to modern poetry.)

"Gerontion" is usually placed high among Eliot's works; but it is not much better than "Mr. Apollinax" and is in fact an extension of that poem in its manner. In order to escape a derivative Symbolism, Eliot has settled on the borrowing of quotations. Without a knowledge of the sources the poems sound more or less unified; the quotations themselves remove some of the author's responsibility for what the poems say. Eliot was here working out a method for a kind of poem which would implant certain ideas and images in the reader's mind, almost as if Eliot himself had nothing to do with the poem. The use of quotation without reference has a further advantage: it creates a specialized class of readers; I am quite serious when I say that Eliot is here providing texts for a new academic faculty. In the same way as Pound he is trying to solve an educational problem. But "Gerontion" is also a personal catechism of the poet's religious hopes and doubts and is part of his spiritual autobiography. Its best feature is the rhetorical accretion of the same grammatical form and the use of meaningless but suggestive names. The theme of the youth-less-ageless man, which is Eliot's one contribution to symbology, is advanced again, as in all his earlier poems. There is in "Gerontion" a careful propaganda for Eliot as a symbolic figure, the poet deep in thought, seated among the ruins of the ages, longing for a salvation which will suit his intellect as well as his desires for spiritual comfort.

The Waste Land is the most important poem of the twentieth century, that is, the one that has caused the most discussion and is said by critics to be the culmination of the modern "mythic" style. The poem, by Eliot's own admission, is a collaboration with Pound. Pound edited it and removed a third or two thirds of it. The "continuity," we can assume, is therefore the work of Pound, who abhorred continuity in his own more ambitious poetry. As everyone knows how to read the poem or can find out by visiting the nearest library, I will say nothing about its meaning. I will speak rather of the success and the failure of the poem. That it is lacking in unity is obvious (assuming, as I do, that unity is a literary virtue). Any part of *The Waste Land* can be switched with any other part without changing the sense of the poem. Aside from the so-called "mythic" form, which is worthless and not even true—for Eliot misread James Joyce's *Ulysses* when he saw it as a parallel to Homer—the underlying unity of the poem is tonal and dramatic, exactly as a Victorian narrative poem would be. Eliot tries to conceal this indispensable literary method by mixing languages, breaking off dramatic passages, and by dividing the poem into sections with titles. But what really keeps the poem moving is its rhetoric, its switches from description to exclamation to interrogation to expletive, sometimes very beautifully, as in the passages beginning "Unreal City." The straight descriptive passages are weak:

"A Game of Chess" is one of the dullest and most meretricious of Eliot's writings, indicating his own dissatisfaction with that kind of verse. The dialogue, on the other hand, is generally good. The best moments of all are the image passages, where the images are set in dramatic tonalities: "What the Thunder Said" is the finest of these. The very worst passages are those which are merely quotes; even Eliot's most abject admirers can find no justification of the last lines of the poem, with its half-dozen languages and more than half a dozen quotations in a space of about ten lines.

The Waste Land, because of its great critical reputation, not because of any inherent worth it might have, is one of the curiosities of English literature. Its critical success was, I dare say, carefully planned and executed, and it was not beyond the realm of possibility that the poem was originally a hoax, as some of the first readers insisted. But hoax or not, it was very shortly made the sacred cow of modern poetry and the object of more pious literary nonsense than any modern work save the *Cantos* of Pound. The proof of the failure of the "form" of this poem is that no one has ever been able to proceed from it, including Eliot himself. It is, in fact, not a form at all but a negative version of form. It is interesting to notice that in the conventional stanzas of the quatrain poems Eliot is more personally violent and ugly about his own beliefs; in his unconventional style the voice of the poet all but disappears and is replaced by characters from his reading.

The emergence of Eliot's piety in "The Hollow Men" and in *Ash Wednesday* takes the form of self-disgust in the one and self-pity in the other. "The Hollow Men" is in every way a better poem than *The Waste Land*, though the parodistic style again enforces a poverty of statement and language which become the marks of self-imitation in Eliot. *Ash Wednesday* is probably even more laden with gratuitous quotation than *The Waste Land*, but its ecclesiastical imagery and richness of music give the poem a beauty which the poet can finally accept as beauty. Eliot here luxuriates in the emotions of piety and surrender which seemed shameful to his Puritan soul in a purely human situation. The Eliot-God equation, once he has made the daring step, gives him an intellectual-emotional balance for the first time in his career. After the publication of this poem, Eliot's former work seems more of a piece and his future work is all laid out for him, everything from church pageants to Christmas-card poems. The *Ariel Poems* are relatively simple and almost narrative. The rest of the poems are shelved under "fragments," minor pieces, and unfinished experiments. Eliot's career as a poet virtually comes to a close with *Ash Wednesday*. After that there is criticism, theology, and drama. The *Four Quartets* is the only attempt at what modern criticism calls a "major" poem—meaning a poem that deals with Culture wholesale. The *Quartets* were hailed by the Eliot critics as his crowning achievement; actually they are evidence of the total dissolution of poetic skill and even a confession of poetic bankruptcy. Eliot is quite open about this in the *Quartets*.

Four Quartets is Eliot's bid to fame as a "philosophical poet." In it he expounds his metaphysics, his poetics, and his own place in the scheme of things. All of this is quite legitimate and not at all surprising; what is disturbing about the poems is their commonplaceness, their drabness of expression, their conventionality, and, worst of all, their reliance on the schoolbook language of the philosophy class.

Eliot has traded poetry for the metaphysical abstraction, as in *The Waste Land* he had traded narrative for "myth." This development is psychologically consistent, a descent from French Symbolism to Metaphysical complexity-for-the-sake-of-complexity, to pastiche, to the myth-science of *The Golden Bough*, to philosophical abstraction without poetic content. It all ends in the complete abandonment of poetry. When he comes to the drama in earnest he knows, of course, that he must use human language and he begins a new ascent into literature and the voices of poetry. But the *Quartets* lies at the bottom of the literary heap. All the so-called lyric sections, with one or two exceptions, are written with such disregard for the ear that one cannot associate them with the Eliot of "Prufrock" or the "Rhapsody." "Garlic and sapphires in the mud/ Clot the bedded axle-tree" is typical of this diction devoid of both image and music. Eliot, who used to condemn poets like Tennyson for what he called crudeness of feeling, here shows an insensitivity toward language which is marvelous. The more prosy passages are even voided of that kind of poetry which rises from the use of imagery or sound. As for the philosophical development, it fails to reach a state of poetry, and it may fail as philosophy—of this I am no judge. The much-quoted third section of "East Coker" about everyone going into the darkness, even people in the Almanach de Gotha and the Stock Exchange Gazette, is possibly the best passage of a long, very bad piece of writing; one feels that here there is an acceptance of the badness of the writing, as if good writing no longer held any meaning for the poet. The "lyric" section that follows contains a stanza ("The whole earth is our hospital/ Endowed by the ruined millionaire . . .") which in its vulgarity of thought and expression is hardly superior to "Only God can make a tree." For the rest there is a kind of narcissistic figure of the aging Eliot lolling through the poem, the climactic Dante imitation in "Little Gidding," and finally the magnificent passage "Sin is Behovely, but/ All shall be well . . ." Unfortunately these glorious lines are not Eliot's but are one of his borrowings. In general, the *Four Quartets* appears to be a deliberately bad book, one written as if to convince the reader that poetry is dead and done with. We should remember Eliot's lifelong interest in the final this and final that, and at least entertain the possibility that the *Four Quartets* were intended to stand as the last poem in the Great Tradition. Eliot and Pound have both shown themselves capable of such arrogance.

I have now said all the wicked things I can think of about Eliot and it remains at last to say something favorable. At the beginning of these remarks I mentioned one phase of Eliot's work in which I regard him as a true poet and a man of rich spiritual insight. While I cannot feel that Eliot has contributed anything to the spiritual advancement of our age, I am convinced that he tried. But why is it that his own poems are rubrics rather than works of art? What are they for? What are they trying to say? Is it really all just sociology, reactionary politics, bitterness, spite and despair? I think not. I have spoken of the apparently deliberate erosion of his great gifts, leading to the final desertion of poetry. And I have touched on Eliot's lapse into religion. Here is a capital puzzle for the critic.

My solution to the puzzle is this. The motivating force in Eliot's work is the search for the mystical center of experience. This search in his case has been fruitless and increasingly frustrating. Eliot's entire career is a history of his failure to penetrate the mystical consciousness. He begins as a youth with Symbolism when it is already a dying religious-esthetic *mystique*. He moves from Symbolism to the Metaphysical poets of the seventeenth century. (Neither the dictionary nor modern criticism explains what it is that interested Eliot in these poets, for it certainly was not extreme metaphorical technique or what the textbook calls the conceit.) Eliot was fascinated by the Metaphysical poem because it is virtually a demonstration of prayer. Nearly all the Metaphysical poets were Divines, men deeply troubled by the new scientific knowledge. What Eliot studied in their poetry was the possibility of fusing sacred with secular knowledge in poetry. Metaphysical poetry lies close to absurdity because it is premised on this peculiar dualism. We recall also that Eliot associated the fairly recent French poet Laforgue with the English Metaphysicals, for at one time it seemed to Eliot that a keen enough wit might serve as a key to the door that refused to open. But neither Symbolism nor Metaphysical sacred poetry offered a way to Eliot, even when he tried a fusion of the two. Third, he attempted secular mythology as a way to penetrate the mystical consciousness. It was in this phase that he wrote *The Waste Land*, a poem which is a jumble of sacred and "profane" myths, adding up to nothing.

Meanwhile, both Eliot and Pound had discovered T. E. Hulme, whose essays provided written authority for them both, in different ways. Every major doctrine of Eliot's can be found in Hulme's *Speculations*, the most basic the one that relates fundamental Christian doctrine to a theory of society and a theory of poetics. Hulme formulated for Eliot the attack on Romanticism and the attack on mysticism (for the Romantic and the mystical are always related, while the Classical and the orthodox are related in their ways, at least in the critical mind). Hulme pointed the way for Eliot to orthodoxy in letters and to ritual and dogma in the spiritual realm. I consider Hulme's book as the *Mein Kampf* of modern criticism and a thoroughly evil work; and it was Eliot's undoing. For after the assimilation of Hulme, the rest is elaboration. Except for one thing: the search for the mystical center of experience goes on. Eliot worries it in Dante, in the Hindu scriptures, in St. John of the Cross, and in Julianne of Norwich. But poets of more recent vintage who come closer to mysticism infuriate Eliot, and he pours out his scorn on Blake, Lawrence, Whitman and our own Transcendentalists. Yet it is eternally to Eliot's credit that he does not fake the mystical (as he seems to accuse Blake of doing) and it is also to his credit that he does not relapse into magic and spiritualism, as Yeats did. It appears that Eliot is not even acquainted with esotericism; at least he does not even seem to be conscious of the esoteric meaning of the Tarot, which he uses in *The Waste Land* for "fortunetelling."

The failure to achieve mystical consciousness (which indeed is one of the rarest achievements in mankind) drove Eliot back to metaphysics proper and to religion proper. This in my view is the great failure of Eliot. Eliot ends up as a poet of religion in the conventional sense of that term. And once having made the religious commitment he tried to visualize a religion-directed society; he thus becomes an official of the most conservative elements of society and a figurehead for all that is formalized and ritualized. Yeats' fascination for the Byzantine betrays the same spiritual conservatism, as does Pound's fascination for the corporate state and the leadership principle. And Eliot ends his quest

with his caricature of the modern poet-priest or psychi-
atrist-priest who alone has power to allay the Eumenides.
Witch-hunting runs through Eliot from beginning to end.

Eliot is a poet of religion, hence a poet of the second or
third rank; he is a thoroughgoing anachronism in the modern world, a poet of genius crippled by lack of faith and
want of joy.

EZRA POUND:

The Scapegoat of Modern Poetry

... the goat shall bear upon him all their iniquities unto a land which is cut off; and he shall let go the goat in the wilderness.

ANY WAY YOU look at it, writing about Ezra Pound and his poetry is an unpleasant business. It is unpleasant for his friends and fellow travelers, who must either by-pass or explain away the various Pound scandals; just as unpleasant for his ill-wishers and critics; and unpleasant as well for the scholars, book reviewers, and historians of the age who find him looming up menacingly from the card catalogue. Pound is not the kind of writer who once did something wrong and can now be forgiven in the mellowness of time. It is hard to forgive him because everything he did wrong he insists was right. He is righteous about his wrongness; he forces his worst upon us wherever we meet him, and there is no escaping it.

People who try to minimize Pound's sins, errors, and

crimes are simply playing a game that Pound himself refuses to play. Critics who would like to shelve the ugly side
of Pound's poetry for its virtues are also playing a game
that Pound refuses to have a hand in. Of all the modern
didactic poets there is none more didactic than this one,
none more "topical," whether the topic is religion, politics,
war, or money and banking. Eliot hopes that his readers
will distinguish between his poetry and criticism, but
Pound demands a thorough identification of his prose with
his poetry. They are one and the same, all a single immense
prose-poem supposedly covering in time all the known civilizations in all their main ramifications. The size, scope,
and style of this prose-poem raises the most embarrassing
question of all about Pound, which I am going to express
my opinion about. This question is whether Pound is insane.

The question of whether Pound is insane is, properly
speaking, none of our business. Many poets and artists have
been, or have been adjudged, insane and have spent terrible years in asylums. But we who are readers and lovers of
poetry are not doctors and it is not within our scope, except
out of human sympathy or curiosity, to dwell upon an artist's worst moments or periods of life. What does concern
us is whether the poet's *poetry* is insane. If it is, and we as
readers should be able to tell that, then we must treat it as
such, as the work of a sick mind, or, sometimes, a dangerous one. I have read Pound's poetry all my life, carefully,
with pain and with pleasure, and I know that his poetry is
anything but insane. People who have termed it so may
know a good deal about insanity but they know little about
poetry. One of the chief defects of Pound's poetry, in fact,
is that it is too *rational*, forced, and wanting in imagination.

Insofar as we can reconstruct the character and intellect of a man from his writings, we can get a fairly whole portrait of Pound. I will be sketching that portrait for you, and you will see that he is a perfectly normal, though badly frustrated, fellow American. He is, in fact, a well-known American type, the provincial overexposed to the guidebook.

But leaving the question of insanity aside, there is also the question of the social dangerousness of Pound. Pound is, or rather wants to be, thought dangerous, but it appears that the danger is now a thing of the past. Eliot, if anything, is a much more dangerous element in society than Pound. He is more persuasive, highly respectable, a better strategist, a theologian, a modernist, and a gentleman saint. No one that I ever heard of has been seriously influenced by the theories of Pound—except Eliot! But Eliot's danger period has also passed, in any case, his job has been done; he has put literature back in the Reference Room and has apologized for his youthful indiscretions about the lower races and popular governments. Eliot today is the kindly Greco-Judaic-Christian gentleman who made good. There is an almost touchingly comic element in the Pound-Eliot team, their spats and undying loyalties to one another, their division of the empires of literature into East and West; but there is a good bit of pathos as well.

The chief difference between Pound and Eliot is one of intelligence. As far as poetic talent goes, Pound sometimes seems the superior poet; but as far as the I.Q. goes, Eliot is head and shoulders above his teacher. In the case of writers like these two, we must speak of intelligence because they make us consider their minds, their ideas, and their opinions, and not simply their poetry. They make a cult of Intelligence. Dylan Thomas, for example, makes no pretenses about his intelligence, and it is hard to tell whether he was or was not a man with a good thinking apparatus. That Eliot has a fine intellect we all somehow agree; it is his chief claim on our attention. Eliot even talks about the importance of the intelligence in such a way that it seems an attribute comparable with poetic artistry. It is one of his tricks of strategy. Following this mode of criticism, W. H. Auden writes an introduction to the poems of Tennyson warning the reader that he must not make the mistake of considering Tennyson intelligent. Auden (mimicking the tone and manner of Eliot) says: "He had the finest ear, perhaps, of any English poet; he was also undoubtedly the stupidest." According to "modern" criticism, Tennyson is unintelligent or stupid because he did not develop a fine critical sensibility. Those are Auden's words. One could wish that a fine critical sensibility (whatever that is) would prevent a critic from calling a poet like Tennyson stupid, if only for the sake of common decency. On the other hand, I am tempted to call Ezra Pound stupid, but in this case I think even Pound's best friends might agree.

The question of the intelligence of the artist is one of those phony questions which have been brought to the fore in our time by critics like Eliot, Valéry, and Auden. Once we begin to debate this question we are in the Dismal Swamp of criticism. It is an endless and irrelevant question, like art and homosexuality, or art and science—questions which belong anywhere but in literature. Was Mozart intelligent or "stupid"? Critics sometimes point out the "stupidity" of Beethoven, based on the laborious evidence of his notebooks. Beethoven was slow, Mozart quick as a flash, but "stupidity" somehow seems the improper term for so great a genius as either. I think we should consider the intelligence of the artist within the framework of art. It is meaningless to call Tennyson stupid while complimenting him on his excellent ear. Ear *is* to a great extent what poetic intelligence means; not "critical sensibility" or a sense of history, and so on. What annoys Auden about Tennyson is that Tennyson had not read sociology or thought deeply enough about Original Sin. (I will deal with this quirk in Auden's thinking in another place.)

But when the poet makes a boast of intelligence like Pound and is defended at the last ditch on the grounds of his *ideas*, and is elevated by T. S. Eliot as the most important critic of the age—what are we to do? For Pound has chosen to be the "poet of ideas" (grotesque and unbeautiful phrase), and it is as a poet of ideas that we have to accept him. The ideas in Pound are not only explicit, they are magnified, repeated and spelled out in block letters. No poet in history has boasted so loudly of what he believes; none has tried harder to convince, without trying to please. So, discussing Pound's intelligence is something one would almost rather not do: it is like taking candy away from the baby.

I have called Pound the scapegoat of modern poetry. This is true in a very real sense. Pound is famed for being the teacher of modern writers: of Eliot, of Joyce, and of Yeats. This reputation, while it is the kind of exaggeration that approaches falsehood, is true in the legendary sense. Yeats must have used Pound in order to avoid certain mistakes which Pound insisted upon making. And to Yeats, Pound must have seemed a voice of the future. Joyce could have learned nothing of consequence from Pound; and Eliot, who evidently learned a very great deal from him, still developed in a direction that seemed to Pound seditious. What all three got from Pound was not so much inspiration as the sanction to use the "poetry of ideas." In return, and possibly out of a sense of guilt, Pound was overpraised, especially by Eliot, without whom Pound's reputation would probably be no greater today than that of, say, Richard Aldington. Eliot's defense of Pound and his wild encomiums are also a self-defense. Eliot has had to bear the brunt of all of Pound's mistakes, poetic, esthetic, and cultural. There is a kind of haggard nobility in Eliot's support of his mentor and friend. But it bears looking into.

There are two large classes of "ideas" in Pound's work; one has to do with works of poetry (his esthetic), and the other with social ideas. The second category comprises whatever he has to say about philosophy, science, history, ethics, and economics. All of the ideas in the second class are exposed, in the worst sense of the word. They are vulnerable. They are vulnerable because they all relate back to source works, other books. This throws Pound into an arena where readers of any description can have a go at him. Purportedly Pound makes connections between his various interests, such as economic theory and esthetics, and this becomes one of the worst burlesques of poetry we know of in modern literature: in Eliot's case, we have a different, more sophisticated element at work. But we cannot understand Pound without Eliot, or Eliot without Pound. One is the wide-awake, cautious scholastic; the other is the wild, noisy, system-crazy Yankee who demands to be a prophet, at any expense. My own sympathies are much more with Pound than with Eliot; and this is the case with William Carlos Williams also, who is revolted by Pound but who is always ready to go bail for him. Eliot uses Pound, not for his own advantage but for the advan-

tage of the intellectual position. There is in Pound something which appeals to every American writer—it is the
super-European drive and the blundering arrogance that
goes with it—and there is also the provincial snobbery. It is
the snobbery that appeals to Eliot, the bluster that makes
him cling to Pound as an American-in-exile and a displaced
European at once. In speaking of Pound's career we should
keep in mind that this man was almost a contemporary of
Henry James and Mark Twain—that he was born in the
twilight of American literature. Pound busied himself with
literature for half a century.

Pound started out as a young poet and scholar who was
not appreciated in the America of about 1905. Having behind him a tradition of cultural expatriation and discon-
tent, he thought he would assail England. But Pound was
not really for England—he was a Romance-language
scholar, not an "Anglo-Saxon man." In England he was the
type of belligerent European-American we know so well
through out literature. He married an Englishwoman
named Shakespear and left for the Continent. Pound became European editor of Harriet Monroe's *Poetry* until he
could no longer stomach her Americanism. He then became
a one-man literary movement—but there is no point in re-
capitulating all this. The only fact of interest about Pound's
biographia literaria is that he managed to capture the es-
teem of such poets as Eliot and Yeats, though almost no
others.

Pound's ideas are neither very complex nor very extensive. In the first place he is without religion and practically
without a *mystique* of any kind. He is a rational poet, a
humanist *manqué*, if one needs a name for him (though not
many humanists would claim him). Pound's humanism is,

of course, a bookish variety and derives from the periods of art and poetry he admires. The eighteenth century is about as far as he wishes to go in time, Jefferson and Adams being the main political figures he admires from our own past. The Italian Renaissance and similar periods in China are his two main focal points. In the twentieth century he tries with miserable results to equate Jefferson with Mussolini; and Mussolini he even compares with Christ. His worship of "the Boss," of course, is partly born of spite, but it contains rational elements also. Mussolini's paternalism and economic program somehow recall Jefferson in Pound's mind. That Pound could not recognize the Chicago-gangster quality of his hero is typical of the humorlessness and childishness of Pound's political ideas. This is the poet who will spend his life writing an epic of world history and culture and who is claimed by Eliot as his peer. As far as a social order goes, Pound has a vestigial idea of a kind of hierarchy based upon the good-ruler-art-patron equation; very likely it is this simple notion which led him to a study of Oriental history. Confucius provides what basis for an ethical-social order there is in Pound's world; Chinese calligraphy and the imagistic character of Chinese writing help convince Pound that an interest in clear definitions leads directly to good government. Finally there is Pound's own economic system, which according to his view could stop war, balance all national economies and bring about something like a terrestrial paradise. His precedents for this belief are a few non-usurious banks tried out here and there in history. Evidently the greatest crime Pound can invent in his world ideology is the crime of Usury; and it is because of Usury that he devotes a good deal of his prose and poetry to imprecations against capitalism and the Jews, whom he associates historically with *Usura*.

Pound's lifelong problem was to establish an equation between poetry and society, between the esthetic and the politick. The nexus is economics. Good economic system and good ruler equal civilization. That is the whole story. His solution is not convincing even to his adherents, and the best of it is based partly on the sayings of Confucius. Pound acts out the pathetic drama of Modern Poetry, that of trying to make a place for the poet in the modern world by remaking the world. It is in this phase that Pound's so-called insanity has been brought to the attention of nonliterary folk. It is his air of conviction rather than any series of acts or writings which has struck the bystander as lunacy.

This brings us to the most unaccountable paradox of all in Pound's writing, that of his own style as the exemplum of precision in language and in ideas. If it is the high responsibility of the poet to clarify the language, as the good ruler clarifies economic life, then certainly we should expect the poetry of Pound to execute this service. But instead of clarity and precision we get an epic poem which not even scholars can read without long study. Once the University of California published an index to the *Cantos* with seventeen thousand references to names, dates and other factual information in the poem. Certain references could not be solved even by the editors; nor would the author lend a helping hand! Clarity, evidently, is not as simple a matter as telling someone what you mean. But the *Cantos* are supposed to be case studies of the economic-esthetic failures of all civilizations, and the quantity of data available is, of course, sizable. The style of the poem represents the brave and hopeless attempt to carry over into poetry all the sad prose of History. These case studies are documented by the use of large image groups. For instance, Ovid's *Metamorphoses* is used to denote change, Dante to denote punishment, Homer to denote the brave exile, etc. This is pretty much what Pound means by the ideogram method— giving one image or anecdote or document after another to build up the total ideogram.

In looking at the vagaries of Pound's various styles we must not lose sight of the fact that he is a Modern, that he is one of the poets who flourished around 1915–25. We must remember his proximity to the James Joyce of *Ulysses*, Eliot of *The Waste Land*, the heyday of the little magazine, and so on. The *Cantos* are an anachronism, or rather a historical phenomenon of a certain decade of long ago. While Eliot abandoned the fads of the twenties, Pound did not. The method of the *Cantos* is precisely the method of *The Waste Land*. Had the so-called mythic method, with all its artificiality, proved successful, we may be sure Eliot would have hung on to it. No other poet has profited by this "form," and only Pound would not give it up. The reason he did not give it up is that he was still searching for the meaning of the form. The *Cantos* are a series of experiments that failed; they are almost scientific in their exhaustive persistence. But this hysterical search for "form" is the chief characteristic of modernism.

If anyone needs proof that there is no form to the *Cantos* he can take Pound's word for it. When the poem was three-fourths finished (1939) Pound wrote to an American poet: "As to the *form* of the *Cantos*: All I can say or pray is, wait till it's there. I mean wait till I get 'em written and then if it don't show, I will start exegesis . . ."

As with the poetry of Eliot, we must look closely before we can find a point of departure to discuss the poetry of Pound. Pound is even more permeated with his own criticism than Eliot, though fortunately almost nobody reads Pound's prose. But Eliot is also intertwined with Pound's poetry and in fact has misled the entire literary world as to the worth of this and that poem and in the total assessment of Pound's work. Looking, for instance, at Eliot's introduction to Pound's *Selected Poems*, a book which every twentieth-century poet will have a copy of, I can see how all of my own early ideas about Pound's work derive from Eliot. I am sorry to revert to Eliot this way, but that is where all the arrows point in modern criticism. And this is Eliot on his favorite subject—Pound. Here Eliot is making some mysterious remarks about Pound and Whitman which are supposed to show why Pound is the better poet. Eliot says that Whitman's originality is spurious as well as genuine. Whitman, says Eliot, speaking of Whitman's poetry, was "a great prose writer," and his originality "is spurious insofar as Whitman wrote in a way that asserted that his great prose was a new form of verse." But Pound, he goes on to say, is original (Eliot slyly changes the subject while he seems to be talking about versification). "Now Pound is often most 'original' in the right sense, when he is most 'archeological' in the ordinary sense." . . . "One of Pound's most indubitable claims to genuine originality is . . . his revivification of the Provençal . . ." Anyhow, in this typical shell game of Eliot's, the pea under the shells is the word "original."

The poems in *Personae* (1909) are nearly all bad, full of the worst "romantic" and sentimental affectations and the most archaic English. Pound has never really stopped

being archaic—it is another of his inherent weaknesses—
and even in the late *Cantos* when he becomes moved he
drops back into the *thee's* and *thou's* and *hadst's* of old.
This becomes painfully ludicrous when he is *theeing* and
thouing about money, as in the much-quoted Usury *Canto*:

> Usura slayeth the child in the womb
> It stayeth the young man's courting
> It hath brought palsey to bed . . .

Pound sentimentalizing over usury in Quakerish English is
almost too painful to read. Many of the *Personae* poems are
translations or adaptations, nearly all in the pre-Raphaelite
manner and different from late Victorian verse only in their
reliance on the erudition of the student of Romance culture. A few of the poems are still repeated in anthologies,
for instance the "Sestina: Altaforte," which is appealing in its
loudness—"May God damn for ever all who cry 'Peace!'"
Pound's good effects are frequently based on volume of
sound. The *theeing* and *thouing* are also forms of loudness,
as in the translation of Leopardi, where he also uses "ye" as
a half-colloquialism, half-archaism for the second person
singular. These may be details but they spoil any quality of
the poetic Pound. Pound so far fails to achieve a style and
covers up its absence with a mixture of noise and gim-
crackery. Even the pretense of a rich tradition underlying
the poems is dissipated by all the flailing around on the
surface.

Ripostes (1912) and *Lustra* are different and contain the
best of Pound's poetry, the best of his experiments and
the best of his "translations." Except for a few passages in the
Cantos, all that is good in Pound as a poet is represented in
these collections. Significantly, one of the books is dedi-

cated to William Carlos Williams. It is in these poems that Pound produces his best epigrammatic verse; the translations and adaptations are still uneven, as they will remain, not so much in their incorrectness but in their failure to convey the quality of the originals. His chief defect is trying to invent a diction which he cannot achieve; throughout his life Pound plays with dialects in all languages. His use of dialects in English is poor, and one can assume they are not much better in Old French, Latin, Greek, or Chinese. Sometimes Pound claims to write in what he calls the American language, with results that few Americans can recognize. His translation of Confucius' *Ta Hio, The Great Learning*, is subtitled "Newly Rendered into the American Language." In this work he renders the Chinese for "make it over" into

"Renovate, dod gast you, renovate!"

Great chunks of the *Cantos* are composed in this pidgin. But in *Lustra* (1916) Pound reaches his best style, possibly because he begins to write about himself (this is also true of the *Cantos*; the *Pisan Cantos* are the best because they are so personal). Many of these poems are on the subject of Pound's "exile" and the sorrows of the artist. They are not very important and they are badly dated but they are honest and clear and to a degree dramatic. If one compares them with poems of the same period by Lawrence, Sandburg, John Gould Fletcher and especially Williams, one will see that Pound is doing the same thing as these poets, almost as well. As for the epigrams and translations from the *Greek Anthology* and such sources, Pound is about on a par with Horace Gregory's *Catullus*, which is saying a great deal. Gregory has done *Catullus* better in English

41

than anyone else in our time. Pound, however, is not content to be a mere translator, because he is always teaching some lesson about history or civilization. Consequently, even his translations have a queer evangelistic ring. His haiku are neither better nor worse than all such Japanese forms in English. English being what it is and Japanese being what it is, the haiku seems destined to sound silly in our language. The general tone of all these poems is that of the world-weary college instructor who writes tweedy poems about the burden of being so horribly well educated. "O God, O Venus, O Mercury, patron of thieves,/ Give me in due time, I beseech you, a little tobacco-shop, . . ." [anything] "save this damn'd profession of writing, where one needs one's brains all the time." One feels for Pound, trying so desperately to justify his existence with such verses. The fact is that Pound has not yet found anything to be heroic about except Romance languages; he is still innocent, still a poet, though the most bookish one we hear about.

The *Cathay* poems (1915) are also at his best level and form the only group of complete poems Pound ever wrote. Chinese was the making of Pound, not in the misleading sense that Eliot means when he says *ex cathedra* that Pound is the "inventor" of Chinese poetry for our time. This is not it at all. Pound's discovery of Chinese poetry was good for Pound but for no one else. As Eliot says, the poems are paraphrases. They lead not to China but to Pound, and that is valid for Pound and for us. Pound can here write complete paraphrases because he is out of Europe, out of America, out of a literature which presumably nobody knows except a few functionaries at the British Museum. It was about this time that Pound wrote conspiratorially to a young lady that it was good for a writer to know a certain large body of knowledge which nobody else did. Any large body of knowledge would do as long as it was more or less unknown, even to experts. China was to be that knowledge for Pound. Parenthetically, I must make mention of the *Letters* of Pound, which like his poetry are almost devoid of human substance, character, and relationship. Pound is a littérateur, even in his letters; the letters are meticulously offhand, each one a specimen for future publication. There is no question about it. Poor James Joyce's letters are human, all too human, with his broken glasses and failing eyesight and poor wages; Joyce poured all his artistry into his novels and stories; but a letter to him was a letter. Not so with Pound. A letter to Pound is a document for the ages, even if it refers to having his shoes half-soled or varnishing his floor.

Let us glance now at the poem *Hugh Selwyn Mauberley*, which Eliot has nominated as a great poem, "genuine tragedy and comedy," etc. Eliot introduces *Mauberley* as a great poem in his typical manner: his opinion worms its way into a discussion of versification, of all things, in which Eliot guffaws that "I only pretend to know as much about versifying as my carpenter knows about woodwork . . ." He does and he doesn't; you can never quite pin Eliot down. Anyhow, *Mauberley* is a great poem, according to Eliot.

Mauberley is a miniature of the *Cantos*; it has all the defects and only a couple of suggestions of the virtues. No one but T. S. Eliot, and that for his own reasons, would ever call it a good, much less a great poem. It has the kind of skill which we associate with putting a full-rigged four-masted schooner, with people on deck, inside a bottle. But there is nothing to be gained by making fun of a very bad poem and the only reason for mentioning it at all is that it has been called a great poem by the critic who has the greatest authority in the twentieth century. There is no question that the poem would never have reached publication, much less "greatness," had it not been for the critical hoodwinking of the Eliot-Pound team. In addition to calling the poem great (as if that weren't enough) he calls it the most advanced portion of what is a textbook of modern versification. Eliot's snide references to versification lead one in two directions: (a) that there is really no such thing as versification for Serious Poets (this is the meaning of his remark that he knows only as much about versification as his carpenter knows about woodwork), and (b) that versification is the real key to the esotericism of poetry. Actually, Eliot is right on both counts: he knows nothing about versification, even though like all good natural poets, it comes naturally to him. He is also right that successful rhythms lie at the bottom of any successful poem. And he is wrong about *Mauberley*, which is a childish work of versification, as well as being a childish work of intellect. In charity to Eliot, one must say that his loyalty to Pound is magnificent.

Hugh Selwyn Mauberley does have some sections which are good poetry: Part IV about the World War, Part V, and the envoi to Part VI. The rest is student poetry which every teacher of Creative Writing sees at least once in a semester, the weighty and deliberate display of what and how much the author knows, put into "poetry." This is not meant as a joke: it is an exact description of *Mauberley*, which is such a poor little poem that one turns away from it with a blush. Everyone, that is, except T. S. Eliot. The poem is a literary critique and an autobiography, very cryptic supposedly, but in reality a ponderous summation

of the literary mistakes of the author. It contains such ju-
venilities as the rhyming of Τροίη with *lee-way* and the
pun of the Greek τίν' with the English *tin*; it contains all
the Baudelairean platitudes about modern commercialism
and the failure of the Esthetes, all decorated with Pound's
linguistic cartouches and pseudo-British harumphing
("Dowson found harlots cheaper than hotels"), all dedicated to a farewell to Style. There are even little provoking
pseudonyms in epigraphs, a variation on the more grim
headnotes of Eliot's poems. Nowhere is there the faintest
note of Versification or Style or anything that would hold
the attention of anyone but a close friend. In a very biographical sense the poem is, among other things, a confession of hopelessness. The cry is against "the faint susurrus
of his subjective hosannah" of whatever Dowsons and Li-
onel Johnsons that Pound was plowing under. He himself
would not succumb to that. But my sole point here is to
remind the reader that this is a poem which Eliot has made
a standard of form and content (evidently) of the modern
canon. There is little proof that anyone, even Eliot followers, has been convinced by this pronouncement of Eliot's;
and yet the record is there, one of the larger stumbling
blocks of modern criticism and modern poetry.

The big poem of the "Age," however, is the *Cantos*, the
modern poem *par excellence*, and I want to relate this big
poem to the shorter ones and to the criticism by Pound.

First, there is no form, plan, or subject matter of the
Cantos except the reading matter of the poet. There is a
very simple proof that Pound himself did not know what
"form" he was using when he began the epic. The first
versions of the *Cantos* which appeared in *Poetry* magazine
are quite intelligible and almost confessedly written in the

manner of Robert Browning. Immediately after these attempts he began the final version which we know. There are ponderous books written about the form of the *Cantos* and it is of interest to note that the obscurity of the criticism is in a direct ratio to the difficulties of the poems. The difficulties of the *Cantos* are, as I have said, entirely encyclopedic and linguistic, and not structural. With a good reference work at hand one can piece together the main names and dates; with a half-dozen foreign dictionaries one can make real headway; with the Pound Index all difficulties evaporate, except those having to do with the relationships in the poet's ideas. Even these are not insurmountable; as all of the poet's ideas are derivative, based upon other books, one has only to compare him with the originals. The only really deep water Pound ever enters is Confucianism; but Confucianism, compared with, say, the Hermetic philosophy of Yeats or the religious symbolism of Eliot, is child's play. The so-called obscurities are then the obscurities of the pedant and the obscurities of pedantic rhetoric, plus certain profundities inherent in the quoted works. The most original cantro is the one which is a malediction against Usury; it is, sadly, the high point of the whole poem. As for the form, it remains invisible.

Critics of Pound, pro and con, have paid him the highest compliments as adaptor and translator. Here lies his strength. As the *Cantos* begin with a translation of a translation, the entire work is a rewriting from language to language of the documents, literary and historical, which the poet tries to organize into a pattern. The use of bits and pieces of other languages is often of great beauty; and the method itself offers possibilities for originality, although the limitations are obvious. Pound also develops a prosody for the poems, which more than anything else suggests a unity. The prosody is an approximation of the Greek heroic dactyl: the most common rhythmic figure through the poem appears in a line like

> And then went down to the ship,
> Set keel to breakers, forth on the godly sea . . .

This is an excellent device, lending itself to some of the properties of modern speech. But it fails to achieve a standard for all the levels of diction and foreign languages the poet uses. Eliot's versification is nearly always a variation of standard iambic, and it is no surprise to see his later dramatic verse falling back into a weak iambic line. Pound's verse is stronger because he reverses the iambic from the beginning, thus opening the way for new forms such as Whitman invented. But Pound is more conservative than Whitman or Williams and falls back on "Greek" rhythms, where Whitman took as his model the English of the King James Bible and the idiom of America. Whitman's free verse is therefore more natural because it is English, not Greek.

But the fatal weakness of Pound's *Canto* style is his inability to relate one passage or "ideogram" or "image cluster" with another. His usual device is simply to use a conjunction at the beginning of the line (there are passages of great length which rely on this weakest of all English structures of grammar. The weakness, however, is inherent in the material; there is no way to relate it because the relations are arbitrary, chaotic, and without design). There is no vision or ideal central to the *Cantos*, only a tangle of data, prejudices and galvanic twitches of emotion. One would think a poem of this kind would plunge into the universe of philosophies, theories, and systems of knowledge which fill most libraries; but Pound has very little of even this kind of intellectual interest. American that he is, he is so bowled over by facts and statistics that he hardly ever pauses to consider the relevance of his data.

Let us keep in mind the place of Eliot in the appreciation of these poems of Pound. It is impossible to separate Eliot from Pound just as, according to Eliot, it is impossible to divide Pound's criticism from his poetry. "His criticism and his poetry, his precept and his practice, compose a single *oeuvre*," says Eliot. They are the least dispensable body of critical writing in our time, he continues, underlining *least dispensable*. Let us glance hurriedly at this least dispensable body of criticism. Incidentally, Eliot warns against quoting Pound out of context, but it is hard to find the context in these jottings. Pound's criticism is no more than a series of maxims repeated over and over again and illustrated with threats and imprecations—all designed to show that poets are the most important people in history. For example: "A civilization was founded on Homer, civilization not a mere bloated empire." This saying supplies the rationale for the poetry of Pound.

"It is as important for the purpose of thought to keep language efficient as it is in surgery to keep tetanus bacilli out of one's bandages." "Efficient language" of course is Pound's way of trying to make poetry as respectable as science.

Or again: "Great literature is simply language charged with meaning to the utmost possible degree." This is a good definition of poetry as far as it goes. Pound makes his definition in order to talk about those who are inventors and those who are masters and those who are "diluters" of language. The only point of interest here is that Pound is trying to invent categories of poetry which can then be applied to a curriculum of books. The language of poetry is also broken down into categories; the three divisions of lyric, image, and idea-poetry imply a theory of psychology which Pound never states.

Pound's simplification of literature and history is convenient for him. Poetry, he tells us, is a science, just as chemistry is a science. Bad art is inaccurate (unscientific) and is therefore immoral. I am not sure how he makes the jump from "inaccurate" to "immoral," but he does. On this basis he can relate a civilization which he dislikes with the art he dislikes. Thus democracy, a form of government which went to pot after the death of Jefferson or thereabouts, would give rise to such degenerate poetry as *Leaves of Grass*.

"Most important poetry has been written by men over thirty," he announces as he approaches his thirtieth birthday. The Eliot-Pound war against the poetry of youth and what they call Romanticism is an attempt to show people that poets can sit at conference tables as well as the next man.

"The disease of the last century and a half has been 'abstraction.'" This is one of Pound's better directives, and makes him, in practice, a better poet than Eliot.

"There is no use talking to the ignorant about lies, for they have no criteria," says Pound, speaking of the hideous "lie" that poetry is made to entertain.

"The twenty-three students of Provençal and the seven people seriously interested in the technique and aesthetic of verse may communicate with me in person." No comment.

"I do not think the rhyme-aesthetic, *any* rhyme-aesthetic,

can ever do as much damage to English as that done by latinization in Milton's time and before." Pound rails against Milton's style but he himself invents a whole new polyglot on the analogy of the Chinese written character!

"A sound poetic training is nothing more than the science of being discontented." (!)

"Democracies have . . . always fallen, because humanity craves the outstanding personality." ". . . there should be definite subsidy of individual artists." These are platitudes, of interest only because of the connections Pound makes between the effect of art on history, the basic premise of his work, unprovable and in any case unexplored by Pound.

"The British public liked, has liked, likes and always will like all art, music, poetry, literature, glass engraving, sculpture, etc., in just such measure as it approaches the Tennysonian tone. It likes Shakespeare, or at least accepts him in just so far as he is 'Tennysonian.' " While intended to be a cute remark, this denotes Pound's contempt for nearly all things British. Speaking of America and her view of the artist he says: "America has not yet realized that never in history had one of her great men abandoned his citizenship out of shame." This is in praise of Henry James and is also an explanation of Eliot's contempt for his native land, as well as Pound's.

These few quotations I have taken from Eliot's edition of Pound's essays, the introduction to which announces Pound's critical supremacy in our time. I have not combed the essays for their worst but for their typical ideas, the ones that appear over and over again in the *Cantos*. On what ground Eliot considers his colleague a great critic it is hard to say. One of the most curious facts of modern poetry is that Pound has had followers such as Archibald Mac-

Leish, men who are in direct opposition to Pound's atrophied political and social views but who use Pound as a symbol of their own literary plight. In looking at such poets we must come to the dismal conclusion that they have been infected by the belief that the poet is the handmaid of History. It was this self-important attitude that led to the infamous Bollingen Prize award to Pound in 1948, when under the leadership of Eliot, a group of his followers presented a prize to Pound (at that time under indictment for treason) in the name of the Library of Congress. I was myself a member of that group and narrowly escaped being pressured into voting the prize to the *Pisan Cantos*, which among other things, contained Pound's wildest anti-American and racial outburst (by that time fused into the same thing). Eliot's criticism had by 1948 so far penetrated the critical mentality of his followers that they dared ignore the plain English in the poems for what they called their magnificent artistry. The insults in the *Cantos*, curiously, are quite clear English, so clear that much of it is given in dots and dashes, which every schoolboy would delight to fill in. One of the judges even informed me sanctimoniously that the award to Pound was a great act of piety, a remark which I am still puzzling about after all these years.

Everything I have thus far written about Pound I have written with a feeling of lassitude and distaste. I do not want to write about Pound; I do not think he is worth my time or yours, but as you can see, there is no escaping him even now. I hope that this essay will help remove Pound from the position of prominence in which Eliot has placed him. I am also aware that all Pound adherents will immediately discount everything I have said about Pound on the grounds that I am a Jew. This is not the place to deny such a motive: I am dealing with the poetry and prose of Pound and not with Pound's ethnological prejudices. It happens that these prejudices occupy a large place in all of Pound's writings and that they are inescapable.

Everything about Pound seems to sum itself up in the photograph that appeared in the papers a few months after his release from the prison asylum. There was Pound back at his home in Rapallo, arm outstretched in the Mussolini salute! Charlie Chaplin couldn't have been more true to life.

I would like to close with an apology and a summary.

The apology is for continuing to hammer away at Eliot. This is tiring, I know, but it is the crux of the matter. I will continue to deal with Eliot wherever he rears his critical influence, and that unfortunately is practically everywhere. I have no apologies for my remarks about Pound himself because I consider him an effect rather than a cause. Actually, I have been gentle with Pound; if you don't believe me, pick up one of his books of criticism, or his pamphlets on economics, or his broadcasts for the Axis, or the *Cantos* themselves: you will see how criticism works with no holds barred and with flowing introductions by the Possum himself, as Pound calls Eliot.

By way of summary: Pound and Eliot meet on the grounds of Education, if that is the right term. They begin as students, one of philosophy, the other of Romance literature. Both are poets and expatriates, anti-American and antidemocratic. The one becomes a monarchist, the other a Fascist. Both gravitate toward orthodoxy, the one toward a national church freighted with tradition; the other toward a ritualism of culture without religious sanction. Both construct theories of literature out of opposition to individualism, "freethinking" and what they label Romanticism. Both

center their attention throughout their careers not on poetry nor on belles-lettres nor on literature proper, but on
the function of these things in a controlled society. As late
as 1940 Pound and Eliot are worrying about the Ideal Curriculum to save civilization via the American university
student. They even try to enlist George Santayana, aged
about eighty at the time, to lend respectability to their
project. What project is this? Is it only Pound's poor old
booklist of Homer, Dante, Ovid, and Confucius, which he
thinks will save the world because it leaves out Virgil and
Milton? Very likely it is no more than that.

But to Pound the great curriculum is the *Cantos*, a manual for princes, as it were, a compendium of history and
culture morphology, as well as guidebook and a bibliography, as well as an exposé of Judaism and Christianity, the
New Deal and the vocabulary of the American Army.

Eliot's part in these schemes has been more frivolous and
irresponsible than Pound's, for Eliot knows better. With
Pound the scheme to save civilization with a poem is true-
blue evangelism and rather poetic to boot. Pound at bottom
shares that American optimism which, when it goes bad,
attempts to destroy itself in a wholesale negation of everything that can be tagged American. We recognize in Pound
that peculiar buffoonery of the frontier American, the intellectual dandyism of the tourist abroad, and the enormous
wasted energy of the crank.

How much of Pound's worst can we attribute to the sol-
emn encouragement of T. S. Eliot? How much to reckless
journalism? How much to criticism itself, which disdains so
haughtily to talk about anything except the poem *in vacuo*?

And yet under it all one feels a flow of sympathy, a kindliness, and a sorrow for Pound. He is such a storybook American, a stereotype, and a scapegoat certainly. To which I wish to add my epitaph:

> Here lies the master of the Modern School,
> A Great Poet and an even Greater Fool.

W. B. YEATS:
Trial by Culture

1
Modern Poetry as a Religion

A CLEVER FRENCH critic once said the nineteenth century began with the poetry of religion and ended with the religion of poetry. This saying sticks in my mind; it is one of those epigrams which would be fascinating for somebody to document and even write a book about. One can see the plan of strategy at once: the nineteenth century begins in France with the Romantic Catholicism of Chateaubriand and ends with the poet-priests Mallarmé and Valéry. It begins in England with the religious mysticism of Blake and Wordsworth and ends with the poetic high seriousness of Arnold, Pater, and Yeats. Even in America the equation works, with the poetic mysticism of Emerson and Whitman turning into the cultural priestliness of T. S. Eliot. Anywhere you look, in fact, it appears that "poetry of religion" resolves into the "religion of poetry."

The trouble with epigrams like the one I mentioned is not that they are false but that they are misleadingly true. And when we analyze such a saying, which is made in good faith certainly, we find that it is not an answer after all but only a new question to be solved. It is an elegant question, and it is hard to resist answering.

The question is whether modern poetry has metamorphosed into a religion. And the answer is: Yes. But then one must define both "modern poetry" and "religion," a tedious business. But like most poets, I have thought about this matter a great deal, and have what I think is a passable answer.

In the first place, "modern" poetry is not synonymous with contemporary poetry. Modern Poetry to my mind refers to a group of writings of about one decade, say 1915-25, and comprises all the works which we refer to mentally when we use the term Modern.

"Modern" poetry is a school, a literary philosophy, with definite and precise aims, all of which have been enunciated boldly by Pound, Eliot, Yeats, and their associates and followers. This philosophy, called "Classicism" in the textbooks, has its own poetics, its own esthetic, and its own world-view. That it has fathered a new pedagogy and a new criticism every sophomore is dismally aware. Modern Poetry is the official poetry of the twentieth century in all English-speaking countries. But properly speaking, it is not a religion; *it is a surrogate for religion.* If we could digest this extraordinary fact, we would have the key to Modern Poetry as a "religion."

Let us look at three or four of the chief Moderns ("Classicists") in relation to religion: Pound, Eliot, Yeats, and Stevens. Stevens sets poetry apart from and above religion. Yeats gingerly dissociates himself from religion, while pursuing occult and mystical studies. Pound comes no closer to religion than an Oriental ethics permits; Christianity he X's out. Eliot alone makes a specific religious commitment. But at the same time, all four poets observe one or another version of the central religious doctrine of Original Sin. It is at this point that Modern Poetry differentiates itself from "Romantic" poetry, whether by Whitman, Blake, Lawrence, or Williams. It is also at this point that Modern Poetry becomes anti-American and anti-twentieth century. All four poets adulate the Tradition, accepting the "fall" of man from Civilization, and an esthetic Ideal which is capable of reinstating the artist as the carrier of Civilization. All four are anti-Humanist (therefore politically pessimistic). All are anti-"Rationalist" (that is, anti-Science).

Modern Poetry (still using the famous decade as the point of reference) recognized the failure of Symbolism, the poetry-religion of the late nineteenth century. It is for this reason that Symbolism is used sparingly, if at all, by our quartet. We note that Eliot takes off not from Mallarmé but from Laforgue, for Symbolism is already bankrupt when Eliot picks it up. Pound denigrates the great Symbolists for the same reason. Yeats remains closer to Symbolism, as Stevens does in a more superficial manner, but neither is a "purist" in the Mallarméan sense. (It is curious to see Eliot use the line from Mallarmé about Poe in which it is said that Poe purified "the dialect of the tribe." Eliot has no admiration for Poe but pays his respects to dead Symbolism in that manner.)

Symbolism in the hands of the French lay close to a proper religion. The Symbolists believed that poetry through symbols apprehended the secret meanings of the world. Symbolism failed as a religion because of its divorce from the commonplace. A bona-fide religion must have a pyramidal base and not merely an apex. Symbolism finally led to its own defeat through its own idealism; it virtually parodied itself out of existence in such works as *A Rebours*, *Un Coup de Dés*, and even in the tragicomic life of Oscar Wilde. When the movement collapsed, poetry found itself once again on the street.

It has always struck me that Eliot's use of Laforgue is somewhat counterfeit. Laforgue did not mean what Eliot meant by banality, for instance. To Laforgue banality was a phase of the landscape. To Eliot it was a religious miasma of some kind, related to spleen, accidie and so forth. Nevertheless, our four poets all recognized the new attraction of the commonplace, the "antipoetic." Their object was not to exalt the commonplace but to explore it as a cultural site. Eliot's empty lots and sputtering lamps all point to the "fall" from civilization. Yeats has it in a perfect epigram in which God takes (not Eve) the spinning jenny out of the side of—Locke. No French Symbolist would have come that close to the history book. Yet Symbolism was a profitable failure for the Moderns. Pound knew that poetry must, according to his lights, descend to history and even politics, and he taught Yeats this message. Eliot's religion is, in fact, a *descent* from Symbolism to a lower plane of poetic endeavor; for religion in Eliot is just another name for Civilization.

Modern poetry claims a moral prerogative which is in effect a religious preorgative; but it does not claim it in the name of religion. Modern poetry claims a moral prerogative in the name of Culture. It is this Culture which is the substitute for religion and which is the cement of Modern Poetry.

There is, of course, no secret about the aims of the culture religion instituted by Modern Poetry. This poetry began, to be sure, as a poetic movement, or a series of poetic movements, such as a new "Classicism," Imagism and so on; it then became a theoretical educational revolt, the more conservative motto of which was to "correct taste." The correction of taste led to a full-scale re-examination of history. It is very important to remember that with Pound, Yeats, and Eliot it is not the history of poetry or of literature that matters, but history itself. Poetry is actually secondary to anthropology and sociology in the writings of Eliot and Pound. Yeats alone tried to escape from this culture revolution with his head; but his own later poetry is much contaminated with cultural theorizing and historical prophecy.

In what seems an innocuous statement in *Notes Toward a Definition of Culture* Eliot says: "The dominant force in creating a common culture between people each of which has its distinct culture is religion." Even so, he spreads his definition of this culture to include the "legacy of Greece, Rome, and Israel." In other words, it is not simply Christianity which the poet must transmit, according to Eliot, but the whole cultural complex of the Western past. This Culture, supposedly derived from religion, is larger than the religion and subsumes it. Culture is therefore the chief business of the poet, his religion in fact.

It is my opinion that Eliot scamps the relationship between Culture and religion, despite his own churchly affiliations. It would be unfair and pointless to accuse Eliot of exploiting religion for the purposes of literary ambition, but even a casual look at Eliot's religious view reveals that it is much more eclectic than the European tradition calls for. The chief object seems to be not religion for its own sake, or even for Eliot's sake, but for the sake of civilization, for Culture. Eliot approaches mysticism from time to time but retreats hurriedly into metaphysics. He quotes the mystics but is not on good terms with them. The mystics are too original, unmanageable, and "home-made," as he says of Blake. Yeats, however, is a better example of the Modernist withdrawal from religion into some cultural substitute. In Yeats' case it is magic and occultism which are the cultural substitues for mysticism.

Yeats begins an essay on magic with these words: "I believe in the practice and philosophy of what we have agreed to call magic, in what I must call the evocation of spirits, though I do not know what they are; in the power of creating magical illusions, in the visions of truth in the depths of the mind when the eyes are closed . . ." And in three doctrines, he adds: that many minds can flow into one another and reveal a single mind; that our memories are part of the Great Memory of Nature herself; and that this great mind and great memory can be evoked by symbols.

This credo represents only one of the phases of Yeats' occultism, but it is one which he never rose above. Yeats' use of magic is closer to primitive science than it is to mysticism. There is in all spiritualist and theosophical activity an element of spite, based on the envy of modern science and its triumphs. Even Blake's cry that "Sir Francis

Bacon is a Liar" partakes of this bitterness against rational science. Blake, however, appears to be more of a true mystic or gnostic than Yeats. Mysticism and magic are two different things, and it is on the latter inferior level that Yeats rested.

We should remember that in the great decade of Modernism, magic in such forms as spiritualism and theosophy reached its greatest popularity among artists and intellectuals; and that it was in fact an acceptable convention of the poet. Eliot's use of the fortuneteller in *The Waste Land* is a very *topical* allusion. Rilke himself indulged in spiritualism, even though he was aware that greater powers lay in himself than outside him. (". . . my greatest, my most passionate wonderment lies with my own achievement . . . and with certain movements in Nature rather than with any mediumistic occurrences, however much they have stirred me on occasion.") But Rilke knew enough as an artist not to enter the lists against Science or to fight battles for Culture. Neither Blake nor Yeats made a distinction between mysticism proper and magic. We gather from this fact that both poets were exploring the possibilities of a cultural *mystique*, a *mystique* lying outside religion and outside modern rationalist science.

I take it that the failure to distinguish between mysticism and magic in Modern Poetry is deliberate and strategic. Religion is not a primary force in modern civilization and some substitute for religion must be found. So reasoned the Pounds and Eliots and Yeatses and Stevenses. Mysticism proper was therefore suspect; it lay at the very heart of religions. The mystical must therefore be intellectualized in some manner. Stevens took the most tentative path, that of employing the minor techniques of Symbolism and doodling with a theory of the Imagination. Imagination is the Providence in this version of the culture religion of the Moderns. It is probably because of Stevens' relatively perfunctory view of a total Culture poetry that he was not "recognized" by Eliot, Pound, and Yeats. "The poet is the priest of the invisible," says Stevens in his notebook, but he goes no further. To do so would be to encourage the sweeping Romantic outlook of, say, Shelley. We cannot understand the anti-Romantic bitterness of Stevens without taking into account his fear of mysticism proper.

Yeats' scrambling of mystics, alchemists, theosophists, neo-Platonists, and so forth, is his attempt to steer clear of both religion and philosophy. "Science" of course is his avowed enemy, but so are clericalism and orderly philosophical speculation. Occultism was to Yeats what anthropology was to Eliot—an instrument for fashioning the culture religion. It is commonly said about Yeats' interest in the magical that it helped him perceive his poetic images, or something equally silly. Yeats himself is responsible for that interpretation of *A Vision* and of most of his culture poetry. In reality, *A Vision*, like the notes to *The Waste Land*, the *Notes Toward a Definition of Culture*, or Pound's book on *Kulchur*, is a highly programmatic, even political work. The occultism suddenly jells into a practical psychology and ethics, providing not "metaphors for poetry" as the spirits whispered to Yeats, but a full-scale commentary on socialism, democracy, famous periods of history, and great men. The object of the book is to help create the culture climate in which the poet can again take up the robes of authority, dethroning rationalism and clericalism. Everyone who loves poetry forgives Yeats this book, although it would be foolhardy to overlook its dangers.

All Modernists, including Eliot, agree unanimously that Pound is the father of the Culture religion of Modern Poetry. And Pound certainly makes no bones about it. He proposes to lay down a "system" and does. It is a way of life, an *Anschauung* dealing with man and with nature. God, significantly, does not come into the system. Pound's anti-Semitism and anti-Christianity, by the way, are his version of the poetic liberation from religion. (I should think that Catholics would complain more about the *Cantos* than the Jews.) Pound is almost charming in his arrogance about the founding of the culture religion—"these are notes for a totalitarian treatise and I am in fact considering the New Learning or the New Paideuma . . ." What this New Learning is everyone knows by now: a full-scale culture revolution in which the end justifies any means at hand, "ideas in action," and the rest. But in the long run Pound turns out to be the weakest link in the cultural chain. Eliot's commitment to him, Yeats' acknowledgments and the tacit approval of the New Critics (students of the New Paideuma) all throw a strong light on their own motivations as culture religionists. It does no good to brush Pound off as old Assen Poop, as Williams calls him; he remains the figurehead of the religion. Eliot does not miss an opportunity to defend him in every phase.

Eliot, however, is the key to the religion of culture. Eliot is the only Modern of any consequence who decided to take the risk of religion. Pound was furious; it was almost as much of a betrayal as Jung's branching away from Freud. I do not pretend to know the ins and outs of Eliot's spiritual biography, for it is a labyrinth. But the most interesting thing about it is that it appears to be a highly suspect commitment and may be no more than an intellectual stratagem to capture confidence. When Pound calls him the Reverend Eliot he is very nearly letting the cat out of the bag; evidently Pound refuses to believe that his prize pupil has really turned respectable.

Eliot's sanction of religion is a parallel to Pound's cultural sanction of Fascism. Religion to Eliot is primarily a social question, and not a *mystique*. It is a dismal crutch for a society he detests. In Eliot's words: "As political philosophy derives its sanction from ethics, and ethics from the truth of religion, it is only by returning to the eternal source of truth that we can hope for any social organization which will not, to its ultimate destruction, ignore some essential aspect of reality." The term *democracy* (says Eliot) "does not contain enough positive content to stand alone against the forces that you dislike . . ." Notice how easily democracy becomes almost incompatible with God in this little recital.

Eliot's cultural development may be sketched in this manner. He begins as an uneasy Symbolist; he knows something is wrong with Symbolism, and that it has not worked. He approaches religion in the typical manner, by negating it (at a time when negating religion is an anachronism). The negation is also typical in its dual anti-Catholicism and anti-Semitism. He then explores the possibility of a relativistic mythology, thus flattering the more rationalistic of the mythologists and anthropologists, such as Sir James Frazer. This is the famous "mythic method" and it is so overwhelmingly a *succès d'estime* that Eliot is suddenly elevated over and above Yeats and Pound and becomes the living incarnation of Modernism. He has now earned the authority to proceed on his own, and it is at this juncture that he makes his extraordinary conversion to the Church of England. It is extraordinary in every respect: the last decision anyone would expect from a twentieth-century American intellectual and poet. Now, with religious authority behind him, and with historical tradition at his side, he begins the elaboration, not of his poetry but of his criticism. He even seems to defend Humanism, though it is a brand which Eliot calls *pure* Humanism.

By fixing his spiritual authorities and antecedents, his literary references and forebears, he manages to rewrite English poetic history, resurrecting the forgotten Metaphysical poets, burying the Romantics and Victorians, removing Walt Whitman to a footnote, and so forth. Finally, departing from Church of England orthodoxy, he scans the mystics. Any suspicion of parochialism is therewith removed, and he is now free to take up his real job of pronouncing about world culture. He becomes in his own lifetime a culture god. This is not the place to delve into the school of literary criticism of which Eliot is godfather. The New Criticism is one of the more noxious by-products of the culture religion and it is too large a subject for me.

Before the coup d'état of the culture religion, readers of poetry tended to think of it as a "secular" art, or a refined amusement, an expression of the national or of the individual psyche. That is, there was at the beginning of the twentieth century very little doctrinaire agreement about the nature and the uses of poetry. Eliot began by explaining the uses of poetry and the uses of criticism, as Pound had begun with his great blast about a total cultural upset. But by 1925, poetry was no longer "secular"; neither was it "religious," nor philosophical, nor rationalist. It had found a way to compete with every other form of intellectual activity: by pronouncing a curse on the century and everything it stood for; by plunging back into the past and "making it new"; by removing the arts from the people and returning them to the classroom; by promulgating new theories of the Imagination, of the State, of the "sensibilities," and of the *Spiritus Mundi*. Systematically this culture faction eradicated as best it could any influence by D. H. Lawrence, William Carlos Williams, Blake, Walt Whitman, and all other "Romantics" and humanists. It ignored the great poetry being written on the Continent by Lorca, by Rilke, by Cavafy (a much finer "traditionalist" than either Eliot or Pound).

It would be interesting to speculate upon the narrowly "Anglo-Saxon" character of this religion of culture, but I had best not go into that. Suffice it to say that this religion has all the earmarks of puritanism at its worst. Its bitterness, its sense of exile from one or another homeland or paradise, its strong theocratic flavor, its sanctimoniousness, its hatred of spontaneity, originality, and freedom, its insistence on orthodoxy—these are all symptoms of the puritanical hatred of poetry and its cynical abuse for purposes of power.

II

Only a few years before his death Yeats paid a visit to Ezra Pound at his home for the purpose of seeking advice about a play he was writing. Yeats had been troubled by loss of creative power and he thought he would see what Ezra would have to offer as an oracle. The anecdote has been repeated now and then for its anecdote value, but no one seems to have taken it more seriously. But the fact that Yeats went to the trouble to print the story as a note to one of his books signifies, to me at least, that Yeats was finally washing his hands of the American panjandrum. Here are Yeats' own words:

A year ago I found that I had written no verse for two years; I had never been so long barren; I had nothing in my head, and there used to be more than I could write. Perhaps Coole Park where I had escaped from politics, from all that Dublin talked of, when it was shut, shut me out from my theme; or did the subconscious drama that was my imaginative life end with its owner? but it was more likely that I had grown too old for poetry. I decided to force myself to write, then take advice. In 'At Parnell's Funeral' I rhymed passages from a lecture I had given in America; a poem upon Mount Meru came spontaneously, but philosophy is a dangerous theme; then I was barren again. I wrote the prose dialogue of *The King of the Great Clock Tower*, that I might be forced to make lyrics for its imaginary people. When I had written all but the last lyric I went a considerable journey, partly to get the advice of a poet not of my school who would, as he did some years ago, say what he thought. I asked him to dine, tried to get his attention. 'I am in my sixty-ninth year,' I said, 'probably I should stop writing verse. I want your opinion upon some verse I have written lately.' I had hoped he would ask me to read it but he would not speak of art, or of literature, or of anything related to them. I had, however, been talking to his latest disciple and knew that his opinions had not changed: Phidias had corrupted sculpture, we had nothing of true Greece but Nike dug up from the foundations of the Parthenon, and that corruption ran through all our art: Shakespeare and Dante had corrupted literature, Shakespeare by his too abounding sentiment, Dante by his compromise with the church.

He said, apropos of nothing 'Arthur Balfour was a scoundrel,' and from that on would talk of nothing but politics. All the other modern statesmen were more or less scoundrels except 'Mussolini and that hysterical imitator of his, Hitler.' . . . He urged me to read the works of Captain Douglas who alone knew what caused our suffering. He took my manuscript and went away denouncing Dublin as 'a reactionary hole' because I had said that I was re-reading Shakespeare, would go on to Chaucer, and found all that I wanted of modern life in 'detection and the wild west.' Next day his judgment came and that in a single word 'Putrid.'

Then I took my verses to a friend of my own school and this friend said, 'Go on just like that. Plays like *The Great Clock Tower* always seem unfinished but that is no matter. Begin plays without knowing how to end them for the sake of the lyrics. I once wrote a play and after I had filled it with lyrics abolished the play.' Then I brought my work to two painters and a poet until I was like Panurge consulting oracles as to whether he should get married and rejecting all that did not confirm his own desire.

Now this seems a lengthy and uncalled-for footnote from the poet who in 1935, when this was penned, was probably the most revered living poet in the world. We notice the graciousness of Yeats' manner even in this footnote and his sly Swiftian style ("Then I brought my work to two painters and a poet until I was like Panurge . . .") but underneath the story and the style we are aware that Yeats' blood is boiling. Because of the little insult or because of the long, slightly unsavory association with Pound? It is hard to tell. But the fact that Yeats ever wandered into the Pound orbit at all is one of the more disturbing facts of modernism.

Yeats takes his place along with Eliot and Pound as the third of the triumvirate of Modern Poets who have made the Modern canon respectable. But Yeats was never happy in the company of either. He had a barely concealed contempt for Eliot and he used Pound as a kind of antithesis of his own being. But the fact remains that Yeats is part of the club.

People generally agree that there are several Yeatses: the youthful romantic poet of love and the Celtic twilight, the Yeats of Ireland reborn, the Yeats of the Hermetic societies, and finally the Yeats of world culture. These appellations are grotesquely crude but in effect they give the well-known departments of Yeats' writings. And they are somewhat related. The love poems are also folklore poems to a degree; the patriotic poems of the Irish revolution are also part of the folklore idealism and part of the esoteric explorations simultaneously; and the Culture poems are the final effort to project the subjective personal Yeats, the national Yeats, and the magus or alchemist Yeats into the figure of the seer of history. It is in this final phase that Yeats writes his occult book *A Vision*, in which he contends that he will adapt the symbolic and mythological techniques of Swedenborg and Blake to an interpretation of history, "historical movements and actual men and women." So here is Yeats acting precisely like Pound and Eliot. Yeats is a poet of true genius and not a mere opportunist, but he's off to make a sociological ass of himself all the same. And with much the same results as we have already seen.

I would like to run through one poem of each of Yeats' main phases as a way of seeing him as a whole. If my observations are right, this bird's-eye view of Yeats should lead us to a complete sketch of him. In any case, Yeats cannot suffer from critical myopia on my part; he is too good a poet; he even escaped the condemnations of Ezra Pound. But did he escape the blandishments of the culture religion? That is the question.

Here is the young poet nostalgically in love with the old

Celtic Ireland before he knows much about the mysteries of the Irish past. He takes a song he has heard a few lines of from a peasant woman, and he rewrites it. The poem is the famous and pretty song "Down by the Salley Gardens" and was printed as long ago as 1889. The book it appeared in contained several pieces of the same exquisite lyric quality which were to make Yeats famous long before the intellectuals arrived on the scene. What Yeats did with the poem was typical of his gift for changing the sense of a line by using an unusual sense of a word. The original song read "Down by my Sally's garden my love and I did meet"—this version evidently being something of a bawdy song. Yeats changes the proper name Sally to the word salley, meaning willow.

> Down by the salley gardens my love and I did meet;
> She passed the salley gardens with little snow-white feet.
> She bid me take life easy, as the leaves grow on the tree;
> But I, being young and foolish, with her would not agree.
> In a field by the river my love and I did stand,
> And on my leaning shoulder she laid her snow-white hand.
> She bid me take life easy, as the grass grows on the weirs;
> But I was young and foolish, and now am full of tears.

What Yeats was doing here besides writing a lovely song was to find and modernize some of that poetry of the past of his country which had evidently died out. This was Yeats' first concern as a poet and a true one: to discover his poetic identity. Forty years later he was using the identical

technique to write the modern poem " 'I Am of Ireland,' "
which is one of the best of all Yeats' poems. Now here, too,
Yeats has had his material given to him, he says, by someone else. He himself never went to the trouble to immerse
himself in the old languages, or that is my understanding.
And I dare say there is a clue here to all of Yeats' later
difficulties, obscurities, and pretenses, namely, that he
never gave himself to that Ireland at all and was afraid of
it. The Irish poets take their pride in Yeats but they know
after all that he is Anglo-Irish in letters. Yeats virtually
exiled himself to England off and on throughout his life.
When we remember that Yeats' life spans the high moments of the struggle for independence and that Yeats
wished to be the spokesman for Ireland, we have the making of a rich conflict. The biographers have handled these
questions well; but I see in Yeats' English-Irish ambiva-
lence the thing that made him a prey for the Pounds and
the Eliots, men without a country. Most important of all,
Yeats never developed completely away from his early
Irish "Celtic" romanticism. It was still the Holy Ireland,
not of St. Patrick but of the pre-Christian religions. Yeats,
of course, spent almost as much time combating the official
religions of Ireland as he did writing poetry. This is the
poem " 'I Am of Ireland' ":

> *'I am of Ireland,*
> *And the Holy Land of Ireland,*
> *And time runs on,' cried she.*
> *'Come out of charity,*
> *Come dance with me in Ireland.'*

> One man, one man alone
> In that outlandish gear,
> One solitary man

Of all that rambled there
Had turned his stately head.
'That is a long way off,
And time runs,' he said,
'And the night grows rough.'

'I am of Ireland,
And the Holy Land of Ireland,
And time runs on,' cried she.
'Come out of charity,
And dance with me in Ireland.'

'The fiddlers are all thumbs,
Or the fiddle-string accursed,
The drums and the kettledrums
And the trumpets all are burst,
And the trombone,' cried he,
'The trumpet and trombone,'
And cocked a malicious eye,
'But time runs on, runs on.'

'I am of Ireland,
And the Holy Land of Ireland,
And time runs on,' cried she.
'Come out of charity,
And dance with me in Ireland.'

Yeats puts a note on this poem telling that he heard a bit of it from someone who told him it was from a fourteenth-century Irish dance song. One would assume as a certainty that Yeats would have at some time made a mad dash for all that old Irish literature which, we are told, is still unexplored, still untranslated, and which only the post-Yeats poets are beginning to get at. Why did Yeats avoid it and yet saturate himself in spiritualism, theosophy, Neo-Platonic cabalism, and finally cyclical theories of history? I think the answer is apparent. Ireland wasn't big enough for Yeats, even mythologically. But in " 'I Am of Ireland' " he is beckoned to come "out of charity," too late, and can do no more than cock a malicious eye. The voice of pagan Ireland never held Yeats the way the poetry and mysticism of Bengal held his friend Tagore. The difference between them is the most vital one possible between two such similar poets: Tagore accepted the mystical content of the folk poetry of Bengal; Yeats rejected the mystical content of the Irish tradition while hanging on to the superficies of the "supernatural" (ghosts on the stair, the wee folk, ectoplasm, etc). There is a lifelong silliness about Yeats' preoccupation with magic which he himself contributed to by not ever quite believing in it; and in the end it weakened his whole structure of thought. Not that the esotericism is inherently weak —it is not; it is one of the most powerful elements of literature, though we are seldom led to literature via the occult. But Yeats dallied with it; he was hangdog about it, or "literary" or affected, as the case might be. He was expelled from one Hermetic society for breaking the discipline; he was rather cavalier about the leaders of magic of his day, though he was in it up to his ears.

I seem to be getting ahead of the early Yeats in mentioning the Yeats of " 'I Am of Ireland,' " but these phases of Yeats do overlap and recur. Here next is Yeats of the Irish revolution, which is his best phase of all. Possibly a fourth of all Yeats' poems deal with modern Irish history and nearly all of them are of the highest caliber of that type of topical verse which almost invariably defeats itself in time. What is it about Yeats' patriotic poems that keeps them readable long after so much other "political" poetry has died? The best answer is that Yeats wrote them; second, that they are not patriotic but that they deal with a more or less imaginary Ireland, Yeats' Ireland. This is an Ireland compounded of Irish mythological heroes, national heroes, literary and political, and personal acquaintances; Yeats' Irish poems all have a closely personal quality; an intimacy which is born of a common cause. And Yeats always managed to extract the dramatic and the heroic from the scene; he was a dramatist and a hero in his Irish political poems, inside and outside the scene at once. Yeats sees the poetry of the rebirth of all Ireland through the firing of a few shots. The most trivial and meaningless persons have become transformed through the Easter Rebellion and the Civil War; Ireland itself becomes a symbol of tragic and noble power in the modern world. Here is a piece of the stirring poem "Easter 1916":

> Too long a sacrifice
> Can make a stone of the heart.
> O when may it suffice?
> That is Heaven's part, our part
> To murmur name upon name,
> As a mother names her child
> When sleep at last has come
> On limbs that had run wild.
> What is it but nightfall?
> No, no, not night but death;
> Was it needless death after all?
> For England may keep faith
> For all that is done and said.
> We know their dream; enough
> To know they dreamed and are dead;
> And what if excess of love

Bewildered them till they died?
I write it out in a verse—
MacDonagh and MacBride
And Connolly and Pearse
Now and in time to be,
Wherever green is worn,
Are changed, changed utterly:
A terrible beauty is born.

I doubt whether any other poet of the English tongue in the twentieth century could have pulled out all those stops without making a mockery of the poem: everything is in it, from mother and childhood to God, England, Ireland, and the names of four of the revolutionaries who were shot by the English, including MacBride who took Yeats' beloved Maud Gonne away from him. But instead of a shambles we get a ringing elegy and something like a battlecry. Yeats has managed to put together a vision of the old listless Ireland and the new, with the sixteen dead men as the metamorphosis and himself as the seer; a wonderful performance.

So far so good. But when Ireland has become a contemporary reality and even a national literature has been brought into being, largely through the efforts of Yeats, when the cause is won (or as much won as it can be), what then? Was Yeats ever really concerned about the political Ireland as much as he was about the "magical" symbolic Ireland?

There is something indeterminate about Yeats' interest in magic and the occult. That he belonged to various Hermetic and spiritualist and theosophical societies off and on from early youth we know. What we are not sure of is whether Yeats was a believer or an experimenter. I am inclined to think the latter. His entire performance as a magus from beginning to end smacks of the literary. The interest itself seems to have grown from the reaction against the modern commonplace world, and is a plunge back into that age when science and alchemy were still undifferentiated. Yeats' distaste for modern scientific progress was another thing that drew him toward Pound. Yeats also shares with Pound a distaste for religions of any description, but he takes religion seriously enough to want to be heretical about it. In the poem "The Magi," Yeats shows the Wise Men slipping away from the revelation of Christ and the "turbulence" of the crucifixion to the dream of a new rebirth. In this poem, too, one can see the rather violent sexual preoccupation of Yeats.

> Now as at all times I can see in the mind's eye,
> In their stiff, painted clothes, the pale unsatisfied ones
> Appear and disappear in the blue depth of the sky
> With all their ancient faces like rain-beaten stones,
> And all their helms of silver hovering side by side,
> And all their eyes still fixed, hoping to find once more,
> Being by Calvary's turbulence unsatisfied,
> The uncontrollable mystery on the bestial floor.

So with all Yeats' poems that touch the religions: he will preserve the symbol, if he can, but not the form of a belief. It is really striking the way he skims over the surface of religion:

> I asked if I should pray,
> But the Brahmin said,
> 'Pray for nothing, say
> Every night in bed,
> "I have been a king,

I have been a slave,
Nor is there anything,
Fool, rascal, knave,
That I have not been . . ."

For an oversimplification of Hindu homiletics this goes pretty far, unless we keep in mind that Yeats is probably not even thinking about religion but about the kind of reincarnation which can be used to explain historical data. Everything in Yeats' esoteric activities points to a search for a plan of history. As a religious agnostic and poet he must gravitate toward one or another system of symbols to explain cause and fate, personality, great events, creativity, himself in the cosmos, and so on. I find Yeats' solutions always charming and brilliant and disappointing; he seems unnecessarily driven to patent a system; his system after all is not much more convincing than Pound's view of history.

Yeats is a modern "Classicist" by virtue of his emphasis on the civilized and the aristocratic. Civilization is the touchstone. He defines it: "A civilization is a struggle to keep self-control, and in this it is like some great tragic person, some Niobe who must display an almost superhuman will or the cry will not touch our sympathy. The loss of control over thought comes towards the end; first a sinking in upon the moral being, then the last surrender, the irrational cry, revelation—the scream of Juno's peacock." Yeats' fear of the mystical revelation weakens him as a poet; and the irrational and the popular become identified in his mind, as in the mind of Pound, with demagoguery, the decline of the West and what not. What he has to say about his extraordinary sonnet "Leda and the Swan," though it may be one of those critical irrelevancies which we are accustomed to nowadays, signifies that Yeats had very little inspiration for poetry outside his historical spec- uations. These are his words: "I wrote 'Leda and the Swan' because the editor of a political review asked me for a poem. I thought, 'After the individualist, demagogic move- ment, founded by Hobbes and popularized by the Ency- clopedists and the French Revolution, we have a soil so exhausted that it cannot grow that crop again for centuries.' Then I thought, 'Nothing is now possible but some move- ment from above preceded by some violent annunciation.' My fancy began to play with Leda and the Swan for meta- phor, and I began this poem; but as I wrote, bird and lady took such possession of the scene that all politics went out of it . . ." The rape of Leda by Zeus in the guise of a swan resulted in the birth of Helen, the symbol of perfected fe- male beauty and the cause of war. Yeats seems to be asking for some violent annunciation or rape, "from above," as he puts it.

> A sudden blow: the great wings beating still
> Above the staggering girl, her thighs caressed
> By the dark webs, her nape caught in his bill,
> He holds her helpless breast upon his breast.
>
> How can those terrified vague fingers push
> The feathered glory from her loosening thighs?
> And how can body, laid in that white rush,
> But feel the strange heart beating where it lies?
>
> A shudder in the loins engenders there
> The broken wall, the burning roof and tower
> And Agamemnon dead.
>   Being so caught up,
> So mastered by the brute blood of the air,

Did she put on his knowledge with his power
Before the indifferent beak could let her drop?

Lucky for this poem, Hobbes and the Encyclopedists and the French Revolution are nowhere to be seen. But Yeats uses the poem as the frontispiece to one of the sections of *A Vision*, the work said to have been dictated to his wife by spirits and taken down by her in a species of automatic writing. *A Vision* is a "system of thought," in Yeats' words, that would leave his imagination free to create as it chose and yet make all that it created part of the universal history. All history is fixed upon a lunar wheel; the individual human personality as well as historic and cosmic events can be plotted according to the twenty-eight phases of the moon. The wheel, its phases, and the gyrations of great and small events make an understanding of past civilizations and their mythologies possible; more important, in the case of Yeats, they make prophecy possible. Yeats took a dim view of the chances of our scientific civilization to survive; he envisioned a new terror abroad in the world which he likened to the Antichrist. He wrote poems to that effect but his prose from *A Vision* is even more explicit; this was written in 1925:

It is possible that the ever-increasing separation from the community as a whole of the cultivated classes, their increasing certainty, and that falling-in-two of the human mind which I have seen in certain works of art is preparation. During the period said to commence in 1927, with the 11th gyre, must arise a form of philosophy, which will become religious and ethical in the 12th gyre and be in all things opposite of that vast plaster Herculean image, final *primary* thought. It will be concrete in expression, establish itself by immediate experience, seek no general agreement, make little of God or any exterior unity . . . Men will no longer separate the idea of God from that of human genius, human productivity in all its forms.

Unlike Christianity which had for its first Roman teachers cobblers and weavers, this thought must find expression among those that are most subtle, most rich in memory; that Gainsborough face floats up; among the learned—every sort of learned—among the rich—every sort of rich—among men of rank—every sort of rank—and the best of those that express it will be given power, less because of that they promise than of that they seem and are. This much can be thought because it is the reversal of what we know, but those kindreds once formed must obey irrational force and so create hitherto unknown experience, or that which is incredible . . . it may grow a fanaticism and a terror, and at its first outsetting oppress the ignorant—even the innocent—as Christianity oppressed the wise . . .

This passage is laden with obscurities, of course, but it is clear that Yeats envisions a turn of the wheel of history which will mean the end of our era. "A decadence will descend" he says; and the new era will bring its stream of irrational force. "I imagine new races . . . each with its own Daimon or ancestral hero . . . history grown symbolic, the biography changed into a myth . . ."

In all of which I detect overtones from T. E. Hulme, Eliot, and especially Pound. But primarily the theme is Yeats' own and goes back to his earliest years when he dreamed romantically of a world made perfect for love. As Yeats matures, this passion for the earthly paradise expresses itself in the extreme symbol of Byzantium. Yeats looked upon Byzantium as next to Heaven. "I think if I could be given a month of Antiquity and leave to spend it where I chose, I would spend it in Byzantium a little before

Justinian opened St. Sophia and closed the Academy of Plato . . . I think that in early Byzantium and maybe never before or since in recorded history, religious, esthetic, and practical life were one . . ." This then is the ideal, that absolute stylization and depersonalization of experience which we associate with the Byzantine mosaic but of which Yeats sang so fervently:

> O sages standing in God's holy fire . . .

To the aged Yeats, the cold fire of the impersonal mosaic was an answer to the unquenchable passions of the flesh. In fact, what keeps Yeats lively and interesting to the very end of his poetic life is this intensity of conflict between body and soul which he could never resolve. The jaunty Crazy Jane poems are a record of that conflict also. Yeats was a Puritan as much as Eliot and Pound; in the Irish Senate he once made a speech defending the divorce laws. Later he felt guilty about it—it was hardly the kind of thing to come from the leading poet of the land—but there you have it. In Byzantium everything is fused together, in Yeats' fine phrase, "into the artifice of eternity."

Altogether, Yeats poses one of the central questions of the modern Classical poet, of which he is one of the gods. That question is also Eliot's question and Pound's question, namely, what is the position of the poet vis-à-vis history? From my point of view, I consider the question unreal and not worth the asking. If the self-consciousness of this attitude and the pompousness of it did not utterly defeat Yeats, that can only be because his genius never completely deserted him even throughout his intellectual soul-searchings. But it is my opinion that Yeats will always remain pretty much a poet of his time, because of his commitment to the historical role. The burlesque magus and spiritualist do not add to his stature; they detract from it; all the pronouncements about history and historical types are so much doodling in the margins of his mind. The poetry itself becomes affected; while the idiom steadily increases in subtlety and beauty, the feeling becomes more violent, turning against himself. Yeats could not make peace with age in any aspect; his central image becomes that of "this caricature," decrepit age tied to him "as to a dog's tail." Even that simple wisdom of reconciliation with age is denied him. That Byzantium symbol is a desperate remedy, no remedy at all. That vision of history is hardly a great vision after all but more of a travesty of the great cosmic systems of emanation which he had borrowed from the Hindus and the Neo-Platonists. The flaw in Yeats is his narrowly conceived idea of civilization; Yeats is quite eighteenth century in the long run. He loved Blake, but did he really learn anything from Blake? It appears not. There is no marriage of heaven and hell in William Butler Yeats—save in Byzantium. Think of the Byzantine mosaic and then try to set beside it the flowing angelography of Blake's pen. There is a complete divergence of imaginations.

The key with Yeats is the word "civilization," the alpha and omega of his culture philosophy. And civilization apparently is—Byzantium. Little wonder that Yeats, a scant generation after his death, is considered a master craftsman of the poem, and nothing else.

The Retreat of W. H. Auden

I DOUBT WHETHER any man living has read everything published by W. H. Auden, probably the most prolific poet-critic of the twentieth century. Not only the quantity but the range of Auden's writing is the most extensive of any contemporary poet's; what is more remarkable, everything he writes is readable. The luxuriance of the Auden bibliography recalls the Victorians, who provided not only the high literature of their time but the popular literature as well. Auden, however, is not popular, any more than T. S. Eliot is popular. Like all Moderns he has eschewed popularity.

The Victorian analogy is a fair one. There is in the quantitative Auden as in the ideal Auden a comfortable paternalism and a sense of cultural responsibility which dates back to the days of Herbert Spencer, Thomas Huxley, and the great novelists who wrote—who must have written—eight hours a day for decades. There is a pervasive and convincing pastness about Auden's writing which always leaves me wondering whether he really is a twentieth-century man or one of those creatures flung over the time barrier by a nineteenth-century time machine.

Auden is probably the most *English* poet since Thomas Hardy died in 1928, the year Auden published his first book. Internationalism has never sat on him well; nor has Americanism (Auden has camped out in America for many years); he is indeed the chief ornament of English letters in the twentieth century. But English poetry is to this day largely "nineteenth century" compared with American or French or Spanish poetry.

In calling these remarks the *retreat* of W. H. Auden I am not referring to the fact that Auden was in his early days a Marxist and later became a poet more involved with theology than with anything else. The fact is that Auden was never as much interested in the social revolution or in religion as he was in psychology; it is Auden's fascination with psychological behavior that makes him readable, charming, and, it may be, lasting. The retreat of Auden is the retreat from poetry to psychology, an almost total sacrifice of the poetic motive to the rational motive. We shall see that Auden is as great a schoolmaster as Pound, though a much more kindly one. Auden is truly a civilized, rational poet (if these are not contradictions in terms), the last of a long line of illustrious "new-classicists" and the father of contemporary poetic style. There is in him nothing of the visionary or the seer, everything of the conversationalist and the classroom wit. Auden, moreover, is an intellectual through and through, and poetry to him is a species of talk. The retreat of poetry into talk, which Auden has made a respectable poetics, is part of the canon of Modernism.

There is no point, in a brief essay of this kind, in trying to sort Auden out into phases, styles, genres, categories of ideas, allegiances, and what not. My aim rather is to determine to what extent Auden takes poetry seriously; and if he does not, what view of it he does hold.

There is one minor matter I would like to dispose of first, namely, the relationship between Auden's earlier social revolutionary poetry and his eventual theological poetry. Readers of Auden have been greatly disturbed (*a*) by the conversion of Auden from humanism to religion, and (*b*) by the fact that Auden has tried to rewrite much of his early humanistic verse to make it conform with his later views. The question of rewriting one's early poems to make them sound ideologically like the later ones is such a curious question of literary morals that we had better not try to deal with it at all. This "police" question has been dealt with in J. W. Beach's book, *The Making of the Auden Canon.* The question of Auden's religious conversion from a youthful revolutionary fervor, on the other hand, is a common literary question, one we meet in poets who live through more than one phase of history. I do not find this question very important, however; a poet's politics and his religion are pretty much his own affair, unless they actually do run afoul of the law, as Pound's did. Auden, as far as this reader knows, has never broken any laws, he is thoroughly law-abiding and is in fact a great respecter of the law, in poetry and elsewhere. A poet's religious and political attitudes are of no concern to the reader unless they become part of the poetry.

From the beginning Auden adopted a position about religion and about history; and this meant a personal encoun-
ter with Eliot. Auden was too much the scholar and the
gentleman ever to be other than respectful to Eliot, but he
presented himself as the chief member of the loyal opposition. By the time Auden began to publish, in the early
thirties, Eliot was so deeply entrenched in his self-styled
Classical revetment that it had become heroic for the
young to adopt the pose of the Romantic poet. One could
not be a simple Romantic like Rupert Brooke or Shelley
(whom Auden always goes out of his way to tell how much
he detests); one must be a Romantic and an intellectual to
boot. The construction of a Romantic program was a simple matter of drawing a diagram of the Eliot-Pound-Hulme
platform and then writing in the opposite terms. Instead of
Classicist there would be Romantic; instead of Monarchist
there would be Socialist; instead of Anglican there would
be Agnostic. Not that Auden was ever so unsophisticated as
to write a manifesto, but he saw the literary opportunity
quite clearly. And he had organizational ability. Social revolution was thick in the air when he began; clinical psychology and "depth" psychologies were all over the place;
and textbooks of every description were as much "experience" to Auden as fields of daffodils to Wordsworth. While
Eliot is a learned poet, one who adjusts his poetry to his
education, Auden adjusts all knowledge to the poem. It is
interesting to note about Auden that he never espouses an
extreme cause; his opinions are extensive in range and thorough in their digestion of the material, but never radical.
In this he differs from his early associates like Spender and
Day Lewis, both of whom were willing to take Causes literally. Auden has always been too detached from people,

one gathers from his poetry, and too excited by theories about people (psychology) to ever become more than a paper Romantic. A more horrendous way of putting it would be to term him a Cultural Romantic. Even his religious poems give the impression that he is concerned with the idea of religion, rather than with the religious experience.

Auden's disinterest in unseating Eliot and the things which Eliot symbolizes is one of the chief factors in the continued pre-eminence of Eliot as a critic. Either Auden failed to see the profoundly reactionary quality of Eliot's poetics, or he was content to compromise with them. The latter is probably the case. In the long run, as we all know, Auden became completely magnetized to the Eliot position and finally only a satellite spinning around him. The fact is that Auden never did develop a poetics of his own, as one would expect the author of so much criticism to do. Auden's poetics are inclusive: they comprise the sum total of poetry in the English tongue, from *Beowulf* through the young poets he chose to appear in the Yale Younger Poets series. This is quite a different thing from Eliot's "Tradition," which excludes practically everybody in English poetry—and includes almost no living poets. Auden's rejections are dislikes rather than principles. When Eliot points his finger at John Milton and says, "Go!" Milton must be gone. When Auden, on the other hand, tells us that Shelley is loathsome, we feel that this is more of a personal than a literary matter. Auden is the editor of the best general anthology in English poetry, among his other numerous anthologies, and he knows the tradition in a true sense, and loves it. He is part of it; he is heir to it. In fact, one can understand Auden best by seeing him in the role of curator of the tradition of English poetry. One of the reasons Auden fled England must have been his fear of being recognized as a traditional English poet to the manner born. He has Poet Laureate written all over him.

But the career of Auden is curiously without center; it is uninteresting. It consists of a series of reports on the goodness and the badness of English poets and their ideas. These reports are sometimes in prose, just as frequently in verse. He arranges and classifies, he is meticulously neat, tireless, painstaking, accurate, patient, polite (except on rare occasions of schoolroom outburst), thoughtful, intelligent, sensitive, and more knowledgeable "in his field" than any other poet of the time. For all of this the world is immeasurably in his debt. Eliot once made the remark, which was quite far from the truth, that Pound's poetry is a kind of textbook of modern versification. But such a remark would be true of Auden; Auden is the teacher of prosody.

There is a consistent ambiguity about Auden's position at whatever point we observe it. We must give him the benefit of the doubt and hope that his uncertainties are not fatal. While Auden has a somewhat ferocious capacity for belief, we can never be sure whether it is belief or love of argument that moves him. Auden is a highly argumentative poet and he is always trying to convince the reader of something; one begins to wonder if he isn't trying to convince himself as well. From the standpoint of poetry this constant debating is foreboding; a poet's beliefs, after all, should be taken for granted in his poetry. A tremendous quantity of Auden's poetry fades quickly; very seldom does it rise above the argument, whatever the argument happens to be at the moment. In Auden one is constantly thrown back on the "content" because the content is never purely taken for granted. He is forever washing his intellectual linen in public. His most interesting poems are those in which he generalizes the troubled "I" into "we"; Auden's preoccupation with pronouns is famous.

In his work we see an enormous mass of unrelated poems and verses covering every possible category of the poem, as the textbook and the anthology classify the English poem. The poet's hallmark is always evident; the turn of phrase, the vocabulary, the rhythms themselves are always distinctively his, so characteristic that one can spot them in a second. And these forms run from the smallest to the largest, from the minutest epigram to the oratorio, libretto, verse play, prose-poem; everything, in fact, except the modern "epic" like the *Cantos* or the straight narrative, like "Roan Stallion." Yet we cannot find a particular form which we identify as Auden's, one he has invented.

As a guide in this essay I will use Auden's *Collected Poetry*, published over a decade ago, with mention of his later works at random. This is not a study of Auden's totality of production but only of his significant books, the most significant being the *Collected Poetry* published in 1945. The book is the first great landmark in his career, his first plateau of achievement. It is in many respects a peculiar book, not so much a collection as a final rewriting of all the nonrejected poetry—an attempt, in other words, at a unity which Auden covets and seems unable to accomplish.

The book, close on to five hundred pages, has as an epigraph a tellingly ambiguous quatrain. It reads:

Whether conditioned by God, or their neural structure, still
All men have this common creed, account for it as you
    will:—
The Truth is one and incapable of contradiction;
All knowledge that conflicts with itself is Poetic Fiction.

In this dedication, as in so many of Auden's poems, it is hard to tell where he stands. There is an antithesis as follows: The Truth (with a capital T) is one. But all knowledge that conflicts with itself (that is, which is not *one*) is Poetic Fiction. What the reader has to dope out is whether Auden is being serious about the meaning of Truth and serious about Poetic Fiction (also capitalized). Or whether he is being serious about one and not the other. Or finally, whether he is being serious at all. Even his initial statement is open to question—that all men have this common creed. It is Auden's typical way of saying that what he believes at the moment, all men believe. The epigram is therefore a subjective statement around a typical dualism. It is at once a justification for his poetry and a kind of poetics. It gives him an aim (Truth) and it rationalizes "conflicting knowledge" as poetry. In what sense of irony Auden uses Poetic Fiction is hard to tell. Evidently he both accepts and rejects the idea of Poetic Fiction. In one of his pastoral poems Auden writes about wanting to live in a cave "with two exits." The epigram I have cited has more than two exits. Notice that Auden does not say that all knowledge that conflicts with itself is Poetry, as Yeats would have it, but Poetic Fiction. Perhaps Poetry is Truth and near-poetry is poetic fiction; it is hard to tell. We rather expect Auden to say something startling like Truth is Beauty, but in a more Modern manner, more subtly. This poem is not important except that it is the frontispiece to the *Collected Poetry* and is a web of dualisms.

The poems themselves are arranged in a manner which every critic has noticed and been annoyed at. Many of the poems did not have titles originally, but are given offhand titles and put in a sequence depending on the spelling of the first word of the first line. The purpose here, aside from the obvious one of scrambling the chronology, is to suggest a unity and spontaneity which lie beyond any preconceived plan. There is a kind of waggery and even tomfoolery about the arrangement which is supposed to bear out the poet's notion of poetry as "play." The notion that it is play is paired with the somewhat desperate hope that this play, this Poetic Fiction, will somehow lead to the Truth.

But a chronological view of Auden's poems will not yield much insight anyway; at any one time Auden can be found practicing a goodly number of "forms." In every case they are retrospective and can be related to a model from the past or the present. He makes no effort to invent in the sense that, say, Hopkins invents or Pound strives to invent; there is a different "prosody" operating in Auden and it is the prosody in the old-fashioned sense of line, stanza, and rhyme. Auden's great achievement, on the other hand, is the modernization of diction, the enlarging of dictional language to permit a more contemporary-sounding speech. In this endeavor he has created a revolution in English poetic speech for our time *which is in effect part of the counter-revolution of T. S. Eliot.* In Auden's case this was an honest and perhaps inevitable development, not a scheme to rule the poetic roost. The Eliot-Pound "form" is, as we know, barren, and nothing new has grown out of it. Its failure permitted Auden to return to the standard forms. English poetry, as I mentioned, has been singularly weak in the aspect of invention for a hundred years in comparison to French or American poetry of the same period. The fact that an inventive poet like Gerard Manley Hopkins went unnoticed in his lifetime is evidence of this. Even Yeats, a basically conventional writer, thought Hopkins a bit queer.

While Auden has no part in the polemics of the American Moderns about schools of poetry, his work in bulk represents a slowing-up of the formal process, through a broadening of the diction for the sake of inclusiveness. The Auden poem is intelligible, with the logic of beginning, middle, and end, and intelligible within the semantics of the dictionary.

Diction is that aspect of style which refers back to wording; its final authority is the dictionary. The inventive poet uses the dictionary, if at all, as a point of departure, not as a resting place. The orthodox poet, or classical poet, or academic poet, or intellectual poet, however you call him, always gravitates toward language in its accepted state. It is his authority. In this respect Auden is a dictionary poet, one who refers to the authority of the lexicon and the authority of the anthology. He is himself a scholar and superb editor, with a tremendous grasp of his material. Even his theorizing is handsomely documented.

But Auden has no poetic direction; his theory as well as his practice of poetry reverts to play; he develops a kind of self-defeating technique which prevents even his followers from making him the center of a poetic cult. He would like to be as dogmatic as Blake, for instance, but cannot; as flamboyant as Byron (or Dylan Thomas); or as desperate as Rimbaud. But he is in fact too much a poet of debts and obligations, too happy with books, and too civilized a man to kick over the card catalogue and run howling to his Muse.

"About suffering they were never wrong, /The Old Masters:" begins his *Collected Poetry*. It is one of his best-known poems and a poem that has become the prototype for younger writers throughout the English-using world.

Everything about it makes it a model poem, a poem for the album. The title is "Musée des Beaux Arts," signifying that the poem is and is not a museum piece. It suggests the poet magnetized to the museum, whose experience is limited to the big city where the masterpieces settle down after their hard careers in the outside world. The poet is not really looking at the picture of Brueghel's *Icarus* but thinking about it as he walks away. The poem is something like a twenty-one line sonnet. It has the grace and structure and smugness of the sonnet. But of course it is not a sonnet, any more than it is a poem about a picture. The theme of the poem is Icarus in relation to the landscape of man as seen in a famous painting and put into a poem. The whole tone of the poem is that of the man walking down the street after having been to the museum, explaining the significance of a certain famous work of art to a young friend. This is the peculiar intimacy of Auden and it is never without its charm. It is serious, accurate, and urbane with the authoritative urbanity of the city-cultivated man. The example of the work of art is indispensable to Auden as a center of value; for he can provide none without the examples of art. Thus Auden has led us back to the art-gallery poem, the poem suffused with the golden light of the museum and the library. It is Browning without the narration. It is what young people mean by "academic."

Auden regards his own book as an anthology, a museum, not out of conceit but because of a confidence that his poetry is part of the great flux of the past, as it is. His earliest poems are the most exciting as experiment, with their play on the rhythms of Skelton and Old English, the primitive movements of a great literature. In these poems the meaning is more approximate than precise and it appears that Auden will try for a breakthrough into new forms, like Williams. But it transpires quickly that Auden is not thinking of poetry in this aspect but of poetry as it has always been; he reverts to the forms, loosening them, making them generally available and comfortable to use. And meanwhile he uses the poem as a blackboard to chalk out his views. Voltaire, Freud, Yeats, places he has been, wars he has lived through, Utopias he has dreamed and which have or have not failed him, psychological types, the great artifacts like the Sphinx, and Oxford. At the same time there is never the poem bound wholly to a subject; the subject in Auden's poetry is always moving away from the subject, toward the psychological monologue. This monologue develops naturally from discussion of societal man to spiritual man, from social science to spiritual science, theology.

One finds it impossible to do more than to praise Auden for his extraordinary competence, and after that to talk about the significance of his competence. Each work of his achieves its own perfection; and there is probably no poet in English who has written so much whose successes are so many. In this excellence Auden is like a superb athlete, unaware of his own agility, and spectacularly lucky. I leave to others the discussion and analysis of Auden's scholasticism, his observations about society and about man's spiritual place in the modern world. The pageantry of Auden's poetry is the pageantry of ideologies; to the degree that Auden makes his poetry serve the ends of argument his poetry is in mortal danger of dying with the century. While *The Waste Land* and the *Cantos* may always be retained in the museum of literary knickknacks, Auden's poetry suggests the fate of period literature. It appears that Auden has already lost touch with a contemporary audience and that even his enormous influence over the diction has been assimilated and forgotten. But it is Auden more than any other poet who has stamped the modern poem with a style. To Auden belongs the honor of having brought to perfection what everyone nowadays calls the Academic Poem.

The academic poem is discursive poetry; it is versified thinking. I am not speaking of Auden now but of Audenesque. Eliot and Pound returned poetry, as William Carlos Williams never tires of saying, to the university by making literary data the center of the poem. Auden followed the cue and made all printed data of every description the center of the poem. This was the revolution in diction that I mentioned earlier. If Pound quotes a saying by an American soldier it is to demonstrate the degeneration of Americans in language. When Auden studies and adopts American journalism, he is not trying to demean it but to see its possibilities as poetic usage. Auden uses all the jargons, from social science to advertising, accepting them as current languages of communication, allowing for just enough irony of tone to save himself from being identified with these jargons. The dictions border on the comic, sometimes even imitating Ogden Nash or Edward Lear. They open the door to the old rhetorical devices like the capitalized abstraction of allegory, which with Auden is an unserious way of being serious. By doing this with such apparent ease, he has made the discursive poem casual and universal.

What distinguishes Auden from, say, the "Georgian" poets is the intellectualizing of emotion. Yeats admired greatly a villanelle of Ernest Dowson's with the refrain "Wine and women and song, /Three things lighten our way." Auden writes "I sit in one of the dives /On Fifty-second Street" and shortly begins to talk about the "low dishonest decade." Dowson mourned in the bar about his fellow artists and his own emotional griefs; Auden in the bar mourns about politics, society, and war. This fusion of personal emotion with intellectual debate was something quite new. Eliot and Pound had rid the poem of emotion completely and talked about "felt" ideas. Eliot advised poets to "feel their thought" like Dr. Donne. Auden reversed the process and showed the poet how to "think his emotions" in poetry. Eliot and Pound failed to create a following because poets *are* enormously emotional animals, and do not want to use thought as an experience, as Eliot advises. Poets would much rather feel sorry for themselves (if that is the only emotion available, as it seems to have been for Ernest Dowson) or generalize their emotion into "universals," like Keats in his somber odes. They do not want to "feel their thoughts" like the Wits and the Metaphysicals Eliot is so fond of. But in a pinch they are quite willing to "think" their feelings, like Auden.

The Auden poem is intellectualized emotion. The academic poem is intellectualized emotion, when there is any emotion to intellectualize. Most often there is only a pretense of emotion and this pretended emotion is intellectualized and versified. Auden's emotion is usually vital and warm, even though he chews it over in the poem. The truly academic poem is cold and clammy; whatever feeling it had to begin with its filtered through the screen of wit until it is unrecognizable as feeling. In the academic poem the reader does not know what the emotional direction is; to this charge the academic critic replies that that is not important: if you want your emotions directed, go to the movies.

I suppose I should give an example of an academic poem, one in which the original feeling is lost through talk about it. For this purpose I might use almost any poem chosen at random from the big literary quarterlies or the small reviews, as this is the type of poem most in favor with editors today. But I do not feel that I should make fun of some other poet's work and I will use a poem of my own. The only thing I want to say in defense of the poem is that I rather like my version of the academic poem. Notice that there is a double meaning of some kind in almost every line of the poem, that some words are used simultaneously as nouns and verbs or adjectives and that there are so many instances of this kind of play in the poem that I find new ones every time I look at the poem. Such a remark would elicit a chuckle from the modern critic to the effect that "I told you so; there is even more to your poem than *you* think."

The poem is titled "A Calder," the title being a play on words for: Alexander Calder, the inventor of mobile art; the article "a," signifying a particular Calder mobile; and also his initial. Here is the poem:

> To raise an iron tree
> Is a wooden irony,
> But to cause it to sail
> In a clean perpetual way
> Is to play
> Upon the spaces of the scale.
> Climbing the stairs we say,
> Is it work or is it play?
>
> Alexander Calder made it
> Work and play:

Leaves that will never burn
But were fired to be born,
Twigs that are stiff with life
And bend as to the magnet's breath,
Each segment back to back,
The whole a hanging burst of flak.

Still the base metals,
Touched by autumnal paint
Fall through no autumn
But, turning, feint
In a fall beyond trees,
Where forests are not wooded,
There is no killing breeze,
And iron is blooded.

No one, I think, could tell from this poem that I am a fervent admirer of Calder. I am. The feeling is almost entirely obscured by paradoxes: an iron tree, a wooden irony, the use of work and play as both nouns and verbs, and so on. I call this an Audenesque poem, a poem in which the emotion is thought to pieces. Auden himself would never be this obvious in a poem; he would think the poem a good deal further along the line than I have. Or he might write one stanza with the mobile in it and then take off into a rarer atmosphere of speculation, as Yeats does in his schoolroom-visiting poem, another model of the age in which the human element is all but snuffed out by Yeats' talk about metaphysics.

To recapitulate what I have said: Eliot and Pound destroyed all emotion for poetry except emotion arising from ideas. (The formula is theirs, not mine, and I take no responsibility for the obscurity of it.) Observing their stigma against emotion, Auden used emotion in the poem as a subject for intellectual speculation. Auden's use of emotion-as-conversation was the model for what we call the academic poem. It was not only Auden's great skill in making this kind of poem readable that turned it into a genre; it was also the fact that people in the twentieth century tend to intellectualize emotion anyway. The curse laid upon emotion by the Moderns was inherited by Auden, who apologizes for his emotions by talking about them in the poem. To use the critical jargon, the academic poem can be recognized by its Objective Form, objective form being anything from jamming the text, the use of concealed metaphor, involved stanzaic form, "personae," to anything else that prevents direct expression of feeling. The modern critic considers the expression of personal or subjective emotion a "fallacy."

Auden is essentially a lyric poet but lyricism also was frowned on by the inventors of Modernism. Pound had expressed some interest in Robert Burns and Villon, it appears mostly for the dialect quality of their poems; but what he called in his terminology "Melopoeia" was not at the top of the poetic heap. At the top of the heap was the "poetry of ideas." People used to speak of Dylan Thomas as a great "lyric" poet, meaning that they liked his work but didn't think it would produce much intellectual aftermath. It didn't; but it produced the first spontaneous audience for good poetry since the moderns ruled out audiences as immaterial. Auden's own lyric talent has been subsumed under his own intellectual talent. Auden, in fact, has created a genre, the intellectual lyric: he says:

> O who can ever praise enough
> The world of his belief?

Every Auden lyric or ballad has an intellectual point to make—there is no story for the story's sake, no song for the song's sake.

The lyricism of Auden is almost always spoiled by self-conscious siftings and ruminations. Many of them are little parables, some are leftovers from plays, but very few are lyrics. Generally Auden treats the lyric too gingerly, like an archeological find which he has just dusted off. Here is an example, using the recently discovered American folk-song idiom, which our poet is a little uncertain about.

"Gold in the North," came the blizzard to say.
I left my sweetheart at the break of day,
The gold ran out and my love turned grey.
You don't know all, sir, you don't know all.

"The West," said the sun, "for enterprise,"
A bullet in Frisco put me wise,
My last words were "God damn your eyes."
You don't know all, sir, you don't know all.

In the streets of New York I was young and swell,
I rode the market, the market fell,
One morning I woke and found myself in hell,
You don't know all, sir, you don't know all.

In Alabama my heart was full,
Down by the river bank I stole,
The waters of grief went over my soul,
You don't know all, ma'am, you don't know all.

In the saloons I heaved a sigh,
Lost in deserts of alkali I lay down to die;
There's always a sorrow can get you down,
All the world's whiskey won't ever drown.

Some think they're strong, some think they're smart,
Like butterflies they're pulled apart,
America can break your heart.
You don't know all, sir, you don't know all.

Many of Auden's lyrics are all that endure of some of his plays. This may be as good a place as any to add a note about the use of drama among modern poets. What do we find is the state of the drama in the hands of modern poets whom we have been talking about?

In the first place, Pound puts a virtual ban on drama. To him the theatre is too public and all sorts of illiterate and noisy folk crowd into the playhouse. Pound turns his back on the Greek dramatists and on Shakespeare, and all other drama except perhaps the Japanese Noh. What Pound understood about the Noh was its subtlety as a spirit-play and dance-play; and it was this element that he recommended to Yeats. Pound's insight was excellent here. But Pound also recommended the "aristocratic" quality of the Noh, a typical Pound misinterpretation. The Noh had been killed off by the Western opening of Japan in the nineteenth century, but it was not aristocratic; it began in fact as a public and even mystical art connected with the sect of Zen Buddhism. Yeats followed up the Noh as best he could and wrote dance plays and closet drama and other "aristocratic" forms, some of them quite beautiful, all of them far out of reach of a living stage. Even the quality of the poetry in the Yeats play is thinned out, and there are no characters in that sense that Synge knew and used character. Yeats' dramatic defect was that of the Modern Poet who does not really recognize the existence of people at all, but only voices and masks.

Eliot's place as dramatist is more interesting. In the absence of any poetic drama in our language for centuries, Eliot approached the problem cautiously and intelligently, experimenting with such simple and traditional forms as the church pageant: *Murder in the Cathedral* is not only his best play; it is one of the best "miracle" plays of the literature. Eliot uses only pre-Shakespearian dramatic forms and post-Shakespearian dramatic forms. The high period of English drama he does not try to duplicate. *Family Reunion* is an attempt to reproduce tragedy in the old sense. The later drawing-room plays are evidently modeled on Oscar Wilde. (Eliot's understanding of character is Wildean and requires a static social atmosphere in which the characters can make epigrams.) The success of some of Eliot's drawing-room plays is based not on any use of character or plot or poetry, for the poetry grows less and less and finally disappears, but on the use of the quasi-supernatural man, in reality a *deus ex machina*. Eliot's inability to deal with true character is similar to that of Yeats, neither poet evidently having had sufficient knowledge of, or sympathy for, people to know what to do with them. The chief virtue of Eliot's plays is that for a moment they reversed the tendency of realism in the theatre.

Auden is more attuned with dramatic literature than any of the foregoing poets and from the very beginning of his career has stayed close to the uses of dramatic poetry and theatre poetry. It is interesting to note that Auden has never had a stage success like Eliot or even Yeats, while his use of dramatic forms *not* intended for the stage is better than that of any other contemporary. He is a librettist, not a dramatist; Auden's use of character is even weaker than Eliot's. There are no characters proper in his plays, only literary voices, or rather radio voices, for Auden prefers not even to delineate the face and form of a character. By far the most brilliant of these voice-poems is *For the Time Being*, which is perhaps the best work of Auden's and one that promises to survive much of his other poetry. This oratorio, as Auden calls it, uses all the lyric forms in a burlesque mode, saucily and with all the voices of wit. Considering the subject, which is the "Christmas story," the whole poem is light and pleasant and enlivened by a great deal of sophisticated talk about society and community. There is no particular unity to the poem; Auden prefers the lyric plus recitative form which allows full use of the intellectual choric voice. *The Age of Anxiety* makes even less pretense of being playable; like *The Sea and the Mirror* and *New Year Letter*, it is discursive poetry in voices. Auden's inventiveness in this realm is another of his contributions to literary form; the basis of the form is again diction and the action is all verbal and psychological. One is reminded of the masque of Jonson or Milton.

Auden has moved drama even further from the stage than Yeats. Eliot has moved it closer to the stage than any other poet since the Jacobeans, but only in a technical sense. The Eliot play is a *tour de force* tending toward the kind of brittle stylization we get in Christopher Fry. A true poetic drama must begin from the theatre as it exists today, not from the poem as it exists today. We have the seeds of this drama in a playwright like Tennessee Williams, really a poet, not in Eliot or in Auden or Yeats. Williams' exaggeration of character and situation is poetic exaggeration; the characters are rooted in reality but are not realistic; Eliot's and Auden's are not rooted in reality but in "ideas." Tennessee Williams represents a beginning of a poetic view of character and circumstance. The lurid and baroque atmosphere of his plays should not distract us from the fact that Williams is dealing with recognizable realities. The popularity of his plays attests to the fact that his audiences see beneath the surface distortions, violences, and perversions of their situations. And in general, what is called "Southern" literature in America is more vital than any other literature, not because of its dark and catastrophic surface but because certain effects of American life are best seen through characters who live closer to the real nature of American violence and passion. This is where the poet comes in. It is not a question of setting a play in New Orleans or Oxford, Mississippi, but of dealing with characters whose daily emotions are forced into overt behavior by the spirit of place. Synge could do this with the Aran islanders; Yeats could not do it because he could not see emotion on the streets; he could see it only in dreams. Some of Eliot's characters are convincing in scenes of domestic altercation but in nothing else. Eliot has to get rid of characters by pushing them off boats or sending them into the tropics to be eaten by ants. Auden's characters, on the other hand, have a kind of Gilbert and Sullivan charm, "real" enough, but only for *opéra bouffe*.

The poetry of Auden thus far has demonstrated one fact over all others, that he has advanced the "Classicism" of Eliot and Pound. With more than half the twentieth century gone it is now possible to see the pattern of poetry as it was established by the founders of Modern Classicism and to see the meaning of the discipleship of Auden.

In the face of the enormous productivity of Auden and the relative success of all his work, it is difficult at first to see his connection with Eliot. Where Eliot and Pound failed to effect a revolution in poetry they succeeded in providing cultural sanctions for poets and critics of the next generation. There is no indication that Pound approved of Auden; he would consider him one of the second category of poets, those who consolidate the "inventions" of their masters. Eliot, of course, would take a much more sympathetic view of Auden. Eliot abandoned the pretense of free verse after it had served his purpose; actually he never used it at all except in a few early "imagistic" poems. Eliot used modified French forms which he admittedly copied; by the time of the *Quartets* he no longer pretends any loyalty to new forms but relapses into a gauche lyricism, alternating with a slack line of prose. Pound has, on the other hand, stuck to his conception of a new form of verse, enough to impress William Carlos Williams, among others. Auden evidently saw through the "experimentation" of his elders to their real purpose, which lay beyond poetry. It may be that Auden took literally the Classicists' talk about Tradition, as later he seems to have taken seriously their talk about religion. In any case, Auden's service to Modernism, Classicism, or whatever you want to call it, is the determinant of the common style of poetry in English today.

All of Auden's talk about Romanticism, the romantic voyage, the quest, loneliness, the romantic artist as *poète maudit*, and so on—is all talk. It is well documented, handsome talk, but it comes from books and nothing but books. The sectarian battles between Romantic and Classic one would have thought had died ages ago, but we find them revived by Eliot and his friends, with Auden providing a little fencing practice for the Romantic team. The great "Romantics"—Nietzsche, Whitman, Rimbaud, Lawrence —do not enter into the game, having been polished off by

Eliot long since. The whole point of Auden's "Romanticism" seems to have been to accommodate that persuasion to the tenets of the Classicists. In any case, this most academic of struggles has simmered down in Auden to textbook discussion and no longer plays any serious role in poetry as a living art.

Ironically, Auden brings to our attention the fact that "modern" poetry still has not come into existence. What has passed for Modern Poetry is in no wise comparable to the painting and music of our time, but a weak imitation of those arts. The new poetry which Eliot and Pound bragged they were bringing into existence has its fruits in the stanzas, sestinas, oratorios, and libretti of Auden, the typical New-Classical and academic literature of our time. Nor has Auden profited from the true modern poetry outside of the English language. Except for one translation of Cavafy, which had already been done quite well, Auden shows little sign of interest in the poetry of modern Spain, Italy, Greece, France, Germany, or South America. Stephen Spender has done far more to introduce the European poets into English than Auden.

It is an astonishing fact about the twentieth century that it is without its poet. Auden set out to be the Poet of the Age: at least he was always inventing slogans which the literary journalists readily picked up. He had the air and authority of a Spokesman, but for whom did he speak? We remember that Auden began as the voice of English revolutionary youth and that the enemy was the entrenched bourgeoisie with its country-club ethics, its smug clericalism, and its imperialist bank account. This was the intellectual fashion in England until after the Spanish Civil War and the famous Moscow trials; Auden was the first of the Marxist poets to slip quietly out of the meeting. By the time he was missed he was already ruminating in New York over the failure of Collective Love and the sad truth of the need for personal love. An extraordinary amount of Auden's poetry of this time is an anguished repetition of the cry that self-love is the only possible love. The recoil from the class-war morality was very severe for Auden; in exile he became an American citizen and a parishioner of the Church of England. Auden has always had to have his papers in order; an intellectual decision to him means signing on the dotted line. He shuffles his papers, or reshuffles them and is ready to begin again. But for whom is he the Spokesman this time? It becomes harder and harder to tell. The tone of conviction is as firm as ever; the generalizations as sweeping as before, but now they are couched in theology. As far as Auden's instinct for the public sensibility goes, he is probably right to switch from the language of anthropology and depth psychology to the language of *Angst*, Eros and Agape, for there is no question that the Dismal Science, Theology, is in the ascendency in the late twentieth century. And I have no doubt that Auden can hold his own among the best of the doctors of religion. But my interest in him stops there.

Auden's achievement is that of the great stylist, not that of the primary poet, the actual creator of poetry like Hopkins or Rimbaud or, among his own contemporaries, Dylan Thomas. Auden is more than a literary movement: he is practically a period of literature all to himself. But his is a period of reexamination—of forms, of vocabularies, of ideologies. He is the great amateur of our time; he has taught us all how to improvise. But one would be hard put to find the small handful of poems which are the core of Auden, the man himself, the poet himself. Auden is already forgotten by the present generation, the poets who have begun to write since about 1940; he has been absorbed completely. This is sad for a poet of such rich talents and a man of such good will; but the reason is at hand: he calls his own integrity into question. I began with Auden's quatrain about Truth and Poetic Fiction and I must end with an example of his Poetic Fiction (or is it his Truth?) contradicting itself.

This is part of the passage from his play *The Dog Beneath the Skin*, which, among other things, is a bitter anti-clerical diatribe. A hypocritical vicar is delivering a sermon and Auden is pulling out all the stops to show how revolting are the vicar and his message. The sermon is, in fact, a violent satire on religion at its worst. But note this: when Auden publishes his *Collected Poetry*, ten years after the play itself, he makes a separate place for this very sermon and calls it "Depravity," introducing it with a strange bit of Pecksniffiana:

> I can only hope that this piece will seem meaningless to those who are not professing Christians, and that those who are, and consequently know that it is precisely in their religious life that the worst effects of the Fall are manifested, will not misinterpret it as simple anticlericalism which always implies a flattery to the laity.
>
> It is concerned with two temptations: the constant tendency of the spiritual life to degenerate into an aesthetic performance; and the fatal ease with which Conscience, i.e., the voice of God, is replaced by "my conscience," i.e., the Super-Ego which . . . holds one variant or another of the Dualist heresy.

In this passage the vicar is attacking the idea of freedom and social revolution which Auden (at least when he wrote the play) was defending. (The stage directions have the vicar in a hysterical frenzy, crying and with saliva flowing from his mouth.)

And so, today, we are here for a very good reason. His enemies have launched another offensive, on the grandest scale, perhaps, that this poor planet of ours has ever witnessed. As on the first awful occasion in Eden, so now; under the same deluding banner of Freedom. For their technique of propaganda has never varied . . . that three-syllable whisper: "You are God," has been, is, and alas, will be sufficient to convert the chapped-handed but loyal ploughboy, the patient sufferer from incurable disease, the tired economical student or the beautiful juvenile mama into a very spiteful maniac indeed . . . [The vicar then draws a picture of what it would be like to live under the slave state in the name of Freedom. Then he exhorts his congregation:]

But mind, God first! To God the glory and let Him reward! God is no summer tourist. We're more than scenery to Him. . . . Oh delight higher than Everest and deeper than the Challenger Gulf! His commodores come into His council and His lieutenants know His love. Lord, I confess! I confess! I am all too weak and utterly unworthy. There is no other want. . . .

Oh Father, I am praising Thee, I have always praised Thee, I shall always praise Thee! Listen to the wooden sabots of Thy eager children running to Thy arms! Admit him to the fairs of that blessed country where Thy saints move happily about their neat, clean houses under the blue sky! O windmills, O cocks, O clouds and ponds! Mother is waving from the tiny door! The quilt is turned down in my beautiful blue and gold room! Father, I thank Thee in advance! Everything has been grand! I am coming home!

Here is Auden in a nutshell. A passage condemning an idea is used ten years later to defend the idea that the passage originally condemned. What was a burlesque of ecclesiastical rhetoric is now presented as a sober sermon. Which is the Truth, which the Poetic Fiction? You will have to decide for yourselves. For as Auden says in one of his poems:

> This might happen any day;
> So be careful what you say
>   And do:
> Be clean, be tidy, oil the lock,
> Weed the garden, wind the clock;
>   Remember the Two.

Thus the master of the Middle Style, the poet who will probably give his name to our age of moral expediency and intellectual retreat—the age of Auden.

WILLIAM CARLOS WILLIAMS:
The True Contemporary

WHEN I WAS twenty years old I published a little book of poems privately. It was a confused book, a mixture of Elizabethan and Modern. This volume I sent to several famous poets, only one of whom took the trouble to reply. He was William Carlos Williams. Williams did not praise my book, but his letter, the first I had ever received from a real writer, was full of sympathy and kindliness for a young man who wanted to be a poet. While he had nothing encouraging to say about my poems, he had a good deal to say about the month of March and his anger at T. S. Eliot. The month of March figures a great deal in Williams' poetry, a violent and beautiful season in Williams' New Jersey, as it was in Maryland, where I lived. The diatribe against Eliot disturbed me deeply. I was a worshiper of

Eliot then and a devout reader of the *Partisan Review*, which, although a highbrow left-wing magazine, took Eliot to be the sovereign poet and critic of the twentieth century. I could not understand how any modern poet, especially Williams, who seemed of an extraordinary freshness and originality, could say unkind things about Eliot. If I had ever developed the habit of reading literary criticism I would have known what he meant. But my natural antipathy for criticism kept me away from it for many years. It was not until I began to teach in universities that I was forced to examine criticism; and it was not until I examined it carefully that I began to appreciate Williams' opinion of Eliot, the true significance of Eliot and everything he has promulgated under the name of criticism.

The radical difference between Williams and, say, Eliot, is that Williams divorces poetry from "culture," or tries to. Williams is fighting for the existence of poetry (while Eliot and Pound fought for the "uses" of poetry). Williams' entire literary career has been dedicated to the struggle to preserve spontaneity and immediacy of experience. His explanations of these aims are certainly not as impressive as Eliot's and in fact lead to such confusing theories as Objectivism. In defense of Williams one can say that his theorizing is innocent, while in the case of the Pounds and Eliots it is calculated and tricky. Williams does not stand or fall on theory; he is willing to void it at a moment's notice. But it is unfortunate for him that he must engage in theory at all. At bottom Williams is not an intellectual, and he is too human, too sympathetic, too natural to become a symbol of the anti-intellectual. Besides, as he says in his published letters, he is illogical. He would never be able to impress the quarterly reviews or the highbrows who consider him a kind of intellectual slob. The literary quarterly follows a party line of Culture, any Culture, but Culture is a *sine qua non* for the poet, according to them.

Williams is a guinea pig of modern poetry. He lends himself to the literature of the laboratory and a thousand trials and errors of criticism. He even writes a "mythic epic" like Pound and Eliot which all the culture critics seize on as proof that Williams is not a literary imbecile but one you can practically write books about. *Paterson* is a typical culture poem, the only full-dressed one Williams ever wrote but, according to the critics, the real thing, a kind of New Jersey *The Waste Land*. Williams is so innocent that he would even do that. In writing his large bad poem Williams was perhaps trying to test the validity of works like the *Cantos* and *The Waste Land*, even to compete with them. While he carried on a lifelong fight against Eliotism—a one-sided fight, for Eliot hardly deigned to notice this gadfly—he maintained a lifelong relationship with Pound. Williams' relationship to Pound is very much like Yeats': an antimagnetic relationship. Pound leaned on Williams in the same way that Eliot and Pound leaned on each other. And Williams remained loyal to Pound because Pound seems to remain American rather than English. Williams is faithful to Pound through thick and thin, always annoyed with him, and always attempting to understand his position. Williams can see the demagoguery of Eliot but not of Pound. Somehow he identifies himself with Pound. Williams was once unseated from the poetry consultantship of the Library of Congress, with no organized protest from writers and scarcely any mention of it in the press. Pound was awarded a prize from the Library of Congress which was backed up by all the self-styled Great Poets of the English-speaking countries. Pound got his prize, was feted in the editorials of the national magazines, and was eventually freed without a trial. Williams went home and had a series of strokes. My point is that because Williams abhors fixed positions in politics as in poetics he cannot impress officialdom.

Williams is the American poet who tries to fight off Europeanism. He fights it off, singlehanded, but he cannot impress the European with his cause. Neither can he impress the American. Lacking the arrogance of an Eliot or a Pound, lacking philosophy or religion or logic, he is battered back and forth by the literati, who are always armed to the teeth with Positions and who can make anything out of him they want, except a bad poet. Eliot tried to polish him off by remarking that he had a kind of "local interest." To Eliot anything that is not of world cultural interest is "local." Eliot was also punning on Williams' theory of the Local.

Williams belongs to the generation of Modern Poetry, those poets who suddenly organized literature in 1920 or thereabouts. He was not a high-powered Modern because he lacked the political instinct, but he was aggressive and fought the distortions of Modernism throughout his life. His letters and essays and even his poems are all "local" in the sense that they are contemporary. He wanted poetry to belong to the present, not the past. This is the clue to his involvements with Ezra Pound and his hatred of Eliot.

Williams has written a good deal of literary criticism himself, but he is not a critic in any accepted sense of that word. He is a poet even in his criticism; he refuses to use terminology and everything terminology stands for. He builds up no system; he abjures "style" in his prose, except when he is not sure of his ground. (In such cases he writes a jaunty, affected lingo reminiscent of Pound or Hemingway.) A good many of his judgments seem to be affected by personal loyalty mixed with an overpowering desire to be fair. One time, because of a letter from Robert Lowell, he seemed about to revise his opinion of Eliot. In Williams' world there are no hard and fast rules; the entire literary process is fluid; the governing principle is contemporaneity —immediacy.

There are basic contradictions of judgment in Williams' appraisals. For instance, he praises Marianne Moore excessively while he sees nothing of importance in Eliot. Williams also places Gertrude Stein with Pound as an important innovator. Pound he is inclined to favor from the start, even to a slight imitation of Pound's ideas of American history and banking. But the treatment of Pound is always anguished. One is inclined to feel that Williams does not look up to Pound but is pleased by Pound's interest in *him*! Williams has little use for Stevens, but this is consistent with Williams' objections to prettified language. At the bottom of Williams' specific poetic judgments lies a theory of language, which is practically a *mystique*. Usually it is referred to as a *prosody*, and in the widest meaning of that term it is.

Compared with Pound's prose, which has the tone of the Public Address System, Williams' critical style is weak and plaintive. At times it contains a note of hysteria, frequently its shrillness gets in the way of the clarity, but on the whole there is the pervading innocence and warmth of personality, heightened by genuine excitement. But when he intellectualizes he follows in the footsteps of the Eliot-Pound faction. He praises Joyce for his clarity and his great interest in form but his basic liking for Joyce has to do with Joyce's humanity. This is not a virtue that the Joyceans usually single out. And of course Williams is attracted by the banality of subject in *Ulysses*.

His allegiances are unstable and extreme. Williams reacts sharply to the immediate political or literary event. He is as prone to follow the Right (where the politics are not too obviously putrescent) as he is to follow the Left. Extremism seems to him worth a diagnosis. His detestation of Eliot seems to be a hatred for compromise; Williams does not compromise but he veers crazily from side to side. He writes about Lorca with a political passion while clinging with one hand to the coattails of Pound. He follows Pound's admiration of Jefferson while taking a "leftist" position on Jefferson. "Let's have a revolution every ten years," is Williams' view of Jefferson. Whereas Pound would say: a solid aristocracy without hereditary rights. At the end of a stirring, almost scholarly essay on Lorca he works in a little stab at Whitman, saying that Whitman was a romantic "in a bad sense." Williams is always looking over his shoulder at Pound; in himself he feels no critical authority. Here he mimics the Modern Classical view of Whitman.

Frequently he takes off into the realm of esthetic speculation, always with a certain desperate gaiety that characterizes his criticism. "The poem alone focuses the world," he says. This pleases the Pound side of Williams. Or in an essay about E. E. Cummings: "We are inclined to forget that cummings has come *from* english to another province having escaped across a well defended border . . ." This is about the difference between English and American, which Williams makes the center of his criticism. But he knows he is on the side of the Romantics, on the side of anyone who is opposed to "lapidary work," anyone who opposes a literary poem. Williams is always more or less on the right track, but he never comes to the point in his criticism. He does in the poems. Again he will buckle down to a first-rate piece of criticism in his bitter essay about the failure of Sandburg to continue as a poet. Here he is on safe ground. Williams is as close to Sandburg as twins but he can tell the difference between himself and the professional Americanism of Sandburg. He understands Sandburg because he has been through the same process of handling Americana. But Sandburg's soft-pedaling is to Williams the worst sort of propaganda verse. Sandburg follows the identical course Williams does in his own "formless" poetry; but Sandburg settles for a "form" and Williams still continues the search. When Williams talks about Auden he can say something as mixed-up and as *true* (reading Williams' criticism one begins to write like him, on both sides of the fence) as: "I wish I could enlist Auden in . . . a basic attack upon the whole realm of structure in the poem. . . . I am sure the attack must be concentrated on the *rigidity of the poetic foot*." When Williams begins to underline something like the "rigidity of the poetic foot" he sounds even more sophomoric than his friend Ezra. It is as though Williams had reduced all the cultural viciousness of modernism to prosody—which in fact he has done. Marianne Moore seems to him to have taken recourse "to the mathematics of art." He adores her persnickety syllable snipping but he cannot abide Auden's much more fluid and graceful "feet." The point of argument seems to be British versus American. Puzzling over Dylan Thomas' poems after his death, Williams said that they smacked of the divine. But having fallen between the two stools of the "divine" Thomas and the agnostic Pound, one is not sure what *divine* is, except, as Williams says, "drunken." Clinging desperately to the only poetic he knows he cries at last: "Without measure we are lost." *Measure* is used prosodically and abstractly, as the rule, the law—one is not sure how it is used.

As a critic Williams has no credit whatever. Eliot puts up a full-scale esthetic which anticipates every question and answer. Pound bludgeons his opinions across to a few listeners. Yeats weaves over the crystal ball in a trance of culture sensibility. And poor Williams is haunted by the two specters of Whitman and Pound, the genius and the crank. All of which ends up as an unresolved internal monologue on *Prosody*! The prosody *mystique* in Williams is the center of all his prose and must be understood if the nature of Williams' poetry is to be vindicated. As my own opinion of Williams as a poet puts him over and above Pound and Eliot and Cummings and Marianne Moore, all the theorists and purveyors of sociological opinion, I will attempt to examine Williams' "prosody."

Williams has no critical reputation but he has somehow maintained the respect of the official literati. Simultaneously, he has maintained the loyalty of the literary "underground." (It was Williams who introduced Allen Ginsberg's *Howl*, and dozens of similar works which only poets have ever heard of.) He is the only modern poet who searches everywhere for new poetry.

Imagine any of the official critics, new critics, or editors of the highbrow quarterlies taking notice of a poem like Siegel's *Hot Afternoons*—which Williams alone had the courage and honesty to reintroduce as one of the best twentieth-century poems. *Hot Afternoons* was one of the last authentically American poems, save Williams' own, before the final triumph of Eliot's culture poetry.

The new schools of criticism have always tried to give Williams the benefit of the doubt as a poet of their persuasion. Especially the poem *Paterson* appeals to them as a work comparable to *The Waste Land* and the *Cantos* or the *Anabase* of St. John Perse. *Paterson* to these critics seems an epic in modern style, a "mythic" poem. Controversy over *Paterson* has been considerable; but at least it is recognized by these critics that Williams is as culturally ambitious as his contemporaries in such an undertaking.

It is a waste of time to discuss this kind of criticism, but it is necessary to set it aside if one is to get at a fair judgment of Williams' poetry. There is one early full-scale intellectual probe of Williams. It is a quibbling book, laden with minor points of pedantry and with a dark knowledge of "structures." It is apparent in this work that the author is not able to read poetry except as "comparative ideology." For instance, in speaking of a character in Williams' *Paterson* named Elsie, the critic says: "Elsie is a kind of Yeatsian 'Crazy Jane' presented without Yeats' idealization of the desecrated woman as the authentic guarantor of some superior wholeness, an authenticity with which Yeats also endowed his fools and lunatics." This gibberish rises from the critic's intense interest in "mythic" character rather than poetry. But one of the funniest examples of this kind of criticism is as follows. A critic takes a delightful little poetic quip by Williams and treats it to the following exposition. Here is the poem, "This Is Just to Say":

> I have eaten
> the plums

> that were in
> the icebox
>
> and which
> you were probably
> saving
> for breakfast
>
> Forgive me
> they were delicious
> so sweet
> and so cold

The irony of this poem, the critic says, "was that precisely that which preserved them (the plums) and increased the deliciousness of their perfection (the refrigeration) contained in its essence the sensuous quality most closely associated with death; coldness. So the plums' death (or formal disappearance and disintegration) was symbolically anticipated in the charm of their living flesh. This is, I believe, the exact pathos of this brief poem. . . ."

Whenever I quote something like this I feel constrained to add that this is a true quotation and not a parody I have made up. Most criticism about Williams is written in this patois: in a discussion of the poem "The Yachts" we are told that "suddenly the physical referents are expanded into universals more overtly than had been Williams' earlier custom when the reader had been given the responsibility for making the concrete particulars yield the universals . . ." etc. What the critic is trying to say is that in this poem Williams is using symbols; she cannot say anything so obvious; and she invents a way of saying the obvious to make it look profound.

A similar "explication" is published by the poetry editor

of *The Nation* about the little wheelbarrow poem. This is the poem, "The Red Wheelbarrow":

> so much depends
> upon
>
> a red wheel
> barrow
>
> glazed with rain
> water
>
> beside the white
> chickens

Says the critic: "The poem's design is a striving for value, for significant realization, against the resistant drag of the merely habitual." This kind of highbrow marginalia was, funnily enough, *sanctioned* by Williams, who was always looking for someone to bestow critical respectability upon him.

Williams' poetry is bounded by *Kora in Hell* (1917) at the beginning of Williams' literary life and the epical *Paterson* at the other end. Pound wrote him about *Kora in Hell* and said, "The thing that saves your work is *opacity*, and don't forget it. Opacity is NOT an American quality." The opaque was something Pound might praise; and there is no telling how deeply influenced Williams might have been by this great literary law of Pound's. There are two books preceding *Kora* but the original preface to *Kora* is a mightily opaque and gossipy monologue in the Pound style. More important, Williams announces that the plan of *Kora* is "somewhat after the A.B.A. formula, that one may support the other, clarifying or enforcing perhaps the other's intention." This is the "form" of the *Cantos, The Waste Land,*

and other "mythic structures" of the twenties. The real precedents for the book, however, are the so-called prose-poem, the *Illuminations* of Rimbaud, the poetic notes of Baudelaire, the abortive prose experiments of Eliot, etc. Probably the model of the poem was the pretty little French poem, for children perhaps, called *Aucassin et Nicolette*. Williams was charmed by this piece and evidently kept it in his mind as a form using both verse and prose. But the official precedent for *Kora*, we are told, is a book called *Varie Poesie* dell'Abate Pietro Metastasio, Venice, 1795, designedly dropped on Williams' desk by Pound.

Kora in Hell is a series of observations about poetry and the stance of the poet, full of little psychological asides about our civilization, not in the Poundian political way but in the Surrealist associational manner. Williams is concerned, like all the *avant-garde* writers of his time, with the feasibility of "associations"—the random use of intellectual and personal experience. Williams simply made it his business to jot down something every night, however nonsensical, and then make a comment on it. The chief and it may be the only fact of interest about *Kora* is that *Paterson*, coming at the apex of Williams' poetry, uses the identical method. The method consists of a free use of poetic languages in various states of excitement, alternating with a free use of prose languages. Eliot, Pound, and Joyce all attempted the same technique, with varying success.

But in between *Kora* and *Paterson* we have close to a thousand pages of some of the best or most interesting American poetry in our history. Almost all of this poetry is in a style which is immediately recognizable as Williams' own; further, it is a workable style, one which permits him to write a poem almost at random. At its best, which is a good bit of the time, it is not "experimental" poetry or crank technique. Naïve it certainly is, even what some writers call primitive; it is precisely Williams' innocence of forms that frees him to respond to daily experience as a poet. Williams went on writing, day after day, year after year, losing manuscripts, not finishing them, giving them away, but never letting up. Poetry to him was a daily function of life, a means of seeing. In a sense, he is our first American poet since Whitman. It hardly matters that his counselors poisoned his mind against Whitman; Whitman is his mentor after all.

Critics and journalists tend to heroize Williams for writing poems late at night after a hard day's work at the hospital. Williams has never felt heroic about being a physician. It is pointless to try to imagine Williams ensconced in some village on the Italian Riviera brooding over the effects of the 1905 nickel on the souls of little children. Williams was a New Jersey doctor and that is that. His poetry is the poetry of a very busy man, as busy, say, as Sir Walter Raleigh or Gerard Manley Hopkins. Not that one can generalize about busy poets and poets of leisure. Williams wanted to be a doctor, have a family, live near New York City, and write poetry. As far as anyone knows, he did all these things very admirably.

But the seeming offhandedness of Williams' poems *is* a condition of his life. Obviously the poems would be different had Williams not been a doctor. New Jersey, New York City, Ezra Pound, the delivery room, the back alleys of charity patients, home, the little magazine, the month of March, these are all the elements in which his poetry moves. Williams accommodates himself to the brutal round of modern professional life. It does not embitter him; it sweetens him. And the poems are "scrappy," as the critics note, but there is a method to their scrappiness. And they are not astrology or economics or theology. The element of speed in composing the poem is part of the technique of his poetry, just as speed is a factor in certain kinds of painting. There is, in fact, a definite "Oriental" tendency in his work, not cultural Orientalism like Pound's but an instinct for the work that is as natural as nature herself. And the daily life has a lot to do with it. He survives as a poet even better than his contemporaries, a consequence, perhaps, of his roots in a pedestrian world. Williams never became an "exile;" how can an obstetrician be an exile?

The earliest poems are marked by the ornate imprint of Pound (the use of foreign exclamations and translation-sounding rhetoric and even the "Browning" dramatics which Pound quickly switched away from when he discovered that he could be opaque with impunity). The character of this style is that of a half-biblical, half-Victorian tone which is the quality of all of Pound's early adaptations. In Williams it sounds like:

> Eight days went by, eight days
> Comforted by no nights, until finally:
> "Would you behold yourself old, beloved?"

Actually Pound never rose above this style, either in the *Pisan Cantos* or in the latest additions of his epic. Williams saw through it more quickly. It goes on intermittently through "So art thou broken in upon me, Apollo" and many such imitations of Style, but soon it stops abruptly. One can see the sudden transition in:

> Your thighs are apple trees
> whose blossoms touch the sky.

which is more or less phony Pound, but is followed by:

> Which sky? . . .
> Which shore? . . .
> what sort of man was Fragonard?

This is the beginning. Williams sheds figurative language as a snake sheds its skin; henceforth he is naked, a poet without decoration, without metaphor.

> March,
>> you remind me of
> the pyramids, our pyramids—

There is still a lot of mincing Italian, Spanish, Latin quotation, but this falls away also.

> a green truck
> dragging a concrete mixer
> passes
> in the street—
> the clatter and true sound
> of verse—
>
>> . . .
>
> Moral
>> it looses me
> Moral
>> it supports me
> Moral
>> it has never ceased
> to flow

(through various series of data, menus, signs on walls and labels on bottles). Then a descent into pure spoken idiom, the rejection of all the devices of poetry for speech, always a sign of the poet's sincerity. Where Eliot ends up snipping philosophy from textbooks, Pound cutting whole chapters from history documents and statistics, Williams dives back into the spoken tongue.

It can never be said of Williams that he writes a well-rounded poem like "Ode on a Grecian Urn" or "The Love Song of J. Alfred Prufrock" or even "my father moved through dooms of love." He loathes the *fait accompli* in poetry or in painting. On the other hand, he does not worship the "fragment" for the fragment's sake. He tries to find the center of his experience in relation to the art of poetry; and he finds it over and over again. His "discoveries" are many more than "The Red Wheelbarrow" or "The Botticellian Trees"—good poems but two of many hundreds which are not repeated in the anthologies.

Williams put his poetry in a direct relationship with daily experience. With Eliot there is no daily experience: there are "symbols" of the quotidian (empty lots, carbuncular young men, sandwich papers along the Thames, the silence in the subway) and with Pound there are stock-market reports, the struggles of artists and war communiqués. Williams tries to accommodate his poetry to what the day brings to a poet in a place like New Jersey, where there is no dazzle of the past or of the cultural present. Williams writes about an apple rotting on the porch rail.

He does not exploit his knowledge. It does not occur to him that what he happens to know as an expert might be turned to the uses of poetry. Yet he himself is the organizing center of the poem, bringing together around him the untold *disjecta membra* of the day. *Without metaphor.* This is the challenge. Hence the directness of all his poems and their somewhat shocking physical quality. Williams is like Catullus in his outspokenness and unthinking sensuality and amorality—for there is no bragging or sexual athleticism (or asceticism either) in the poems. Pound is sexless, Eliot ascetic, Yeats roaring with libidinal anguish and frustration. Williams includes the physical in the day's work; he meets it at every turn, being a doctor, and is not obsessed.

> The young doctor is dancing with happiness
> in the sparkling wind, alone
> at the prow of the ferry! He notices
> the curly barnacles and broken ice crusts . . .

or

> I bought a dishmop—
> having no daughter—

There is very little twentieth-century poetry like this except outside the English language. But Williams does not "translate" or "adapt" except infrequently. He refuses to improve upon the language—this is the whole secret of his flatness of style and the inconclusiveness of the forms. He writes in his speaking voice.

In his autobiography, Williams refers to the publication of *The Waste Land* as "the great catastrophe." Looked at from Williams' point of view and from that of all the *avant-garde* of his time, it was indeed the great catastrophe. "It wiped out our world," says Williams, "as if an atom bomb had been dropped upon it . . . I felt at once that it had set me back twenty years . . . Critically Eliot returned us to the classroom just at the moment when I felt that we were on the point of an escape . . . I knew at once that in certain ways I was most defeated." Williams' recognition of the true nature of *The Waste Land* marks him as first-rate prophet in criticism. And the effects of Eliot's poem were even more far-reaching than Williams said; not only was it the poem the academy needed as a pseudomodern example; it was a poem that made poetry and criticism one and the same thing, and that provided a justification for a new critical philosophy. Williams was also right in seeing that he was more damaged by this poem than anyone else. He was left high and dry: Pound, who was virtually the co-author of Eliot's poem, and Marianne Moore were now polarized to Eliot. Williams felt all this and would feel it for another twenty years. His own poetry would have to progress against the growing orthodoxy of Eliot criticism.

At first glance, Williams' remarks about poetic form seem superficial and even inane. One thinks, well, here is a nice man who is sick and tired of effeminate poeticizing and who would like American poets to display some gusto and originality. On second glance, one thinks, the old boy is becoming a bore with his din about prosody and "the line." All that shrieking about the "language" in *Paterson* is as bad as "the precise definition" in the *Cantos* or the "way of saying it" in the *Four Quartets*. And because Williams refuses to use the standard terminology of criticism, because he has a sincere interest in an American poetry, and because he is so suggestive, at least in his early years, to the literary politics of his fellow writers, he generally sounds half unintelligible. But there is a lot more to his "prosody" than that, much more, in fact, than exists in the new criticism.

Prosody is the science of verse. In English there is not and there has never been such a science. English scholars have long since given up prosody studies as a hopeless task. Because prosody and versification have such a justifiably bad name in English literature, no reader is apt to prick up his ears when William Carlos Williams or anyone else introduces the subject. Prosody is a mare's nest. Eliot and Pound took care not to identify themselves as prosodists, even while they were quietly laying down laws for it. In public they always guffawed at the mention of the word.

By prosody Williams does not mean versification. If you examine his own poems or his own remarks about what he calls mysteriously "the line," you will see the following things: He neither preaches nor practices "foot" prosody; he does not preach or practice meters; nor syllabic versification, such as Marianne Moore adopted; nor is his prosody accentual; nor is it "typographical" or what one critic calls grandly "spatial" form; nor does he base versification on rhyme nor on the internal figurations which rhyme may produce. The prosody of Pound is based on cadence which runs close to foot prosody—an imitation of Homeric and English trisyllabic. Eliot's prosody is extremely conservative, either a copy of Laforgue, at its most daring, or of Milton's *Samson Agonistes* (though I have never examined this closely) and it degenerates easily into modified "iambic." Williams' prosody is more advanced than any of these: it consciously departs from every intonation of the past. This is also its danger, as it is its advantage.

The thing to remember about Williams' "line" is that it is not a prosodic line at all. The word "prosody" for him is a metaphor for the whole meaning of the poem. Iambics to him mean cottages all in a row: sameness, standardization of things and of lives. His refusal to write iambic is therefore the same thing as Whitman's. It means that the iambic is not a language for the American poet. Pound and Eliot maintained the same doctrine, each in a less convincing way.

A good start for understanding the significance of Williams' belief about prosody and language (they are the same thing) is to consider his contempt for the modern sonnet. The virtue of the sonnet (which is the only "set" form in the English language) is that it prescribes a kind of syllogism. A sonnet in its simplest form makes a statement, develops or contradicts it, then resolves it. It is a game; hence its popularity with lovers. Eliot began by rejecting the sonnet; Pound rejected it after a few acrobatic flops. On the other hand, a poet like Cummings has advanced the sonnet to a new fame. With him it becomes the most ironical sonnet in English literature. What Williams resents about the sonnet form, even in the hands of Cummings, is the neatness of it. That is what the sonnet is for. The sonnet "line" can lead to nothing but a trick poem or exercise. A poem, according to Williams, should not be that closed, should not click like a box (which was Yeats' way of describing his own metrical poetry). The "closed" poem—the poem that clicks like a box—is the type of poem which has lately become a standard in the twentieth century; the most recent models were made by W. H. Auden.

All the appurtenances of the closed poem, especially the stanza, became anathema to Williams from the beginning. Rhyme itself seems to him meretricious; when he uses it (and he uses it as well as anybody), it is with a slur. The poem must not be governed by meters—any meters—nor by periods and paragraphs (stanzas), nor by the figures of speech. What is left? Nothing. The raw material of the poem is all. It is the same process that Whitman went through: a rebirth.

But Williams had even rejected Whitman's line. (We must try to remember that Williams uses the word "line" in the metrical sense, and in the linguistic sense at once.) The turning away from Whitman is all but fatal in Williams, but he manages to do pretty well in his own way. Williams grew up in the day when Whitman seemed incorrigibly nineteenth century and Emersonian. How Williams could have missed the lesson of Whitman is beyond me. But Williams started over, too. No ideas, no meters, no forms, no decorations; only the search for the raw poetry of experience.

"No ideas but in things," Williams said over and over, for a time. He became an "Objectivist," a man on the search for objects instead of thoughts. But this was just a variation of Pound's Imagism; for there could be no object-poetry that would lead anywhere; any more than Imagism could stand on its own legs. Williams dropped the Objectivist idea, just as he dropped the "antipoetic." These were harmful simplifications. Williams' larger conception of poetry is based on the understanding that a thing is neither poetic nor antipoetic, neither prose nor poetry: there is something else which cannot be so bound. To write a poem about a rotten apple is not "antipoetic"; people laugh at such a poem and love it precisely because it is the poetry of the thing. The poetry of the rotten apple lies outside prosody, outside what is proper for apple-poetry, and outside what is called Symbolism (if you say *apple* to a modern critic you will be pelted with religion, mythology, and Freud before you can duck—but to Williams an apple is an apple).

As for Williams' versification, it goes entirely by ear, and luckily for him he has a good ear most of the time. It is not cadenced, not accentualized, not syllabified, not metered. It may or may not have a "typographical" form: sometimes it has, sometimes it hasn't. For certain periods Williams will print in "couplets"; at other times in tercets; he is not averse to the single word per line nor the long line. Generally (and this is the significant thing) he accommodates the "line"—that is, the typographic or verse line—to the sense of the whole poem. Thus he is doing approximately what Hopkins did in sprung rhythm, creating a total form rather than a unit form. It was a horror to Williams to see *The Waste Land*, partly because of Eliot's use of the old "unit" forms: an iambic passage here; a trochaic passage there; an image poem here; a long rhetorical build-up there and so on, with no organic principle anywhere.

But Williams himself in his desperate moments does the same thing. *Paterson* is just as artificial as *The Waste Land* when it comes to the "line."

Williams and his contemporaries had been schooled to despise "narrative poetry." To tell a tale in verse seemed to the early modern poets of our century the weakest excuse for writing a poem. They tried to get rid of tale-telling altogether and switch to Ideas, which are much more "masculine" than narratives. There is a large residue of narration in Williams' collected poetry which for years he did not know what to do with. The wonderful episode 17 in *Paterson*, one of the most powerful passages Williams ever wrote, was without a context until he stuck it in *Paterson*. But true to his Modernist upbringing, he could not even then *narrate* it, any more than he could narrate *Paterson*. Williams' "epic" poem is thus just another example of *The Waste Land* technique. He is better when he writes about Sacco and Vanzetti (a theme which could not move the great culture poets to even a single word) or about the death of D. H. Lawrence (which the culture poets also avoided like the plague). An interesting thing about Williams' poems is that they move from one to the next easily.

The "secret of that form," as Williams calls it somewhere, is to make poetry natural, not literary. This is, in fact, the secret of his "prosody," the sectet of his "antipoetic" line, the secret of his concentration upon objects as ideas. *The "secret of that form" is the eradication of the line between poetry and prose, between life and art.* Eliot speaks of an art emotion, an emotion reserved for the moments when one turns on the esthetic faucet. And it is precisely this attitude toward poetry that Williams condemns.

At the end of his long struggle with prosody, Williams turned to something very like a "form" but so loose that one can hardly call it a form. Perhaps it began with an admiration of a little quatrain by Byron Vazakas which resembled typographically a toy pistol or the State of Oklahoma. Vazakas managed this thing for speaking in his own voice. Williams hit upon a step-down kind of typography which he used constantly in his later years. But it is not a be-all and end-all; he could drop it any time he liked. It is not a syllogistic sonnet or sestina at any rate. This style differs from Williams' earlier style only in that it appears to conform to a certain regularity. But there is none, except the regularity of thought as it progresses in the poem.

Had Williams been as good a theoretician as he was a poet he would probably be the most famous American poet today. But Williams cannot explain, fortunately for him, or he explains badly when he does. It is the poem he is after. His kind of poem may be the chief development of the American poem since *Leaves of Grass.* When it is successful, as it is an amazing number of times, it abolishes the dualism of form-content, expression-artistry, and all those other dualisms which get in the way of art. Williams' almost mystical repetitions about "the line" (and somewhat wildly in *Paterson* about the *Language*) are a decree against critical speculation about forms. He knows that forms are not predetermined, not inherited, not traditional. He knows, too, that forms do not matter for the honest artist, whether he uses them or not. It is when form becomes a fetish that he draws back and howls.

Speaking of howling, Williams has been the sole example in twentieth-century poetry, along with Lawrence, for hundreds upon hundreds of poets, the majority of whom are Americans who oppose the Eliot "line." Williams knows too much about poetry to set up a critical shop or lay out a curriculum like Pound. He is the godfather, all the same, of nearly all the existent *avant-garde* poetry, all the free poetry that exists in the English world today. This is recognized by the young poets who long ago branched away from the cultural highway and took to the backstreets and bohemias of the land. Williams is no bohemian; he is a serious man of letters (as the stuffy expression goes) but he is closer to the life of the poet than any of his contemporaries. By the life of the poet I mean the man to whom the daily life is the poetry itself, whatever his occupation. Williams may have been trying to do the impossible in taking for granted the unity of expression and artistry in the early years of the century, but he was one of the few who accepted this high premise of the poet. When the "great catastrophe" (the publication of *The Waste Land*) occurred, most of Williams' friends dropped by the wayside or split into little groups or went over to the enemy, as Williams put it. It is curious that through all the ensuing years Williams remained loyal to Pound and could not perceive that it was Pound who was the lever for the catastrophe and would continue to be.

One book by Williams serves better than anything I have ever read about him to clarify and sum up his poetry and his poetics. It is a strange and charming work called *I Wanted to Write a Poem*. The book is an informal bibliography which is also a kind of autobiography. The editor (Edith Heal) lists the books chronologically, fifty of them, and gets the poet to discuss their inception. Mrs. Williams, the poet's editor throughout his career, makes additional comments. Throughout this running commentary one can follow the fifty-year search for form which has been Williams' lifelong preoccupation. I would like to conclude by condensing and commenting upon his own findings, after which I will give my evaluation of his achievement.

His earliest influences, he says, are Keats and Whitman. He would rather be a painter than a poet (his mother is an artist) but cannot because of the medical profession. He finds his contemporaries quickly: Wallace Stevens, Marianne Moore, Hilda Doolittle, Ezra Pound. Pound is the only one of these to whom he feels literary loyalty. Stevens tags him with the label "antipoetic," which Williams resents ever after. (Mrs. Williams, curiously enough, does not understand the poet's rage over this designation.) He abandons rhyme and meter in his second book (1913). While he is writing *Kora*, "Prufrock" appears; Williams says: "I had a violent feeling that Eliot had betrayed what I believed in. He was looking backward; I was looking forward. He was a conformist, with wit, learning which I did not possess . . . But I felt he had rejected America and I refused to be rejected . . . I realized the responsibility I must accept. I knew he would influence all subsequent American poets and take them out of my sphere. I had envisioned a new form of poetic composition, a form for the future. It was a shock to me that he was so tremendously successful; my contemporaries flocked to him—away from what I wanted. It forced me to be successful . . ." He consciously rejects free verse, simultaneously rejecting metered verse. "The greatest problem [he says] was that I didn't know how to divide a poem into what perhaps my lyrical sense wanted." *Paterson* seems to him the answer: he personifies a city and follows its river (the Passaic) and the river-of-history from Paterson down to the sea. Documentary prose breaks the flow of the poetry. Evidently it is the formless form that he has been searching for. In *Paterson, II* he hits upon the step-down form in which all his subsequent poems are written. The line he now refers to as the "variable foot."

What then is the "prosody" of the Williams poem? If we can believe that every good poem ever written in form is good despite the form, and that every formless (free verse) poem that succeeded has succeeded despite its formlessness, then we will be getting close to the idea of Williams' form. It is the purest theory of poetry I have ever heard of and I take it to be the ideal of all poets, formalists or *vers librists*. For meter has nothing to do with it; meter is an aftereffect. Metaphor and simile have nothing to do with it. "The coining of similes is a pastime of very low order, depending as it does upon a merely vegetable coincidence . . ." Structure has nothing to do with it: you cannot remove the parts from the whole; or rather you cannot find the structure. Beautiful language has nothing to do with it any more than the antipoetic. And finally, poetry is a secular art "free from the smears of mystery."

I am not sure I understand all this (assuming I've got it down accurately) but I know in my bones it is right. It is not theory; it is the laborious explanation of an artist stammering out the reasons why his poem came out the way it did. Each poem is its own form, as it must be. The poem is unique and unrepeatable; it is when you repeat that form arises, for form is imitation, as in Eliot, precedent heaped upon precedent. With Williams the poem is raw, quivering, natural, an *objet trouvé*, something you look at twice before you pick it up. It is the extreme of the original, the condition of poetry which frightens off most poets, a complete breakthrough to his own language. It is the kind of poetry which it may take years to see but once seen remakes all other poetry and conceptions of poetry.

But I do not mean that Williams' works are perfection or even that he has written a score or two of poems which will set him beside Milton or Catullus or Marlowe. It is hard to judge such work comparatively; it is too new, too unlike anything else. But there is one sure sign of its value; it has already penetrated the poetry of a whole generation of American poets, not the ones we read month after month in the apple-pie-order journals of letters or the fat anthologies, but in the less-known, less-official magazines and pamphlets strewn over the countryside, which Williams has always lent his hand to. With D. H. Lawrence, Williams is the leader of what authentic American poetry is being written today. Little enough of it is up to his mark, yet the tendency is the right one. The example is there in Williams' poems, not in his criticism. And it is being followed. When I read his poems I feel I am reading a foreign language, my language. After all, there is practically no American poetry to speak of, and nearly all of it has come in the twentieth century, and a good portion of that has been written by William Carlos Williams.

I call him the true contemporary because he saw the challenge from the beginning and saw it whole: to create American poetry out of nothing, out of that which had never lent itself to poetry before. To do this without betraying the present to the past (like Eliot) and without exploiting the present (like Sandburg) and without trying to force the future (like Pound). I call him the true contemporary also because he could not resist trying to write the Great American Epic. But in Williams' case this can be overlooked: he has written enough true poetry to show the twentieth century that *American* and *poet* are not contradictions in terms.

Dylan Thomas

THE DEATH of Dylan Thomas in 1953 was the cause of the most singular demonstration of suffering in modern literary history. One searches his memory in vain for any parallel to it. At thirty-nine Thomas had endeared himself to the literary youth of England and America, to most of the poets who were his contemporaries, and to many who were his elders; he was the master of a public which he himself had brought out of nothingness; he was the idol of writers of every description and the darling of the press. (The Press scented him early and nosed him to the grave.) Critics had already told how Thomas became the first poet who was both popular and obscure. In an age when poets are supposed to be born old, everyone looked upon Thomas as the last of the young poets. When he died, it was as if there would never be any more youth in the world. Or so it seemed in the frenzy of his year-long funeral, a funeral which, like one of Thomas' own poems, turned slowly into a satanic celebration and a literary institution.

When Yeats and Valéry died, old and wise and untouchable, there were held, so to speak, the grand state funerals. It was Civilization itself that mourned. When Thomas died, a poet wrote wildly how, to get him up in the morning, he plugged Thomas' mouth with a bottle of beer—"this wonderful baby." All the naughty stories were on everybody's lips; all the wrong things began to be said, and the right things in the wrong way. Someone quoted bitterly: Kill him, he's a poet! and this childishness was the signal for a verbal massacre of the bourgeoisie, reminiscent of the early decades of our century.

The death of a young poet inflicts a psychic wound upon the world and is the cause among poets themselves of frightening babbling and soothsaying. Such doings may be likened to a witches' Sabbath, and some have seen in these morbid celebrations the very coming-to-life of Thomas' poems. It is his death as an occasion for literary and psychological insurrection that must interest us today, if we are to understand the meaning of Thomas' poetry and the significance his contemporaries have given it. It is one thing to analyze and interpret poetry and keep it all in a book; it is another to watch that poetry enter an audience and melt it to a single mind. I want to speak about the second thing, the live thing, the thing that touched the raw nerve of the world. The poetry of Thomas is full of the deepest pain; there are few moments of relief. What is the secret of his pain-filled audience? How are we to place Thomas among the famous impersonal poets of our time,

140

when this one is so personal, so intimate and so profoundly grieved? Thomas was the first modern romantic you could put your finger on, the first whose journeys and itineraries became part of his own mythology, the first who offered himself up as a public, not a private, sacrifice. Hence the piercing sacrificial note in his poetry, the uncontainable voice, the drifting, almost ectoplasmic character of the man, the desperate clinging to a few drifting spars of literary convention. Hence, too, the universal acclaim for his lyricism, and the mistaken desire to make him an heir to Bohemia or to the high Symbolist tradition.

Writers said of Thomas that he was the greatest lyricist of our time. The saying became a platitude. It was unquestionably true, but what did the word mean? It meant that, in contrast to the epic pretensions of many of the leading modern poets, he was the only one who could be called a singer. To call him the best lyric poet of our time was to pay him the highest, the only compliment. Nearly everyone paid him this splendid compliment and everyone knew its implications. Few realized, however, that this compliment marked a turning point in poetry.

During his life there were also the armed camps who made him honorary revolutionary general; and we cannot be sure Thomas refused the homemade epaulets of these border patrols. I rather think he was proud to be taken in. Who were these people? First there was the remnant of Bohemia. These are people who exist in the belief that everyone is dead except themselves. I saw one of these poets lately; he had just come from England and he informed me casually that everyone in England is dead. To change the subject I asked him if he was glad to be home; but it turned out that everyone in America is also dead.

Among these poets there is a sincere belief in the death of our world, and it is curious to speculate upon their adoption of Thomas as a leader and a patron saint. In the same way nearly all of Thomas' followers have spoken of him as a Symbolist. The Symbolists praise the love of death as the highest order of poetic knowledge. "Bohemian" and Symbolist are never far apart.

All the same, this theory of posthumous vitality seems to make sense when we speak of Thomas. How much did Thomas subscribe to official Symbolism? Just enough to provide ammunition for those people. How much did he love death as his major symbol? As much as any poet in the English language. These factions have a claim on Thomas which we cannot contradict.

Thomas is in somewhat the relation to modern poetry that Hopkins was to the Victorians—a lone wolf. Thomas resisted the literary traditionalism of the Eliot school; he wanted no part of it. Poetry to him was not a civilizing maneuver, a replanting of the gardens; it was a holocaust, a sowing of the wind. And we cannot compare Thomas, say, with Auden, because they are different in kind. Thomas' antithesis to Auden, as to Eliot, is significant. Thomas grew up in a generation which had lost every kind of cultural leadership. The poets who began to write during the Depression, which was worse in Wales than in America, were deprived of every traditional ideal. The favorite poem of this generation was Yeats' "The Second Coming." Yeats' poems gave to a generation of prematurely wise young poets an apocalypse, a vision of Antichrist and a vision of the downfall of civilization. The theatricality of the Yeats poem was a great convenience to a poet like Thomas who, having nothing of true philosophical or religious substance to fall back upon, could grasp this straw. The acknowledged precedence of Yeats in modern English literature—in world literature perhaps—has been a makeshift consolation to all modern poets. Yeats, with his cruel forcing of the imagination, his jimmying of the spirit, is a heroic figure in modern poetry. Yet he belongs to the past, with all its claptrap of history and myth. Thomas' poetry was born out of the bankruptcy of the Yeats-Pound-Eliot "tradition" and all it stood for. It was born out of the revulsion against the book-poetry of Auden and the system-mongering of the social revolutionaries. Thomas' poetry was orphaned from the start.

Thomas suffers from the waifishness imposed upon his generation. The so-called Apocalyptic poets, which he was supposed to be a member of, never existed. Nor is he one of the Metaphysical school. One can see that he plays around with copying the superficies of Vaughan and Herbert and Traherne and maybe David ap Gwilym (who in English is not much better than James Whitcomb Riley) and Yeats and Hopkins. But Thomas was outside the orbit of the English poets and maybe the Welsh. He was antitradition by nature, by place, by inclination. Certainly Thomas' grisly love for America can also be seen in this light; America is the untraditional place, the Romantic country *par excellence*.

Thomas' technique is deceptive. When you look at it casually you think it is nothing. The meter is banal. It is no better and no worse than that of dozens of other poets his age. There is no invention and a great deal of imitation. There is no theory. But despite his lack of originality, the impress of Thomas' idiom on present-day English poetry is incalculable. One critic said not many years ago that

143

Thomas had visited a major affliction on English poetry. This was an unfriendly way of saying that Thomas had captured the young poets, which he certainly had. How did he do this? He did it through the force of emotion, with the personal idiom, a twist of the language, bending the iron of English. Once he had bent this iron his way everybody else tried it.

Yet even when we examine the texture of his language we fail to find anything original, although we find something completely distinctive. It is hard to locate the distinctiveness of Thomas' idiom. There are a few tricks of word order, a way of using a sentence, a characteristic vocabulary, an obsessive repetition of phrase, and so on—things common to many lesser poets. Again, if we scrutinize his images and metaphors, which are much more impressive than the things I have mentioned, we frequently find overdevelopment, blowziness, and euphemism, on the one hand, and brilliant crystallization on the other. But no system, no poetic, no practice that adds up to anything you can hold on to. The more you examine him as a stylist the less you find.

What does this mean? It means that Thomas is a quite derivative, unoriginal, *unintellectual* poet, the entire force of whose personality and vitality is jammed into his few difficult half-intelligible poems. To talk about Thomas as a Symbolist is dishonest. Once in Hollywood Aldous Huxley introduced a Stravinsky composition based on a poem of Thomas'. Huxley quoted that line of Mallarmé's which says that poets purify the dialect of the tribe. This, said Huxley, was what Thomas did. Now anybody who has read Thomas knows that he did the exact opposite: Thomas did everything in his power to obscure the dialect of the tribe—

whatever that high-and-mighty expression may mean. Thomas sometimes attempted to keep people from understanding his poems (which are frequently simple, once you know the dodges). He had a horror of simplicity—or what I consider to be a fear of it. He knew little except what a man knows who has lived about forty years, and there was little he wanted to know. There is a fatal pessimism in most of his poems, offset by a few bursts of joy and exuberance. The main symbol is masculine love, driven as hard as Freud drove it. In the background is God, hard to identify but always there, a kind of God who belongs to one's parents rather than to the children, who do not quite accept Him.

I went through the *Collected Poems* recently to decide which poems I would keep if I were editing the best poems of Dylan Thomas. Out of about ninety poems I chose more than thirty which I think stand with the best poems of our time. If this seems a small number, we should remember that there are not many more poems upon which the fame of Hopkins rests; of Rimbaud; or, for that matter, of John Donne. And yet we expect a greater volume of work from such an exuberant man. Thomas' sixty poems that I would exclude are short of his mark, but they are not failures. I would like to name by name those poems which I think belong to the permanent body of our poetry—or most of them anyway: "I see the boys of summer"; "A process in the weather of the heart"; "The force that through the green fuse drives the flower"; "Especially when the October wind"; "When, like a running grave"; "Light breaks where no sun shines"; "Do you not father me"; "A grief ago"; "And death shall have no dominion"; "Then was my neophyte"; "When all my five and country senses see"; "We lying by sea-sand"; "It is the sinners' dust-tongued bell"; "After the funeral"; "Not from this anger"; "How shall my animal"; "Twenty-four years"; "A Refusal to Mourn"; "Poem in October"; "The Hunchback in the Park"; "Into her Lying Down Head"; "Do not go gentle"; "A Winter's Tale"; "On the Marriage of a Virgin"; "When I woke"; "Among those Killed in the Dawn Raid"; "Fern Hill"; "In country sleep"; "Over Sir John's hill"; and "Poem on his birthday." I leave out the sonnets, which I think are forced, and the "Ballad of the Longlegged Bait," and the "Prologue," and many others. My list is probably off here and there, but I think it is the substantial list of works by which Thomas will be remembered.

The "major" poems, that is, the more pretentious poems, such as the ten sonnets (called "Altarwise by owl-light"), reveal most of what we know of Thomas' convictions and what we can call his philosophy. He believed in God and Christ; the Fall and death, the end of all things and the day of eternity. This is very conventional religion and Thomas was uncritical about it. Add to this the puritanism which runs through his whole work, and, finally, the forced optimism in the last poems such as "In country sleep," in which, although the whole sequence is unfinished, there is a recognizable affirmation of faith in life. But one feels that these matters are not of paramount importance in the poetry of Thomas. Thomas was not interested in philosophical answers. Religion, such as he knew it, was direct and natural; the symbolism of religion, as he uses it, is poetry, direct knowledge. Religion is not to be used: it is simply part of life, part of himself; it is like a tree; take it or leave it, it is there. In this sense, one might say that Thomas is more "religious" than Eliot, because Thomas has a natural religious approach to nature and to himself. The language of Thomas, not the style, is very close to that of Hopkins, not only in obvious ways, but in its very method. Hopkins, however, arrived at his method philosophically, abstractly, as well as through temperament and neurosis. Thomas, with no equipment for theorizing about the forms of nature, sought the "forms" that Hopkins did. The chief difference between the two poets in terms of their symbols is that Hopkins draws his symbology almost entirely from the God-symbol. God, in various attributes, is the chief process in Hopkins' view of the world. Sex is the chief process in Thomas' view of the world.

Thomas' idea of process is important. The term itself is rather mechanistic, as he uses it. He always takes the machine of energy rather than some abstraction, such as spirit or essence. Hence the concreteness of his words and images; obscurity occurs also because of the "process" of mixing the imagery of the subconscious with biological imagery, as in Hopkins. But there is also a deliberate attempt to involve the subconscious as the main process: Thomas' imagination, which is sometimes fantastic, works hard to dredge up the images of fantasy and dreams. Very often the process fails and we are left with heaps of grotesque images that add up to nothing. I would equate the process in Thomas' poetics with his rather startling views of the sexual process. Aside from those poems in which sex is simply sung, much as poets used to write what are called love poems, there are those poems in which sex is used as the instrument of belief and knowledge. Using the cliché of modern literature that everyone is sick and the whole world is a hospital, Thomas wants to imply that sex will make us (or usually just him) healthy and whole again. And there are suggestions of

147

Druidism (perhaps) and primitive fertility rites, apparently still extant in Wales, all mixed up with Henry Miller, Freud, and American street slang. But sex kills also, as Thomas says a thousand times, and he is not sure of the patient's recovery. In place of love, about which Thomas is almost always profoundly bitter, there is sex, the instrument and the physical process of love. The activity of sex, Thomas hopes in his poems, will somehow lead to love in life and in the cosmos. As he grows older, love recedes and sex becomes a nightmare, a Black Mass.

Thomas moves between sexual revulsion and sexual ecstasy, between puritanism and mysticism, between formalistic ritual (this accounts for his lack of invention) and vagueness. In his book one comes, on one page, upon a poem of comparative peace and lucidity, and on the next page upon a poem of absolute density and darkness. His dissatisfaction with his own lack of stability is reflected in his devices which tend to obscure even the simple poems; he leaves out all indications of explanation—quotation marks, punctuation, titles, connectives, whether logical or grammatical. In addition he uses every extreme device of ambiguity one can think of, from reversing the terms of a figure of speech to ellipsis to overelaboration of images. There is no poetic behind these practices—only catch-as-catch-can technique. One is always confused in Thomas by not knowing whether he is using the microscope or the telescope; he switches from one to the other with ease and without warning. It is significant that his joyous poems, which are few, though among his best, are nearly always his simplest. Where the dominant theme of despair obtrudes, the language dives down into the depths; some of these complex poems are among the most rewarding, the richest in feeling, and the most difficult to hold to. But, beyond question, there are two minds working in Thomas, the joyous, naturally religious mind, and the disturbed, almost pathological mind of the cultural fugitive or clown. On every level of Thomas' work one notices the lack of sophistication and the split in temperament. This is his strength as well as his weakness. But it is a grave weakness because it leaves him without defense, without a bridge between himself and the world.

Thomas begins in a blind alley with the obsessive statement that birth is the beginning of death, the basic poetic statement, but one which is meaningless unless the poet can build a world between. Thomas never really departs from this statement, and his obsession with sex is only the clinical restatement of the same theme. The idealization of love, the traditional solution with most poets, good and bad, is never arrived at in Thomas. He skips into the foreign land of love and skips out again. And he is too good a poet to fake love. He doesn't feel it; he distrusts it; he doesn't believe it. He falls back on the love-process, the assault, the defeat, the shame, the despair. Over and over again he repeats the ritualistic formulas for love, always doubting its success. The process is despised because it doesn't really work. The brief introduction to the *Collected Poems* sounds a note of bravado which asserts that his poems "are written for the love of Man and in praise of God." One wishes they were; one is grateful for, and slightly surprised by, the acknowledgment to God and Man, for in the poems we find neither faith nor humanism. What we find is something that fits Thomas into the age: the satanism, the vomitous horror, the self-elected crucifixion of the artist.

In the last few years of his life Thomas was beginning to find an audience. No one, I think, was more taken aback than he at this phenomenon, because most of the poems which the audience liked had been in books for five or ten years already. Thomas was the one modern poet who by his *presence* created an audience. His audience was the impossible one: a general audience for a barely understandable poet. His way of meeting this audience, at the end, was no solution for Thomas as a poet. He became a dramatist, a writer of scenarios, a producer. What he wrote in this phase was not negligible by any means; but it was probably not what he wanted and not what his audience wanted. His audience wanted the poetry; they wanted the agony of the process.

The frenzy that attended Dylan Thomas' death was a frenzy of frustration. Many times, in his stories and letters and his talk, Thomas tried to leap over this frustration into a Rabelaisian faith; but it never rang true enough. After the gaiety came the hangover, the horrible fundamentalist remorse. Yet through the obscurity of the poetry everyone could feel the scream of desperation: not a cry of desire; on the contrary, it was the opposite; it was the cry of the trapped animal; the thing wanting to be man; the man wanting to be spirit.

He is a self-limiting poet and an exasperating one. He runs beyond your reach after he has beckoned you to follow; he arouses you and then slumps into a heap. He knows, more than his readers, that he has no bridge between life and death, between self and the world. His poetry is absolutely literal (as he himself insisted all the time). But its literalness is the challenge to literature which is always significant. He is too honest to rhapsodize or to intone over the great symbols; rather he growls or rages or more often hypnotizes himself by the minute object, which he is likely to crush in his anger. Unlike Hopkins, he has no vision of nature and cannot break open the forms of nature; he cannot break open words. He focuses madly on the object, but it will not yield. He calls a weathercock a bow-and-arrow bird. Metaphor won't come and he resorts to riddle, the opposite of metaphor. A good half of his poetry is the poetry of rage; not rage at the world of society or politics or art or anything except self. He is impatient for a method and the impatience early turns into desperation, the desperation into clowning. He is another naïf, like Rimbaud, a countryman, who having left the country wanders over the face of the earth seeking a vision. He is running away from his fame, which he does not feel equal to. He is running away from the vision of self, or keeping the integrity of self by fleeing from the foci of tradition. I interpret the life and work of Thomas this way: the young poet of natural genius and expansive personality who recoils from the ritual of literary tradition and who feels himself drawn into it as into a den of inquity. This is both the puritanism and the wisdom of Thomas. Such a man can never acquire the polish of the world which is called worldliness, and he turns to the only form of behavior, literary and otherwise, permissible both to society and to self. That is buffoonery. All the literary world loves a buffoon: the French make a saint of the clown. But folklore has it that the clown dies in the dressing room.

It is the most certain mark of Thomas' genius that he did not give way to any vision but his own, the one authentic source of knowledge he had—himself. And it is the most certain mark of his weakness that he could not shield himself from the various literary preceptors who buzzed around him. He became immobile, I think, out of pure fright. He wrote personal letters (which are now being published) apparently meant for publication, in which he adopted the modern clichés about modern life. He pretended to be horrified by the electric toaster, or maybe he really was.

The doctrinaire impersonality of our poetry demands allegiance to a Tradition, any tradition, even one you rig up for yourself. Thomas represents the extreme narrowness of the individual genius, the basic animal (one of his favorite symbols) in man. The animal to Thomas is everything and we listen because he calls it animal, not spirit or essence or potentiality or something else. It is the authentic symbol for a poet who believes in the greatness of the individual and the sacredness of the masses. It is Whitman's symbol when he says he thinks he could turn and live with animals, because they are natural and belong to nature and do not try to turn nature out of its course. They do not try to believe anything contrary to their condition.

But Thomas is drawn away from his animal; he becomes brute. And this he knows. In the brute phase of his poetry (which is the phase loved by the modernists who picked up his scent) the poetry is a relentless cutting down to the quick—surgery, butchery, and worse. And as Thomas is the one and only subject of his poems, we know what is being destroyed.

It is some of the saddest poetry we have. It leaves us finally with grief. The pathos of Thomas is that he is not diabolical, not mystical, not possessed; he has not the expansive imagination of Blake nor even the fanatical self-control of Yeats. He is the poet of genius unable to face life.

Like D. H. Lawrence he is always hurling himself back into childhood and the childhood of the world. Everyone speaks of Thomas as a child. He became a child.

It is easy to dismiss him but he will not be dismissed. He was a tremendous talent who stung himself into insensibility because he could not face the obligations of intellectual life, which he mistakenly felt he must. He could not take the consequences of his own natural beliefs; and he could not temporize; there was no transition, no growth, only the two states of natural joy and intellectual despair, love of trees and fascination of the brute process. He said everything he had to say: it had little to do with wars and cities and art galleries. What he said was that man is a child thrust into the power of self, an animal becoming an angel. But becoming an angel he becomes more a beast. There is no peace, no rest, and death itself is only another kind of disgusting sex.

But something happened to his poems. Somehow the spark escaped; it leapt out of the hands of literature and set a fire. Thomas, I think, did the impossible in modern poetry. He made a jump to an audience which, we have been taught to believe, does not exist. It is an audience that understands him even when they cannot understand his poetry. It is probably the first nonfuneral poetry audience in fifty years, an audience that had been deprived of poetry by fiat. Thomas' audience bears certain characteristics of the mob—but that, under the circumstances, is also understandable. The audience understands Thomas instinctively. They know he is reaching out to them but cannot quite effect the meeting. The reaching ends in a tantalizing excitement, a frenzy. It is not a literary frenzy, the kind that ends in a riot with the police defending Edith Sitwell after a reading of *Façade*. On the contrary, it is the muttering of awakening, a slow realization about poetry, a totally unexpected apocalypse. This audience sees Thomas as a male Edna St. Vincent Millay, or perhaps a Charlie Chaplin; they hear the extraordinary vibrato, a voice of elation and anguish singing over their heads. They know it is acting. They know this is poetry and they know it is for them.

He is like the old cliché of vaudeville in which a tragicomic figure engaged in some private act (such as keeping his pants from falling down) wanders onto a stage where a highly formal cultural something is in progress. Naturally the embarrassed clown steals the show. One must remember Thomas' own story about himself in which he gets his finger stuck in a beer bottle. He goes from place to place, beer bottle and all, meeting new people. The beer bottle becomes Thomas' symbol of his natural self: it is his passport from the common people to the literary life, and back again. It is both his symbol of self and his symbol of other-self. But to Thomas it is mainly a horror symbol. It is the key to No Man's Land. Because Thomas is an uncivilizable Puritan and a hard-shell fundamentalist of some undefinable kind, the puritanism sets up the tension in his poetry— a tension based upon love and fear of love: the basic sexual tension, the basic theological tension. The greatness of Thomas is that he recognizes the equation; and the weakness of Thomas is that he takes to his heels when he has to grapple with it.

Everything I have said can be said better in the little poem by Thomas that takes nine lines. The last line of the poem is so much like a line of Whitman's that I have searched through Whitman's poems to find it. I am sure it

is there and yet I know it isn't. The line reads "I advance
for as long as forever is."

> Twenty-four years remind the tears of my eyes.
> (Bury the dead for fear that they walk to the grave
>   in labour.)
> In the groin of the natural doorway I crouched like
>   a tailor
> Sewing a shroud for a journey
> By the light of the meat-eating sun.
> Dressed to die, the sensual strut begun,
> With my red veins full of money,
> In the final direction of the elementary town
> I advance for as long as forever is.

The First White Aboriginal

D. H. LAWRENCE has more in common with Walt Whitman than any other man has, and it was Lawrence who called Whitman the first white aboriginal. Coming from Lawrence, the epithet was the highest praise. Lawrence's quest was for the aboriginal, the pure energy of the soul. Being an Englishman, he fled from the white man and his white religions and the terrible whiteness of consciousness (which he called mentality) and raced with all his strength to the dark races and beyond, to the blood religions, the spirit of the serpent, and all that. Lawrence made a magnificent leap across civilization into the aboriginal darkness. He is one of the supreme heretics of white, modern civilization. And so for him to bless Walt with the title of the first white aboriginal is a matter of tremendous import. Lawrence is one of the great spirits of our age, as Whitman is, although from Lawrence stems a good deal of the negativity of modern creative life. From Whitman stems much of what there is of the opposite. Lawrence sprang from a modern industrial hell which he never forgave and was never far enough away from to understand. Whitman did not have to spring; he sprouted, he vegetated, he loafed out of nowhere into the role of prophet and seer. At a single stroke, apparently without preparation, he became the one poet of America and Democracy. He is the one mystical writer of any consequence America has produced; the most original religious thinker we have; the poet of the greatest achievement; the first profound innovator; the most accomplished artist as well (but nobody says this nowadays). Yet in the twentieth century Walt Whitman is almost completely shunned by his fellows. He has no audience, neither a general audience nor a literary clique. Official criticism ignores him completely; modern Classicism, as it calls itself, acknowledges him with embarrassment. (Ezra Pound "forgives" Whitman because he "broke the new wood," meaning he broke iambic pentameter). And modern scholars, happily confused by the scholarly complexities of contemporary poets, look upon Walt as a grand failure and an anachronism or a bit of Americana, the prow of a clipper ship, perhaps.

Lawrence, in his search around the world for a pure well of human energy, acknowledged Whitman with love. It is a rare thing for Lawrence. He says:

> Whitman, the great poet, has meant so much to me. Whitman the one man breaking the way ahead. Whitman, the one pioneer. And only Whitman. No English pioneers, no French. No European pioneer-poets. In Europe the would-be

pioneers are mere innovators. The same in America. Ahead of Whitman, nothing. Ahead of all poets, pioneering into the wilderness of unopened life, Whitman. Beyond him, none. His wide, strange camp at the end of the high-road. And lots of new little poets camping on Whitman's camping ground now. But none going really beyond. . . .

But at this point Lawrence changes his tune and explains how Whitman failed. He says that Whitman fell into the old fallacy of Christian love, confusing his great doctrine of Sympathy with Love and Merging. Nothing was more loathsome to the puritanical Lawrence than Merging, and when Whitman merged Lawrence disgorged. How Lawrence longed to merge! And how the mere shake of the hand horrified him! Lawrence in thousands of passages obsessively records his taboo against touching. *Noli me tangere!* It is the opposite of Whitman's obsession *for* touching:

> Is this then a touch? quivering me to a new identity,
> Flames and ether making a rush for my veins,
> Treacherous tip of me reaching and crowding to help them,
> My flesh and blood playing out lightning to strike what is hardly different from myself,
> On all sides prurient provokers stiffening my limbs,
> Straining the udder of my heart for its withheld drip,
> Behaving licentious toward me, taking no denial,
> Depriving me of my best as for a purpose,
> Unbuttoning my clothes, holding me by the bare waist. . . .

(This is the passage in "Song of Myself" which, after a parenthesis, "What is less or more than a touch?" leads into "I think I could turn and live with animals, they are so placid and self-contained, I stand and look at them long and long . . ."—one of the greatest moments of poetry.)

Lawrence, with his deep love of animals and his irritable suspicion of mankind, was the inferior of Whitman. Whitman had the natural love of man which Lawrence, rightly, called American. Lawrence was fascinated, hypnotized, and slightly sick in the stomach. Lawrence says if Walt had known about Charlie Chaplin he would have assumed one identity with him too. What a pity, Lawrence sneers. He'd have done poems, paeans and what not, Chants, Songs of Cinematernity. "Oh, Charlie, my Charlie, another film is done—"

But in the end Lawrence gives in; he knows a kindred spirit when he sees one. He looks down his nose at Whitman's paeans upon Death—Lawrence, who is one of the true poets of Death—and then adds:

> But the exultance of the message remains. Purified of merging, purified of Myself, the exultant message of American Democracy, of souls in the Open Road, full of glad recognition, full of fierce readiness, full of joy of worship, when one soul sees a greater soul.—The only riches, the great souls.

That is the last line of Lawrence's book called *Studies in Classic American Literature*, and I submit that it is a fine concession to be wrung from Lawrence, the archetype of tortured modern man, the man without heroes. Lawrence and Whitman are two modern poets with the deepest concern for mankind, the furthest insight, the widest sympathy, the simplest and best expression. They are scriptural writers in the long run, despising professionalism and literary fashion. But Lawrence fails to do more than pose the problem of modern civilization versus the individual intelligence. He has no answer. He half invents fascism; he is torn between the image of the free natural male (the father who is always leaving home to become a Gypsy) and the image of the leader, the aristocrat. He had it both ways: he remains unresolved. But he also had the vision. He became, in effect, an American, an American among Red Indians and rattlesnakes, close to that darker America betrayed by the white religions, Mexico, which he also loved. But it was Whitman's America that he held out for, "the true democracy [as Lawrence said] where soul meets soul, in the open road. Democracy, American Democracy where all journey down the open road. And where a soul is known at once in its going." Strange words coming from the author of *Kangaroo* and *The Plumed Serpent*.

Lawrence suffers somewhat the fate of Whitman today. He is declassed. He enjoys a kind of underground popularity among writers, but he is outside the pale of the Tradition. He is too violent, too special, too original. And he is too outspoken. But Lawrence could never survive within a tradition, any more than Whitman. And he has, at his best, a style so lean, it matches the burnt-away clean language of prophets. Most of Lawrence's disciples, it seems to me, misunderstand him; but at least he has disciples. Whitman has no disciples and practically no living literary reputation He is only a name.

What has happened to Whitman in the century since *Leaves of Grass* was published? There were the usual false praises and the usual false deprecations, and enough of the true acclaim to give us a little faith in criticism. There has never been anything we could call popularity for Whitman. Publishers are inclined to prepare elaborate editions of

Leaves of Grass, in the same way that they release erotic editions of The Song of Songs: in a wrong-headed way it is a compliment to Whitman. But the best minds of the present century have not closed with Whitman, in my opinion. And the leading poets of the twentieth century have coolly and with relentless deliberation suppressed Whitman and kept him from exerting his force. Any Whitman advocate of great talent, for example Hart Crane, is forced to apologize for this allegiance before he is admitted to the company of Moderns. There is no question that an Act of Exclusion has been in perpetual operation against Whitman since 1855 and is carried on today by the leading "Classicists" of English and American poetry. Walt just won't do. He is vulgar; he is a humbug; he copies the names of rivers out of the sixth-grade geography book; he is an optimist; he is unlettered; he is a theosophist; he abhors institutions; he is auto-erotic; he loves everybody; he is a Rotarian; he goes to the opera; he can't distinguish between good and evil; he has no sense of humor; he cannot solve his own paradox about the greatness of the individual and the greatness of the En-Masse; he has no style—etc., etc.

All such accusations are true, and one could multiply them for pages and pages. Yet in the last analysis, they do not matter. Emerson saw a little humor in Whitman, though he called it wit. But Whitman thought he was writing a kind of bible! And it is the biblical quality of Whitman (as with Lawrence) that is so offensive to lovers of Literature. What insolence! they say, and they are right. For neither Whitman nor Lawrence were "writers"; they were prophets. Literature makes it its business to stone prophets.

Whitman is indeed full of humbug, as when he talks about his experiences as a wound dresser:

One night in the gloomiest period of the War, in the Patent Office Hospital in Washington city, as I stood by the bedside of a Pennsylvania soldier, who lay, conscious of quick approaching death, yet perfectly calm, and with noble, spiritual manner, the veteran surgeon, turning aside, said to me, that though he had witnessed many, many deaths of soldiers, and had been a worker at Bull Run, Antietam, Fredericksburg, etc., he had not seen yet the first case of a man or boy that met the approach of dissolution with cowardly qualms or terror. . . . Grand common stock! to me the accomplished and convincing growth, prophetic of the future; proof . . . of perfect beauty, tenderness and pluck, that never feudal lord, nor Greek, nor Roman breed, yet rivalled. Let no tongue ever speak disparagement of the American races, north or south. . . .

This sounds like Winston Churchill at his worst.

Whitman is not a complicated case of poor manners, confusions and paradoxes; of philosophical muddle and literary naïveté; of good intentions, high passages and bad dreary bogs. He is the one and only poet of America who has ever attempted to adumbrate the meaning of America. The twentieth-century American poet avoids this commitment, by and large: he considers it fitting and proper to take refuge in History against the horrors of progress; or in pure dialectic; or in the catacombs of established faith; or, failing that, in what is called the Language. Whitman's vision has degenerated into a thing called the Language; that is, the American Language, the natural nonhieratic language out of which a mythos might germinate. But Whitman contended that the mythos was at hand. He defined it; he sang it; he argued it; he poured it out. To no avail.

Twentieth-century poetry is a poetry of perfections. It is the least spontaneous poetry since—whatever date for the birth of artificiality you call to mind. It is the pride of twentieth-century poetry that even Yeats was brought to heel by critics who called for a "hard brittle technique." It is the pride of twentieth-century poetry that one publishes a poem once a decade. It is the boast of our poetry that it is impersonal, and that it can mean more or less what you think it means, and be right in the bargain. All of which is "traditional." Whitman and Lawrence were death to Tradition. Yet Whitman did not repudiate the past; nor did he look with any unctuousness upon the present, the America of a hundred years ago.

Never was there . . . more hollowness at heart than at present, and here in the United States. Genuine belief seems to have left us. The underlying principles of the States are not honestly believed in . . . The spectacle is appalling. We live in an atmosphere of hypocrisy through-out. The men believe not in the women nor the women in the men. A scornful superciliousness rules in literature. The aim of all the literateurs is to find something to make fun of. A lot of churches, sects, etc., the most dismal phantasms I know, usurp the name of religion . . . The depravity of the business classes of our country in not less than has been supposed, but infinitely greater. The official services of America, national, state, and municipal, in all their branches and departments, except the judiciary are saturated in corruption, bribery, falsehood, mal-administration; and the judiciary is tainted. . . . In business, (this all-devouring modern word, business), the one sole object is, by any means, pecuniary gain. . . . I say that our New World democracy . . . is, so far, an almost complete failure in its social aspects, and in really grand religious, moral, literary, and esthetic results . . .

Whitman sees the corruption and persists in his faith that the principle of democracy will overrule the corrupt.

Let us call it the romantic position. But Whitman (like Jefferson) does not feel that the written word of democratic principle is sacrosanct. He goes to the heart of the matter. Man must do good, he says, because that is his ultimate nature. The man who falls a prey to corruption, dandyism, superficiality, selfishness, is a fallen man. Whitman despises him. He believes it natural to be pure: nature purifies. He has a kind of worship of chemistry, shared by his countrymen, an animal faith in the god of the sun, and the god of water. It is precisely his contempt for ideas of sin and evil which places him among the great teachers of mankind.

> What chemistry!
> That the winds are really not infectious,
> That this is no cheat, this transparent green-wash of
>   the sea which is so amorous after me,
> That it is safe to allow it to lick my naked body all
>   over with its tongues,
> That it will not endanger me with the fevers that
>   have deposited themselves in it,
> That it is all clean forever and ever,
> That the cool drink from the well tastes so good,
> That blackberries are so flavorous and juicy. . . .
> That when I recline on the grass I do not catch any
>   disease . . .

He did not have a simple faith in the frontiers of "science"; on the contrary, he held a limited belief in physical achievements.

> Not to you alone, proud truths of the world,
> Nor to you alone, ye facts of modern science,
> But myths and fables of eld, Asia's, Africa's
>   fables,

> The far-darting beams of the spirit, the unloosed
>   dreams,
> The deep diving bibles and legends
> . . . You too with joy I sing.

America to Whitman was not a laboratory, but a place in the journey of mankind where the best in man might flower. America was not the goal; it was a bridge to the goal. In "Passage to India" he says of Columbus:

> Ah Genoese thy dream! thy dream!
> Centuries after thou art laid in thy grave,
> The shore thou foundest verifies thy dream.

But the dream is not satisfying enough. We must steer for the deepest waters and take passage to the skies themselves. We must go where mariner has not yet dared to go, risking the ship, ourselves and all. It is not a geographical poem or a historical poem, much less a "war poem," although when Whitman talks about the Atlantic cable and its eloquent gentle wires, he sounds silly enough. But the physical achievement is his symbol of, not progress but goodness! It is axiomatic to Whitman that we shall lay cables, build the Union Pacific Railroad, and fly airships to Jupiter. That is the childlike and wonderful faith of the ordinary modern man who is not thrown into reverse by the terror of it all. Whitman is not even talking about that. It is the twentieth-century "classical" poet who is materialistic and who writes scathing books of poems against the electric toaster. For Whitman says in the same poem that the seas are already crossed, weathered the capes, the voyage done. Everything is already known. The advancement of man physically seems to him good but only a trifle. What really concerns him is that man shall explore the soul.

> Passage indeed O soul to primal thought, . . .
> Back, back to wisdom's birth, to innocent intuitions,
> Again with fair creation.

Whitman is a mystic and he admits it. This is one more reason for his unpopularity. The best modern poets are allowed to admire the mystic but aren't allowed to be one. Whitman is too close for comfort. Furthermore, he has no theology worth sorting out, except a kind of Quakerism, and religion isn't his concern. Man is his concern. And not American man. Whitman is not only the first white aboriginal; he is the first American; or that may be the same thing. When I read Whitman, good or bad, I always feel that here is first and foremost an American. The fundamental religiosity of Whitman plus the contempt for religion is American.

Whitman dissociated himself from mere poets and other writers. Who touches his book touches a man and men of all faiths.

> I do not despise you priests, all time, the world over,
> My faith is the greatest of faiths and the least of
>   faiths,
> Enclosing worship ancient and modern and all between
>   ancient and modern,
> Believing I shall come again upon the earth after five
>   thousand years,
> Waiting responses from oracles, honoring the gods,
>   saluting the sun,
> . . . Helping the lama or brahmin as he trims the
>   lamps of the idols,
> Dancing yet through the streets in a phallic procession,
>   rapt and austere . . .

166

and so on, down to the Mississippi Baptists with the jerks and spasms.

Whitman is too faithful in his belief in man to lay down the rules for a creed. It is unnecessary. If man is of Nature, and Nature is good, good will triumph. Evil is the failure of man to be as good as he can. For man to become all that is utterly possible is divine. And as every man is divine, inside and out, even the lowest are divinities. What is commonly looked down on nowadays in Whitman's talk about the divine average, is the average. Whitman emphasized the *divine*, rather than the average. Each person to him possessed divinity, and to repudiate that divinity was criminal. It is the god in each man and woman (which Lawrence called the Holy Ghost) that we can communicate with. I have *rapport* with you (Whitman's hieratic terminology is always couched in some kind of American French)—I have rapport with you because my divinity has a mouth to speak with. My lower self cannot speak; it can only commit acts of instinct. Yet there is a hierarchy of acts. Each thing to its nature:

> The moth eggs are in their place.
> The bright suns I see and the dark suns I cannot
>   see are in their place,
> The palpable is in its place and the impalpable is in
>   its place.

And Whitman says he is not stuck up and is in his place. Being "in place," of course, is not humility; nor is it a sign of any known orthodoxy.

Whitman asserts his divinity and he cannot evade it, despite a passing show of humility. He has the vision of himself as well in the scale of things. But he acknowledges the god in oneself—and here he makes a break with conventional poetry and conventional thought which is the core of his philosophy.

> Divine am I inside and out, and I make holy whatever
>   I touch or am touched from.

It is Whitman's creed of the equality of the body and the soul. The body is not cursed; it is the miraculous materialization of the soul. The origin of this body-soul Whitman does not explain; he merely states that it is holy and the holy of holies. If he can find an object of worship more worthy than another it shall be his body or a part of his body. And while he is doting on himself he slips without warning into sun worship, nature worship, love worship, and then back to himself.

> If I worship one thing more than another it shall be
>   the spread of my own body, or any part of it,
> Translucent mould of me it shall be you!
> Shaded ledges and rests it shall be you!
> Firm masculine colter it shall be you!
> Whatever goes to the tilth of me it shall be you!
> You my rich blood! your milky stream pale strippings
>   of my life!
> Breast that presses against other breasts it shall be
>   you!
> My brain it shall be your occult convolutions!
> Root of washed sweet-flag!
> Timorous pond-snipe! nest of guarded duplicate eggs!
>   it shall be you!
> Mixed tusseled hay of head, beard, brawn, it shall be
>   you! Trickling sap of maple, fibre of manly
>   wheat, it shall be you!

Sun so generous it shall be you
Vapors lighting and shading my face, it shall be you!
You sweaty brooks and dews it shall be you!
Winds whose soft-tickling genitals rub against me it
    shall be you!
Broad muscular fields branches of live oak, loving
    lounger in my winding paths, it shall be you,
Hands I have taken, face I have kissed, mortal I have
    ever touched, it shall be you.
I dote on myself, there is that lot of me and all so
    luscious. . . .

He begins with his own corpus, which he finds so lus-
cious; he forgets himself and begins looking around the
park, then he recalls the amorous uses of parks; and after a
breath, he comes back to himself and "the lot of him." If
you read on and on you see that Whitman is not talking
about himself at all and acting like a baby discovering its
toes—but that is the superficial trick of it; he is talking
about the primal discovery of self. He is talking about consciousness in the only way it can be talked about: physically. I do not think for a second that Whitman was either
narcissistic or egomaniac; he was trying to obliterate the
fatal dualism of body and soul. All his monotony about
keeping as clean around the bowels ("delicate" was the
word he used) as around the heart and head is not a swipe
at Victorian convention; it was his way of acknowledging
the physicality of the soul, or the spirituality of the body.
Lawrence shied away; and most American writers in more
or less the same Puritan tub get the backwash of revulsion
from this physical "obsession" of Whitman's.

But this is only the beginning. Whitman wanted to create the full individual *in order to put this free man into the*

world. The dialectical conflict in Whitman, as in everyone
else I suppose, is the free individual versus the crowd of
mankind. The twentieth-century poet slinks into his study
and says, No crowds for me. But Whitman took it on. He is
the only modern poet who has the courage to meet the
crowd. And falling back into his demotic French he deliv-
ers the abstraction En-Masse. "Endless unfolding of words
of ages! And mine a word of the modern, the word En-
Masse." This becomes one of the most ridiculed passages in
Whitman, in which he drunkenly chants: "Hurrah for positive science! long live exact demonstration!" and "Gentle-
men, to you the first honors always!" But these funny passages of Whitman are there, not because he is a fool, but
because he has the courage of his convictions. For just after
this idiotic hurrahing for exact demonstration comes another of the great bursts of poetry, the one beginning "Walt
Whitman am I, a kosmos, of mighty Manhattan the son,
/Turbulent, fleshy, sensual, eating, drinking, and breeding.
. . ." (Whitman is always aware of the comic possibilities of
his position, like many prophets.) The balanced man, the
free man, the man who meets his potentiality is a fit man
for the new world, the democracy he envisions. "The purpose of democracy," says Whitman in prose, "is, through
many transmigrations, and amid endless ridicules, argu-
ments, and ostensible failures, to illustrate, at all hazards,
this doctrine or theory that man, properly trained in sanest
highest freedom, may and must become a law, and series of
laws, unto himself, surrounding and providing for, not only
his own personal control, but all his relations to other individuals, and to the State; and this as matters now stand in
the civilized world, is the only scheme worth working from,

as warranting results like those of Nature's laws, reliable
. . . to carry on themselves."

The concept of En-Masse is not absurd and not laugh-
able, as other expressions of his certainly are, such as Democracy, Ma Femme. But even Whitman's tendency to
view Democracy as feminine is penetrating. Whitman was
the first great American feminist.

A great poet is not merely a poet of his nation but a poet
of all peoples. Whitman, who had little enough reward for
his book, and has little enough today, looked beyond literature and beyond the greatness of art. His true personality
went out beyond America, beyond religions and even beyond mankind. His poems about the self and the mass of
America were written before the Civil War, but the war
between the North and South brought everything home to
Whitman. His vision might well have been destroyed, but
with his natural passion for unity he embarked on a new
discovery, not of the body and soul, or rapport, or the En-
Masse, but of the exploration of Death. Whitman had always believed in Death as the purposeful continuity of existence, but he had had no significant experience of it. One
can barely imagine what the Civil War was to Whitman,
this fanatically intense American, this New World man, the
first white aboriginal, with his lusty physical joy of life, his
love of comrades, his genius for poetry, and his natural
mysticism. Whitman was stricken by the war but he was
recreated by it. Columbus had been a rather nebulous
hero; Lincoln was the reincarnation of the American god to
him. Half of Whitman's great poetry is war poetry and
poetry on Lincoln and his death, and death poetry, though
it cannot all be dated from the war. Whitman accepted
death as he did sex and otherness, self and not-self. The

171

war returned to him the particularity of death, and it produced in him not bitterness but love. He triumphed over it. He saw beyond history and beyond America. But what he saw was with the American vision. In Whitman's dialectic, you do not give up the past for the vision: the past is of the vision as much as the future. In the open air "a great personal deed has room" and it is such a deed that seizes upon the hearts of the whole race of man. And this deed is not discovery or triumph or a formula of belief: it is the giving oneself—the Whitman in oneself—to the other, the comrade. Whitman knew that giving in the past had always been a form of taxation and protection. This new kind of giving is reckless and mystical, differing from the old giving because Whitman gives body and soul without sacrificing one to the other. Whitman is no "humanist" and no ordinary libertarian but a seer who dreams of free individuality in a world of free souls. The open road may be a commonplace symbol, but it is a deliberate symbol, and it stands for an actuality. That actuality is America as Whitman sees America in himself. The anti-Whitman party of our time attempts, of course, to deny the vision of the New World with its physical materialism, experimentalism, and the whole concept of man for the world of the present. It turns out that Whitman is not for the "people" and not for the impressively learned poets of our time. He is for man who begins at the beginning—all over again. There is more to poetry than books, he says.

> I think heroic deeds were all conceived in the open
>   air, and all free poems also,
> I think I could stop here myself and do miracles. . .
> Here a great personal deed has room. . .

Here is realization . . . here is adhesiveness. . .
Do you know what it is as you pass to be loved by
    strangers? . . .
These are the days that must happen to you:
You shall not heap up what is called riches. . .
What beckonings of love you receive you shall only
    answer with passionate kisses of parting,
You shall not allow the hold of those who spread
    their reach'd hands toward you. . .
Allons! after the great companions, and to belong to
    them!
They too are on the road—they are the swift and
    majestic men
They are the greatest women. . .
They go, they go! I know that they go, but I know
    not where they go,
But I know that they go toward the best—toward
    something great. . ."

It is all there: the greatness of the body and the greatness
of the soul; the touching of the world and the heroism of
departure; the magnificent motion of death; the expanding
cycle of consciousness; the essential holiness of all things.
And always at the center, the self, the moment of incarnation, the Walt Whitman of oneself. The aboriginal or, if
you like, the American.

The power of Whitman in the world is incalculable. In
literature it has long been calculated as nothing. It is because of poets like Whitman that literature exists but it is
always Literature that determines to exterminate its Whit-
mans, its Blakes, its Lawrences. The probability is that
Whitman will never be "accepted" as one of the great writers of mankind; acceptance is always a function of the writ-

ers who assume the power of literature, for whatever reasons, and who make literature one of the arms of the law. Because Whitman is beyond the law of literature he is condemned to extinction from generation to generation. Like Lawrence, who rescued him in our century, Whitman is beyond the reach of Criticism, beyond the library and the curriculum, beyond Congress and Church, and yet there, right under your nose.

The Greatest Living Patagonian

I WILL INTRODUCE Miller with a quotation from the *Tropic of Cancer*: "I sometimes ask myself how it happens that I attract nothing but crackbrained individuals, neuroesthenics, neurotics, psychopaths—and Jews especially. There must be something in a healthy Gentile that excites the Jewish mind, like when he sees sour black bread." The "healthy Gentile" is a good sobriquet for Miller, who usually refers to himself as the Happy Rock, Caliban, "just a Brooklyn boy," "Someone who has gone off the gold standard of Literature" or—the name I like best—the Patagonian. What is a Patagonian? I don't know, but it is certainly something rare and *sui generis*. We can call Miller the greatest living Patagonian.

How is one to talk about Miller? There are authors one

cannot write a book or even a good essay about. Arthur Rimbaud is one (and Miller's book on Rimbaud is one of the best books on Rimbaud ever written, although it is mostly about Henry Miller). D. H. Lawrence is another author one cannot encompass in a book "about" (Miller abandoned his book on Lawrence). And Miller himself is one of those Patagonian authors who just won't fit into a book. Every word he has ever written is autobiographical, but only in the way *Leaves of Grass* is autobiographical. There is not a word of "confession" in Miller. His amorous exploits are sometimes read as a kind of Brooklyn Casanova or male Fanny Hill, but there is probably not a word of exaggeration or boasting to speak of—or only as much as the occasion would call for. The reader can and cannot reconstruct the Life of Henry Miller from his books, for Miller never sticks to the subject any more than Lawrence does. The fact is that there isn't any subject and Miller is its poet. But a little information about him might help present him to those who need an introduction. For myself, I do not read him consecutively; I choose one of his books blindly and open it at random. I have just done this; for an example, I find: "Man is not at home in the universe, despite all the efforts of philosophers and metaphysicians to provide a soothing syrup. Thought is still a narcotic. The deepest question is *why*. And it is a forbidden one. The very asking is in the nature of cosmic sabotage. And the penalty is—the afflictions of Job." Not the greatest prose probably, but Miller is not a writer; Henry James is a writer. Miller is a talker, a streetcorner gabbler, a prophet, and a Patagonian.

What are the facts about Miller? I'm not sure how important they are. He was born in Brooklyn about 1890, of German ancestry, and in certain ways he is quite German. I have often thought that the Germans make the best Americans, though they certainly make the worst Germans. Miller understands the German in himself and in America. He compares Whitman and Goethe: "In Whitman the whole American scene comes to life, her past and her future, her birth and her death. Whatever there is of value in America Whitman has expressed, and there is nothing more to be said. The future belongs to the machine, to the robots. He was the poet of the body and the soul, Whitman. The first and the last poet. He is almost undecipherable today, a monument covered with rude hieroglyphics, for which there is no key . . . There is no equivalent in the languages of Europe for the spirit which he immortalized. Europe is saturated with art and her soil is full of dead bones and her museums are bursting with plundered treasures, but what Europe has never had is a free, healthy spirit, what you might call a MAN. Goethe was the nearest approach, but Goethe was a stuffed shirt, by comparison. Goethe was a respectable citizen, a pedant, a bore, a universal spirit, but stamped with the German trademark, with the double eagle. The serenity of Goethe, the calm, Olympian attitude, is nothing more than the drowsy stupor of a German bourgeois deity. Goethe is an end of something, Whitman is a beginning."

If anybody can decipher the Whitman key it is Miller. Miller is the twentieth-century reincarnation of Whitman. But to return to the "facts." The Brooklyn Boy went to a Brooklyn high school in a day when most high schools kept higher standards than most American universities today. He started at CCNY but quit almost immediately and went to work for a cement company ("Everlasting Cement"), then for a telegraph company, where he became the personnel manager in the biggest city in the world. The telegraph company is called the Cosmodemonic Telegraph Company in Miller's books, or in moments of gaiety the Cosmococcic Telegraph Company. One day while the vice-president was bawling him out he mentioned to Miller that he would like to see someone write a sort of Horatio Alger book about the messengers.

> I thought to myself [said Miller]—you poor old futzer, you, just wait until I get it off my chest . . . I'll give you an Horatio Alger book . . . My head was in a whirl to leave his office. I saw the army of men, women and children that had passed through my hands, saw them weeping, begging, beseeching, imploring, cursing, spitting, fuming, threatening. I saw the tracks they left on the highways, lying on the floor of freight trains, the parents in rags, the coal box empty, the sink running over, the walls sweating and between the cold beads of sweat the cockroaches running like mad; I saw them hobbling along like twisted gnomes or falling backwards in the epileptic frenzy . . . I saw the walls giving way and the pest pouring out like a winged fluid, and the men higher up with their ironclad logic, waiting for it to blow over, waiting for everything to be patched up, waiting, waiting contentedly . . . saying that things were temporarily out of order. I saw the Horatio Alger hero, the dream of a sick America, mounting higher and higher, first messenger, then operator, then manager, then chief, then superintendent, then vice-president, then president, then trust magnate, then beer baron, then Lord of all the Americas, the money god, the god of gods, the clay of clay, nullity on high, zero with ninety-seven thousand decimals fore and aft . . . I will give you Horatio Alger as he looks the day after the Apocalypse, when all the stink has cleared away.

And he did. Miller's first book, *Tropic of Cancer*, was published in Paris in 1934 and was immediately famous and immediately banned in all English-speaking countries. It is the Horatio Alger story with a vengeance. Miller had walked out of the Cosmodemonic Telegraph Company one day without a word; ever after he lived on his wits. He had managed to get to Paris on ten dollars, where he lived more than a decade, not during the gay prosperous twenties but during the Great Depression. He starved, made friends by the score, mastered the French language and his own. It was not until the Second World War broke out that he returned to America to live at Big Sur, California. Among his best books several were long banned: the two *Tropics* (*Tropic of Cancer*, 1934, and *Tropic of Capricorn*, 1939); *Black Spring*, 1936; and part of the present trilogy *The Rosy Crucifixion* (including *Sexus*, *Plexus*, and *Nexus*).

Unfortunately for Miller he is a man without honor in his own country and in his own language. When *Tropic of Cancer* was published he was even denied entrance into England, held over in custody by the port authorities and returned to France by the next boat. He made friends with his jailer and wrote a charming essay about him. But Miller has no sense of despair. At the beginning of *Tropic of Cancer* he writes: "I have no money, no resources, no hopes. I am the happiest man alive."

George Orwell was one of the few English critics who saw his worth, though (*mirabile dictu*) T. S. Eliot and even Ezra Pound complimented him. Pound in his usual ungracious manner gave the *Tropic of Cancer* to a friend who later became Miller's publisher, and said: Here is a dirty book worth reading. Pound even went so far as to try to enlist Miller in his economic system to save the world. Miller retaliated by writing a satire called *Money and How It Gets That Way*, dedicated to Ezra Pound. The acquaintanceship halted there, Miller's view of money being something like this (from *Tropic of Capricorn*): "To walk in money through the night crowd, protected by money, lulled by money, dulled by money, the crowd itself a money, the breath money, no least single object anywhere that is not money, money, money everywhere and still not enough, and then no money, or a little money or less money or more money, but money, always money, and if you have money or you don't have money it is the money that counts and money makes money, *but what makes money make money?*" Pound didn't care for that brand of economics.

But all the writers jostled each other to welcome Miller among the elect, for the moment at least: Eliot, Herbert Read, Aldous Huxley, John Dos Passos and among them some who really knew how good Miller was: William Carlos Williams, who called him the Dean, Lawrence Durrell, Paul Rosenfeld, Wallace Fowlie, Osbert Sitwell, Kenneth Patchen, many painters (Miller is a fanatical water colorist). But mostly he is beset by his neuresthenics and psychopaths, as any cosmodemonic poet must be. People of all sexes frequently turned up at Big Sur and announced that they wanted to join the Sex Cult. Miller gave them bus fare and a good dinner and sent them on their way.

Orwell has written one of the best essays on Miller, although he takes a sociological approach and tries to place Miller as a Depression writer or something of the sort. What astonished Orwell about Miller was the difference between his view and the existential bitterness of a novelist like Céline. Céline's *Voyage au Bout de la Nuit* describes the meaninglessness of modern life and is thus a prototype of twentieth-century fiction. Orwell calls Céline's book a cry of unbearable disgust, a voice from the cesspool. And

Orwell adds that the *Tropic of Cancer* is almost exactly the opposite! Such a thing as Miller's book "has become so unusual as to seem almost anomalous, [for] it is the book of a man who is happy." Miller also had reached the bottom of the pit, as many writers do; but how, Orwell asks, could he have emerged unembittered, whole, laughing with joy? "Exactly the aspects of life that fill Céline with horror are the ones that appeal to him. So far from protesting, he is *accepting*. And the very word 'acceptance' calls up his real affinity, another American, Walt Whitman."

This is, indeed, the crux of the matter and it is unfortunate that Orwell cannot see past the socio-economic situation with Whitman and Miller. Nevertheless, this English critic recognizes Miller's mastery of his material and places him among the great writers of our age; more than that, he predicts that Miller will set the pace and attitude for the novelist of the future. This has not happened yet, but I agree that it must. Miller's influence today is primarily among poets; those poets who follow Whitman must necessarily follow Miller, even to the extent of giving up poetry in its formal sense and writing that personal apocalyptic prose which Miller does. It is the prose of the Bible of Hell that Blake talked about and Arthur Rimbaud wrote a chapter of.

What is this "acceptance" Orwell mentions in regard to Whitman and Henry Miller? On one level it is the poetry of cosmic consciousness, and on the most obvious level it is the poetry of the Romantic nineteenth century. Miller is unknown in this country because he represents the Continental rather than the English influence. He breaks with the English literary tradition just as many of the twentieth-century Americans do, because his ancestry is not British, and not American colonial. He does not read the favored British writers, Milton, Marlowe, Pope, Donne. He reads what his grandparents knew was in the air when Victorianism was the genius of British poetry. He grew up with books by Dostoevsky, Knut Hamsun, Strindberg, Nietzsche (especially Nietzsche), Elie Faure, Spengler. Like a true poet he found his way to Rimbaud, Ramakrishna, Blavatsky, Huysmans, Count Keyserling, Prince Kropotkin, Lao-tse, Nostradamus, Petronius, Rabelais, Suzuki, Zen philosophy, Van Gogh. And in English he let himself be influenced not by the solid classics but by *Alice in Wonderland*, Chesterton's *St. Francis*, Conrad, Cooper, Emerson, Rider Haggard, G. A. Henty (the boy's historian—I remember being told when I was a boy that Henty had the facts all wrong), Joyce, Arthur Machen, Mencken, John Cowper Powys, Herbert Spencer's *Autobiography*, Thoreau on "Civil Disobedience," Emma Goldman—the great anarchist (whom he met)—Whitman, of course, and perhaps above all that companion piece to *Leaves of Grass* called *Huckleberry Finn*. Hardly a Great Books list from the shores of Lake Michigan—almost a period list. Miller will introduce his readers to strange masterpieces like Doughty's *Arabia Deserta* or to the journal of Anaïs Nin which he (and other writers) swears is one of the masterpieces of the twentieth century. I imagine that Miller has read as much as any man living but he does not have that religious solemnity about books which we are brought up in. Books, after all, are only mnemonic devices; and poets are always celebrating the burning of libraries. And as with libraries, so with monuments, and as with monuments, so with civilizations. But in Miller's case (*chez* Miller) there is no vindictiveness, no bitterness. Orwell was bothered when he

met Miller because Miller didn't want to go to the Spanish
Civil War and do battle on one side or the other. Miller is
an anarchist of sorts, and he doesn't especially care which
dog eats which dog. As it happens, the righteous Loyalists
were eaten by the Communists and the righteous Falang-
ists were eaten by the Nazis over the most decadent hole in
Europe; so Miller was right.

Lawrence Durrell has said that the *Tropic* books were
healthy while Céline and D. H. Lawrence were sick. Lawrence never escaped his puritanism and it is his heroic try
that makes us honor him. Céline is the typical European
man of despair—why should he not despair, this French-
man of the trenches of World War I? We are raising up a
generation of young American Célines, I'm afraid, but
Miller's generation still had Whitman before its eyes and
was not running back to the potholes and ash heaps of
Europe. Miller is as good an antiquarian as anybody; in the
medieval towns of France he goes wild with happiness; and
he has written one of the best "travel books" on Greece ever
done (the critics are unanimous about the *Colossus of
Maroussi*); but to worship the "tradition" is to him the
sheerest absurdity. Like most Americans, he shares the
view of the first Henry Ford that history is bunk. He cannot
forgive his "Nordic" ancestors for the doctrines of righteousness and cleanliness. His people, he says, were painfully
clean: "Never once had they opened the door which leads
to the soul; never once did they dream of taking a blind
leap into the dark. After dinner the dishes were promptly
washed and put in the closet; after the paper was read it
was neatly folded and laid away on a shelf; after the clothes
were washed they were ironed and folded and then tucked
away in the drawers. Everything was for tomorrow, but

tomorrow never came. The present was only a bridge and on this bridge they are still groaning, as the world groans, and not one idiot ever thinks of blowing up the bridge." As everyone knows, Cleanliness is the chief American industry. Miller is the most formidable anticleanliness poet since Walt Whitman, and his hatred of righteousness is also American, with the Americanism of Thoreau, Whitman, and Emma Goldman. Miller writes a good deal about cooking and wine drinking. Americans are the worst cooks in the world, outside of the British; and Americans are also great drunkards who know nothing about wine. The Germanic-American Miller reintroduces good food and decent wine into our literature. One of his funniest essays is about the American loaf of bread, the poisonous loaf of cleanliness wrapped in cellophane, the manufacture of which is a heavy industry like steel.

Orwell and other critics tend to regard Miller as a kind of hedonist and professional do-nothing. And morally, they tend to regard him as one of that illustrious line of Americans who undermine the foundations of traditional morals. Miller quotes Thoreau's statement, which might almost be the motto of the cosmic writer: "Most of what my neighbors call good, I am profoundly convinced is evil, and if I repent anything, it is my good conduct that I repent." One could hardly call Thoreau a criminal, yet he had his run-ins with the law, just as Miller has, and for the same reasons. The strain of anarchism and amorality is growing stronger in American literature, or that branch of it that I am talking about, and Miller is one of its chief carriers. It is not only Emma Goldman, Thoreau, Mark Twain, Whitman and such, but that whole literature of Detachment from political hysteria and overorganization. I am influenced enough by these people and by Miller to tell my students, the poets at least, to cultivate an ignorance of contemporary political and military events because they do not matter. I tell them not to vote, to join nothing. I try to steer them toward their true leaders and visionaries, men almost unknown in the polite literary world, Reich for instance. Wilhelm Reich furthered a movement in Germany called "Work Democracy"; not machine politics, no politics at all, but democracy within one's immediate orbit; democracy at home. America is still the only country where social idealism and experimentation have elbow room; there are still communities that practice primitive Christianity, such as the Catholic anarchists; and just plain little homemade gardens of Eden such as Miller's cliff at Big Sur. The life he describes in *Big Sur and the Oranges of Hieronymus Bosch* is a far cry from the little fascist dreams of the New Classicists. And it is a far cry from the bitter isolationism of Robinson Jeffers or even of Lawrence. Morally I regard Miller as a holy man, as most of his admirers do—Gandhi with a penis.

Miller says in a little essay on Immorality and Morality: "What is moral and what is immoral? Nobody can ever answer this question satisfactorily. Not because morals ceaselessly evolve, but because the principle on which they depend is factitious. Morality is for slaves, for beings without spirit. And when I say spirit I mean the Holy Spirit." And he ends this little piece with a quotation from ancient Hindu scripture: Evil does not exist.

Whitman, Lawrence, Miller, and even Blake all have the reputation of being sex-obsessed, Miller especially. Whereas Whitman writes "copulation is no more rank to me than death is," Miller writes hundreds of pages describing in the

minutest and clearest detail his exploits in bed. Every serious reader of erotica has remarked about Miller that he is
probably the only author in history who writes about such
things with complete ease and naturalness. Lawrence never
quite rid himself of his puritanical salaciousness, nor Joyce;
both had too much religion in their veins. It is funny to
recollect that Lawrence thought *Ulysses* a smutty book and
Joyce thought *Lady Chatterley* a smutty book. Both were
right. But at least they *tried* to free themselves from literary morality. Miller's achievement is miraculous: he is
screamingly funny without making fun of sex, the way
Rabelais does. (Rabelais is, of course, magnificent; so is
Boccaccio; but both write against the background of religion, like Joyce and Lawrence.) Miller is accurate and poetic in the highest degree; there is not a smirk anywhere in
his writings. Miller undoubtedly profited from the mistakes
of his predecessors; his aim was not to write about the
erotic but to write the whole truth about the life he knew.
This goal demanded the full vocabulary and iconography
of sex, and it is possible that he is the first writer outside
the Orient who has succeeded in writing as naturally about
sex on a large scale as novelists ordinarily write about the
dinner table or the battlefield. I think only an American
could have performed this feat.

We are dealing with the serious question of banned
books, burned books, and fear of books in general. America
has the most liberal censorship laws in the West today, but
we have done no more than make a start. I have always
been amused by the famous decision of Judge Woolsey,
who lifted the ban on *Ulysses*, although it was certainly a
fine thing to do and it is a landmark we can be proud of.
Woolsey said various comical things, such as that he could

not detect the "leer of the sensualist" in Joyce's book, and that therefore (the logic of it escapes me) it is not pornographic. In excusing the use of old Saxon words he noted that Joyce's "locale was Celtic and his season Spring." And, in order to push his decision through, Judge Woolsey stated that *Ulysses* "did not tend to excite sexual impulses or lustful thoughts," and he closed his argument with the elegant statement that although the book is "somewhat emetic, nowhere does it tend to be an aphrodisiac." Emetic means tending to produce vomiting and I doubt that Joyce savored that description of his masterpiece. The implication, of course, is that vomiting is good for you, and lustful thoughts not. Now everyone who has read *Ulysses* knows that the book is based largely on the lustful thoughts and acts of its characters and that Joyce spared no pains to represent these thoughts and deeds richly and smackingly. *Ulysses* is, since the Judge used the word, a pretty *good* aphrodisiac, partly because of Joyce's own religious tensions. Miller, on the other hand, is no aphrodisiac at all, because religious or so-called moral tension does not exist for him. When one of Miller's characters lusts, he lusts out loud and then proceeds to the business at hand. Joyce actually prevents himself from experiencing the beauty of sex or lust, while Miller is freed at the outset to deal with the overpowering mysteries and glories of love and copulation.

Miller has furthered literature for all writers by ignoring the art forms, the novel, the poem, the drama, and by sticking to the autobiographical novel. He says in *The Books in My Life* (one of the available works), "The autobiographical novel, which Emerson predicted would grow in importance with time, has replaced the great confessions. It is not a mixture of truth and fiction, this genre of literature, but an expansion and deepening of truth. It is more authentic, more veridical, than the diary. It is not the flimsy truth of facts which the authors of these autobiographical novels offer but the truth of emotion, reflection and understanding, truth digested and assimilated. The being revealing himself does so on all levels simultaneously." Everything Miller has written is part of this great amorphous autobiographical novel and it must be read not entirely but in large chunks to make sense. Many of the individual works are whole in themselves, one dealing with his life in Paris, one with his life as a New Yorker, and there is, in fact, a definite span of years encompassed in the works. But the volumes of essays are also part of the story and there is no way to make a whole out of the parts. Miller is easy to quote if one quotes carefully; the danger is that one can find massive contradictions, unless there is some awareness of the underlying world and the cosmic attitudes of the author. What makes Miller unique is his time and place; he is the only American of our time who has given us a full-scale interpretation of modern America, other than the kind of thing we find in the cultural journals. Incidentally, we do not find Miller in these journals, which, presuming an interest in letters and art, are really organs of social and political opinion.

Readers of Whitman recall that Whitman was blistering about the materialism of this country a century ago, and its departure from the ideals of the founding fathers. Miller is worse. Now it is a commonplace of modern poetry that the poet dissociates himself from life as it is lived by the average American today. Whitman and Miller heap abuse on the failure of the country to live up to its promise. Miller writes as a poet about the demonic hideousness of New

York City, Chicago, the South, or he rhapsodizes when there is anything to be rapturous about. But it is not Art that he cares about; it is man, man's treatment of man in America and man's treatment of nature. What we get in Miller is not a sense of superiority but fury, even the fury of the prophet of doom.

Miller knows America from the bottom up and from coast to coast. In the same way he knows Paris as few Frenchmen do. But when Miller describes slums it is usually with the joyous eye of the artist, not with the self-righteous sneer of the social reformer. Here, too, one might describe his psychology as "Oriental" rather than modern. The cultural situation is a matter of complete indifference to him. Miller frequently immerses himself in such modern Indian mystics as Krishnamurti and Ramakrishna, but without any of the flapdoodle of the cultist. He is himself one of the foremost of the contemporary men of Detachment. His influence (like that of Lawrence) comes as much from his life as from his writings. Here it is better to quote. This is Myrtle Avenue in Brooklyn:

> But I saw a street called Myrtle Avenue, which runs from Borough Hall to Fresh Pond Road, and down this street no saint ever walked (else it would have crumbled), down this street no miracle ever passed, nor any poet, nor any species of human genius, nor did any flower ever grow there, nor did the sun strike it squarely, nor did the rain ever wash it. For the genuine Inferno which I had to postpone for twenty years I give you Myrtle Avenue, one of the innumerable bridlepaths ridden by iron monsters which lead to the heart of America's emptiness. If you have only seen Essen or Manchester or Chicago or Levallois-Perret or Glasgow or Hoboken or Canarsie or Bayonne you have seen nothing of the magnificent emptiness of progress and enlightenment. Dear

reader, you must see Myrtle Avenue before you die, if only to realize how far into the future Dante saw. You must believe me that on this street, neither in the houses which line it, nor the cobblestones which pave it, nor the elevated structure which cuts it atwain, neither in any creature that bears a name and lives thereon, neither in any animal, bird or insect passing through it to slaughter or already slaughtered, is there hope of "lubet," "sublimate" or "abominate." It is a street not of sorrow, for sorrow would be human and recognizable, but of sheer emptiness: it is emptier than the most extinct volcano, emptier than a vacuum, emptier than the word God in the mouth of an unbeliever.

This is a man describing his own neighborhood, but the street is a type that runs from the Atlantic to the Pacific, with variations:

The whole country is lawless, violent, explosive, demoniacal. It's in the air, in the climate, in the ultra-grandiose landscape, in the stone forests that are lying horizontal, in the torrential rivers that bite through the rocky canyons, in the supranormal distances, the supernal arid wastes, the overlush crops, the monstrous fruits, the mixture of quixotic bloods, the fatras of cults, sects, beliefs, the opposition of laws and languages, the contradictoriness of temperaments, principles, needs, requirements. The continent is full of buried violence, of the bones of autediluvian monsters and of lost races of man, of mysteries which are wrapped in doom. The atmosphere is at times so electrical that the soul is summoned out of its body and runs amok. Like the rain everything comes in bucketsful—or not at all. The whole continent is a huge volcano whose crater is temporarily concealed by a moving panorama which is partly dream, partly fear, partly despair. From Alaska to Yucatan it's the same story. Nature dominates, Nature wins out. Everywhere the same fundamental urge to slay, to ravage, to plunder. Outwardly they seem like a fine, upstanding people—healthy, optimistic, courageous. Inwardly they are filled with worms. A tiny spark and they blow up.

The passages on Times Square repeat and catalogue, like Whitman; they are a little too painful to read out of context. Here is a bit of Chicago; Miller is wandering in the Negro slums with a fellow visitor:

> We got into the car, rode a few blocks and got out to visit another shell crater. The street was deserted except for some chickens grubbing for food between the slate of a crumbling piazza. More vacant lots, more gutted houses; fire escapes clinging to the walls with their iron teeth, like drunken acrobats. A Sunday atmosphere here. Everything serene and peaceful. Like Louvain or Rheims between bombardments. Like Phoebus, Virginia, dreaming of bringing her steeds to water, or like modern Eleusis smothered by a wet sock. Then suddenly I saw it chalked upon the side of a house in letters ten feet high:
>
> GOOD NEWS! GOD IS LOVE!
>
> When I saw these words I got down on my knees in the open sewer which had been conveniently placed there for the purpose and I offered up a short prayer, a silent one, which must have registered as far as Mound City, Illinois, where the colored muskrats have built their igloos. It was time for a good stiff drink of cod-liver oil but as the varnish factories were all closed we had to repair to the abattoir and quaff a bucket of blood. Never has blood tasted so wonderful! It was like taking vitamins A, B, C, D, E in quick succession and then chewing a stick of cold dynamite. Good news! Aye, wonderful news—for Chicago. I ordered the chauffeur to take us immediately to Mundelein so that I could bless the cardinal and all the real estate operations, but we only got as far as the Bahai Temple . . .

Or, again—in explanation:

Oh, Henry, what beautiful golden teeth you have! exclaimed my four-year-old daughter the other morning on climbing into bed with me. (That's how I approach the works of my confreres.) I see how beautiful are their golden teeth, not how ugly or artificial they are.

Combating the "system" is nonsense. There is only one aim in life and that is to live it. In America it has become impossible, except for a few lucky or wise people, to live one's own life; consequently the poets and artists tend to move to the fringes of society. Wherever there are individuals, says Miller (like Thoreau) there are new frontiers. The American way of life has become illustory; we lead the lives of prisoners while we boast about free speech, free press, and free religion, none of which we actually do enjoy in full. The price for security has become too great; abundance has become a travesty. The only thing for nonenslaved man to do is to move out to the edge, lose contact with the machines of organization which are as ubiquitous in this country as in Russia. "Instead of bucking your head against a stone wall, sit quietly with hands folded and wait for the walls to crumble . . . Don't sit and *pray* that it will happen! Just sit and *watch* it happen!" These sayings the culture litterateur condemns as irresponsible. Miller follows through with the complete program of nonparticipation in our machine society, which is organized from the cradle to the grave. "Just as Gandhi successfully exploited the doctrine of nonresistance, so these 'saints of the just' practiced non-recognition—non-recognition of sin, guilt, fear and disease . . . even death." Whitman also believed in nonrecognition of death. His view of death as part of life is one of the many reasons for his unpopularity in America, where death is considered a crime against society. "Why try to solve a problem? *Dissolve* it! [says Miller]. Fear not to be a coward, a traitor, a renegade. In this universe of ours there is room for all, perhaps even need for all. The sun does not inquire about rank and status before shedding its warmth; the cyclone levels the godly and the ungodly; the government takes your tax money even though it be tainted. Nor is the atom bomb a respecter of persons. Perhaps that is why the righteous are squirming so!"

All of this is about modern America and the high cost of security. Do we really have a high standard of living? Miller says not, as most poets do. If living means appreciation of life we have the lowest standard of living in the world, in spite of the fact that it costs more to live in America than in any country in the world. Miller says "the cost is not only in dollars and cents but in sweat and blood, in frustration, ennui, broken homes, smashed ideals, illness and insanity. We have the most wonderful hospitals, the most fabulous prisons, the best equipped and highest paid army and navy, the speediest bombers, the largest stockpile of atom bombs, yet never enough of any of these items to satisfy the demand. Our manual workers are the highest paid in the world; our poets the worst . . ."

And Miller gives this answer, letting Krishnamurti say it:

The world problem is the individual problem; if the individual is at peace, has happiness, has great tolerance, and an intense desire to help, then the world problem as such ceases to exist. You consider the world problem before you have considered your own problem. Before you have established peace and understanding in your own hearts and in your own minds you desire to establish peace and tranquility in the minds of others, in your nations and in your states;

whereas peace and understanding will only come when there is understanding, certainty and strength in yourselves.

To place the individual before the state, whether the Russian state or the American state, is the first need of modern man. To interpret Miller, man is like the common soldier on the battlefield; he can know nothing of the battle at large or of its causes; he can know only the fifty feet or so in his immediate vicinity; within that radius he is a man responsible for himself and his fellows; beyond that he is powerless. Modern life, having made everyone state conscious, has destroyed the individual. America has as few individuals today as Russia, and as many taboos to keep the individual from coming to life as the USSR. First, we have contaminated the idea of society; second, we have contaminated the idea of community. Miller writing about his little community at Big Sur frowns on the idea of community itself. "To create community—and what is a nation, or a people, without a sense of community—there must be a common purpose. Even here in Big Sur, where the oranges are ready to blossom forth, there is no common purpose, no common effort. There is a remarkable neighborliness, but no community spirit. We have a Grange, as do other rural communities, but what is a 'Grange' in the life of man? The real workers are outside the Grange. Just as the 'real men of God' are outside the Church. And the real leaders outside the world of politics."

"We create our fate," says Miller. And better still: "Forget, forgive, renounce, abdicate." And "scrap the past instantly." Live the good life instantly; it's now or never, and always has been.

Miller is "irresponsible" as far as official and popular politics go, or as far as common church morality goes, and as far as literary manners go. But he is not a poseur, he has no program, yet he has a deep and pure sense of morality. I would call him a total revolutionary, the man who will settle for nothing less than "Christmas on earth." In his remarkable study of Rimbaud, a prose-poem of one hundred and fifty pages called *The Time of the Assassins*, Miller discourses on the spiritual suicide of modern youth.

I like to think of him as the one who extended the boundaries of that only partially explored domain. Youth ends where manhood begins, it is said. A phrase without meaning, since from the beginning of history man has never enjoyed the full measure of youth nor known the limitless possibilities of adulthood. How can one know the splendor and fullness of youth if one's energies are consumed in combating the errors and falsities of parents and ancestors? Is youth to waste its strength unlocking the grip of death? Is youth's only mission on earth to rebel, to destroy, to assassinate? Is youth only to be offered up to sacrifice? What of the *dreams* of youth? Are they always to be regarded as follies? Are they to be populated only with chimeras? . . . Stifle or deform youth's dreams and you destroy the creator. Where there has been no real youth there can be no real manhood. If society has come to resemble a collection of deformities, is it not the work of our educators and preceptors? Today, as yesterday, the youth who would live his own life has no place to turn, no place to live his youth unless, retiring into his chrysalis, he closes all apertures and buries himself alive. The conception of our mother the earth being "an egg which doth contain all good things in it" has undergone a profound change. The cosmic egg contains an addled yolk. This is the present view of mother earth. The psychoanalysts have traced the poison back to the womb, but to what avail? In the light of this profound discovery we are given permission . . . to step from one rotten egg into another. . . . Why breed new monsters of negation and futility? Let society scotch its own rotten corpse! Let us have a new heaven and a new earth!—that was the sense of Rimbaud's obstinate revolt.

Miller calls for an end to revolt once and for all. His message is precisely that of Whitman, of Rimbaud, of Rilke: "Everything we are taught is false"; and "Change your life." As a writer Miller may be second- or third-rate or of no rating at all; as a spiritual example he stands among the great men of our age. Will this ever be recognized? Not in our time probably.

The Rimbaud book ends with a Coda, a little recital of the literature of despair which has surrounded us for a hundred years.

Rimbaud was born in the middle of the nineteenth century, October 20th, 1854, at 6:00 A.M., it is said. A century of unrest, of materialism, and of 'progress,' as we say. Purgatorial in every sense of the word, and the writers who flourished in this period reflect this ominously. Wars and revolutions were abundant. Russia alone, we are told, waged thirty-three wars (mostly of conquest) during the 18th and 19th centuries. Shortly after Rimbaud is born his father is off to the Crimean War. So is Tolstoy. The revolution of 1848, of brief duration but full of consequences, is followed by the bloody Commune of 1871, which Rimbaud as a boy is thought to have participated in. In 1848 we in America are fighting the Mexicans with whom we are now great friends, though the Mexicans are not too sure of it. During this war Thoreau makes his famous speech on Civil Disobedience, a document which will one day be added to the Emancipation Proclamation. . . . Twelve years later the Civil War breaks out, perhaps the bloodiest of all civil wars. . . . From 1847 until his death in 1881 Amiel is writing his *Journal Intime* . . . which . . . gives a thoroughgoing analysis of the moral dilemma in which the creative spirits of the time found themselves. The very titles of the book written by influential writers of the 19th century are revelatory. I give just a few ... *The Sickness unto Death* (Kierkegaard), *Dreams and Life* (Gérard de Nerval), *Les Fleurs du Mal* (Baudelaire), *Les Chants de Maldoror* (Lautréamont), *The Birth of Tragedy* (Nietzsche), *La Bête Humaine* (Zola), *Hunger* (Knut Hamsun), *Les Lauriers Sont Coupés* (Dujardin), *The Conquest of Bread* (Kropotkin), *Looking Backward* (Edward Bellamy), *Alice in Wonderland*, *The Serpent in Paradise* (Sacher-Masoch), *Les Paradis Artificiels* (Baudelaire), *Dead Souls* (Gogol), *The House of the Dead* (Dostoiefsky), *The Wild Duck* (Ibsen), *The Inferno* (Strindberg), *The Nether World* (Gissing), *A Rebours* (Huysmans). . . .

Goethe's *Faust* was not so very old when Rimbaud asked a friend for a copy of it. Remember the date of his birth is October 20th, 1854 (6:00 A.M. Western Standard Diabolical Time). The very next year, 1855, *Leaves of Grass* makes its appearance, followed by condemnation and suppression. Meanwhile *Moby Dick* had come out (1851) and Thoreau's *Walden* (1854). In 1855 Gérard de Nerval commits suicide, having lasted till the remarkable age of 47. In 1854 Kierkegaard is already penning his last words to history in which he gives the parable of "The Sacrificed Ones." Just four or five years before Rimbaud completes *A Season in Hell* (1873), Lautréamont publishes privately his celebrated piece of blasphemy, another "work of youth," as we say, in order not to take these heartbreaking testaments seriously. . . . By 1888 Nietzsche is explaining to Brandes that he can now boast three readers: Brandes, Taine, and Strindberg. The next year he goes mad and remains that way until his death in 1900. Lucky man! From 1893 to 1897 Strindberg is experiencing a crise . . . which he describes with magisterial effects in the *Inferno*. Reminiscent of Rimbaud is the title of another of his works: *The Keys to Paradise*. In 1888 comes Dujardin's curious little book, forgotten until recently. . . . By this time Mark Twain is at his height, *Huckleberry Finn*

197

having appeared in 1884, the same year as *Against the Grain* of Huysmans. . . . By the fall of 1891 Gissing's *New Grub Street* is launched. It is an interesting year in 19th century literature, the year of Rimbaud's death. . . .

What a century of names! . . . Shelley, Blake, Stendhal, Hegel, Fechner, Emerson, Poe, Schopenhauer, Max Stirner, Mallarmé, Tchekov, Andreyev, Verlaine, Couperus, Maeterlinck, Madame Blavatsky, Samuel Butler, Claudel, Unamuno, Conrad, Bakunin, Shaw, Rilke, Stefan George, Verhaeren, Gautier, Léon Bloy, Balzac, Yeats. . . .

What revolt, what disillusionment, what longing! Nothing but crises, breakdown, hallucinations and visions. The foundations of politics, morals, economics, and art tremble. The air is full of warnings and prophecies of the debacle to come —and in the 20th century it comes! Already two world wars and a promise of more before the century is out. Have we touched bottom? Not yet. The moral crisis of the 19th century has merely given way to the spiritual bankruptcy of the 20th. It is "the time of the assassins" and no mistaking it. . . .

Rimbaud is indeed the symbol of the death of modern poetry. This seer, this visionary deserts poetry at the age of eighteen to make money, by gunrunning, even by slave-trading, ending with a death-bed conversion. His is a life of slander, beginning with the motto "Death to God" chalked on the church door and ending with extreme unction and the money belt under the bed. I think the message of Rimbaud to Miller is the death of poetry, the death of history. The whole romantic agony of the nineteenth century is summed up in this adolescent genius, a curse laid on us. Miller obliterates the curse; he pronounces the benediction over Rimbaud, over the death of poetry, over the death of civilization itself but with a sidesplitting laugh without an iota of animosity in it. Miller leads us away from the charnel house of nineteenth-century poetry; he does not even recognize the existence of twentieth-century poetry. For poetry has lost its significance, its relevance, and even its meaning in our time. To begin again it must repair to the wilderness, outside society, outside the city gates, a million miles from books and their keepers. Almost alone of the writers of our time Henry Miller has done this; I would guess that his following is just beginning to grow. Like Nietzsche, like Lawrence, his word somehow spreads abroad and somehow cleanses the atmosphere of the mind of its age-old detritus of tradition, its habits of despair, its hates.

One word more: at the close of his beautiful clown story, "The Smile at the Foot of the Ladder," Miller talks about the clown, the hero of so much of the best contemporary literature.

> Joy is like a river, it flows ceaselessly. It seems to me that this is the message which the clown is trying to convey to us, that we should participate through ceaseless flow and movement, that we should not stop to reflect, compare, analyze, possess, but flow on and through, endlessly, like music. This is the gift of surrender, and the clown makes it symbolically. It is for us to make it real.
>
> At no time in the history of man has the world been so full of pain and anguish. Here and there, however, we meet with individuals who are untouched, unsullied, by the common grief. They are not heartless individuals, far from it! They are emancipated beings. For them the world is not what it seems to us. They see with other eyes. We say of them that they have died to the world. They live in the moment, fully, and the radiance which emanates from them is a perpetual song of joy.

And Miller is certainly one of these who have died to the world, like the clown. The ponderous absurdities of modern literature and the world it perpetuates dissolve in the hilarities of this almost unknown American author; this poet who dissociates himself from the so-called modern age and whose one aim is to give literature back to life. There are not many of these emancipated beings left in our world, these clowns and clairvoyants, celebrants of the soul and of the flesh and of the still-remaining promise of America. And of these few great souls the greatest is—the Patagonian.

The Decolonization
of American Literature

AMERICAN LITERATURE has been in the throes of decolonization since America first put pen to paper.

This literature began as a country-cousin literature of England. We were beholden to England for "culture" and broke with that culture through politics. For the great literature of this country until lately is political. In fact, it is the great political documents of America which have broken the back of cultural slavery all over the world. The writings of Jefferson, the Constitution, the Emancipation Proclamation are the basic artifacts of American literature. Decolonization is born in these documents. We are just beginning to feel the consequences. We are still at the dawn of those fabulous political words.

Three hundred years passed before the first words of cultural independence were set down, three centuries of holding on to the Old World, the European mother. We might have been a French country or a Spanish country or English like Canada, but we turned out to be none of those. One of the main reasons was that we had slaves, we had Negroes. The presence of slaves forced the ideal of liberty to its conclusion.

When America decolonized itself from Europe, from England, it opened the door to decolonization everywhere. We pressed a button and opened Pandora's box. It is this country that gave France the example of revolution. And even today we are the admiration and the horror of the Old World. We have not broken with those documents.

We were England's, Robert Frost said; we were colonials. When we stopped being colonials, all hell broke loose.

To be colonial means to live in a faraway place and to long for home. American literature was this way until little more than a century ago—until a few writers began to say, like Emerson, Europe is not home; until Thoreau pulled back even from the village of Concord; until Whitman rewrote the Constitution in poetry and sang the one great poem about the death of Abraham Lincoln.

To be colonial means not to cut the umbilical cord with Home and also to create the Native. America created two Natives, the Indian and the Negro. The Indian was banished to the unconscious mind of America (what is left of the Indian is a record of cultural shock which is phenomenal in modern history). But the Negro could not be banished. He was an industrial army, fuel to be burned and to be replenished of itself. He was the American "native." Richard Wright called his first novel *Native Son*; he understood "native."

But we were still colonial when we began to write. We would even send a Negro slave girl to England as a poet in the eighteenth century! I want to quote verbatim the biographical note from an old anthology of Negro poetry, edited by Langston Hughes and Arna Bontemps in 1949. This is colonialism in a nutshell.

Phillis Wheatley (Senegal, West Africa, 1753–84) was captured and sold into slavery in early childhood and brought to Boston in 1761. She became the property of John Wheatley of Boston whose wife and daughter soon noted the alert sensitivity of the young African girl and encouraged Phillis's efforts to acquire learning. Within a few years she was completely at home in the language and literature of her captors. She began writing poetry, and in 1770, at the age of seventeen, published, "A Poem, by Phillis, A Negro Girl in Boston, on the Death of the Reverend George Whitefield." When her health began to fail, Phillis was advised by doctors to take a sea voyage. This was arranged by the kindly mistress, who also gave the girl her freedom before she sailed for England. In London, Phillis was a success. It was there that her only collected volume of verse was first issued under the title *Poems on Various Subjects, Religious and Moral*, 1773. Then one by one the patrons of this talented ex-slave girl died and she returned to Boston. Her marriage was unhappy, and she died as a servant in a cheap lodging house at the age of thirty-one.

The ironies of this footnote are staggering and would require a Dostoevsky to handle them. Phillis Wheatley's poetry is as bad as all eighteenth-century colonial poetry, though better than that, say, of the Hartford Wits, which isn't saying much. Yet this experiment in colonial "culture" contains a message. The message is negative all down the line: slave girl, Boston at the dawn of revolution, guilt about rebellion from the Old World, neo-classical poetry, "the kindly mistress," and so on.

In every case except ours, a new culture is based on Home Country, Settler, and Native. But in America nobody knows where the Home Country is, for the Settlers come from Home Countries all over the world; and the Natives are no more. We have no Natives and no common Home Country. We have no peasantry. We have only expatriates and ex-slaves. This is a country of Runaways and Captives.

When the literature of America got under way it fascinated the world: runaways and captives, cops and robbers, cowboys and Indians, palefaces and blackskins, Jews and Goyim, Syndicate and Chamber of Commerce. Nobody wanted to be a native—the natives were dead and done for; everybody wanted to be a "settler." Those who would not "settle" went back to some Old Country of the mind: Eliot, Santayana, Pound, Hemingway, Henry James. Others mourned their "rootlessness"; we have a whole literature of that.

The cultural history of our country is one of decolonization, every element trying to sever itself from its origins. We are something like the white Australians, who are not eager to trace their ancestry back more than three or four generations because their original ancestors will have been sent over in the "hulks," the convict ships that were sent from England to the farthest place England could think of. Every FFV in Australia was a convict. We are in the same boat; we have only a paper aristocracy, and our aristocrats were revolutionaries who fought for their lives. In this sense the Daughters of the American Revolution are subversive. Only they have forgotten what their ancestors were subversive about.

Our literature took a long time to decolonize from English literature, and the process hasn't ended yet. In the beginning we were "Anglo-Saxon," about 90 per cent, for the blacks were not counted in the population and the immigrants hadn't arrived. Excuse a few sentences of facts, which I think mean so much. A generation after independence the Germans and Irish began to arrive in force. Before the Civil War, hordes of Irish, Dutch, Danes, Swedes, Norwegians, Swiss, and Jews swarmed in. Toward the end of the century came larger waves of Italians, Russians, Poles, Bohemians, and Hungarians. A smaller number of Asiatics seeped in, for this country is still anti-Asiatic (we invented our first concentration camps for American citizens of Japanese ancestry during the Second World War). In all this the English element was inundated and, so to speak, contaminated. The language of the King was lost in the shuffle.

A language in itself is nothing. A literature in itself is nothing. A literature is the expression of a nation's soul, and a great literature leaves nothing out—that is its greatness. But to leave nothing out means to go against the grain; it means to dissent. Our modern literature is a literature of dissent, monotonous and endless dissidence. This dissidence gives modern literature its authenticity. Yet this literature of dissent is only in its infancy. Dissent is contagious, and every day we find new areas of eruption everywhere in the world. But dissent is also a drop in the bucket of literature, a drop of pigment in the skin or in the blood.

American literature is unique; it is the only literature I have ever heard of in which all elements have tried, more or less simultaneously, to decolonize themselves. It is the only literature which practices cultural amnesia as a doctrine. The few famous American writers who refused to surrender the past, who insisted on memory (Henry James or Eliot), surrendered their nationality to the idea of European cultural supremacy. They could maintain a continuity with Europe only by becoming Europeans again.

English literature is a dead literature in America, a memory. The English language is practically a memory. Only a few English professors in America pretend that English and its great literature are continuous with ours.

A decolonized literature in an African country or in a free Arab country or in Israel is different from ours. Those nations have a culture to go back to. They go back to where they began when history interrupted their life. In Israel the Hebrew language was reinvented overnight after a sleep of two thousand years. It seemed the most natural thing in the world, for it was that language and its great book which held those people together who became the new Israelites. In India people fight in the streets to retain their ancient tongues, the source of their culture. In Africa, French and English will not long remain the medium of literature, not in the European forms at least. But in America we have only vestiges of culture *to which we do not wish to return.* The first thing the American immigrant tried to do was to prevent his children from inheriting the old language, the old culture. (In my case, for instance, Yiddish was used as a private language of jokes and confidences which we, third-generation Americans, were not supposed to know. I have found the same to be true with students of mine who are of Czech descent or German or Swedish or Dutch or Greek.)

In a sense, all cultural languages are banished from America. A country settled by runaways and slaves did not carry much high culture with it. And the tides of immigration engulfed what high culture there was. The half-educated American has long been a byword abroad; in fact, it is impossible for the American to be educated in the European sense. We cannot be nor do we have to. As I ask my fellow teachers: In what way am I to present, say, English poetry to the grandson of a Latvian farmer from a ranch in western Nebraska? As the poetry of his culture? In what way am I to present Chaucer or T. S. Eliot to my Negro students? Is that their heritage? Is the great complex of European culture their heritage? And do they have any such heritage at all? Even to me, an English professor and a writer of the English tongue, all things English are somewhat foreign.

I gather from Sartre's writings about Africa that European culture is no longer capable of influencing world culture. Europe is now the colony. It is European culture which is thirsty for replenishment from outside. American culture shows a similar thirst for replenishment but can slake this thirst from within.

The great theme of American literature is rootlessness. And this fact also makes us unique. Many writers have even said that there is no relationship between the American and the land. It is as if the spirit of place were hostile to us. We become the greatest technicians and mechanics because we fight the spirit of place; we are bent upon conquering place by force. We have never made peace with the land but have taken it by storm. D. H. Lawrence felt this about us; Henry Miller and Faulkner have it in their books; the urban poets, who have forgotten what a tree looks like, substantiate it in their dusty poems.

The price our writers have had to pay for rootlessness,

for cutting ties with all the different pasts behind us, is the neuroticism we know so well in our literature. And yet we have no choice; insofar as the American writer is true to his situation, he is a neurotic, ridden with the anxieties of separateness from the past. Freedom is one of the beneficent symptoms of this anxiety. We are suddenly confronted with an alphabet of freedoms ranging from civil rights to freedom of the banned book and the spoken obscenity. Our literature is engaging in a Socratic dialogue with all previous values; we do this with increasing recklessness and frequently with cynicism, for what is there to lose? The fact is, there is no place to go back to; we have nowhere to go but forward. We cannot help ourselves; that is our condition.

So long as America held on to the mother literature it was colonial. This was the case until the twentieth century and even into it. The criterion of the poem was the English poem; of the novel, the English novel. The exceptions are few and can be counted on one hand. It was only with the recognition of rootlessness that a strong and massive American literature came into being. This theme coincided with all the forms of radicalism that swept through the intelligentsia in the early years of the century. Anarchism, various forms of Marxism, and more recently existentialism are all expressions of the rootless, those peoples set adrift by history who have nevertheless become articulate. The Jewish writer was among the first to speak from this void.

The Jew is the mythic wanderer, but the American Jew is the one who has forgotten where he wandered from. The American Jew has no longing for Israel and possibly only an intellectual sympathy with it. He has little or no cultural memory of the religion or of the tradition. All he has is the invisible yellow badge, which still shows up in certain lights. This badge, this psychology of self-consciousness, makes the Jew want to be absolutely visible. He insists on his identification. He is the opposite of Ellison's "invisible man." If the Jew does not stick out like a sore thumb he is very restless. Hence all these books by and about Jews. Why does the Irishman James Joyce choose a poor, uninteresting Jew to be his main character in *Ulysses*? Because Leopold Bloom not only has a faulty memory of his fabulous past as a Hebrew but is lost. Bloom is a symbol of the modern bourgeois drifter. He doesn't belong in Ireland or anywhere else. He is cultural ectoplasm.

In America we are all cultural ectoplasm; and the Jew can stick out his sore thumb, look in a mirror, and say like Job: Whence cometh thou?

What is the fascination for the Jewish-American writer today? It is the fascination of the American for one of his own type, the man who at last debates with himself the question, What does it mean to be a Jew, an American, a Negro, an American Jew, an American Negro, an Afro-American, an American of Jewish descent, and so on?

What it means, of course, is that the question has been raised. The question was not raised in the nineteenth century, except perhaps by Walt Whitman. And the question refers art back to the political artifacts: Are those things real? Do they mean what I think and hope they mean? The Constitution of the United States has been backed into a corner by writers. No constitution can answer all the questions we are asking it. Every time the Constitution answers a question it asks a new one.

But American-Jewish writing is already obsolete. The Jew qua Jew is no longer a major premise in the creative equation. The Jewish writer can in effect sit back and chew his cud and watch the Negro. The Jew has achieved decolonization in America; though not by himself, it was going to happen somehow. I lived through it and even had a hand in it. Maybe I should explain that.

Very early in life I decided upon being a poet. (I won't go into the motivations of "being a poet," which are very complex and also irrelevant here.) I knew only one language, English, and so fell in love with English poetry. Falling in love with English poetry, which is still my old flame, meant living an imaginary English life. Living an imaginary English life meant living a phony life of the mind, for I was not English in any sense of the word. And living a phony life of the mind meant eventually becoming an English professor. One day, when I had learned how to write poetry, I had to make a decision about my name. Nobody in the *Oxford Book of English Verse* was named Shapiro. In fact, nobody was named Shapiro except tailors and junk dealers. What was I to do? Change my name? This was my first crisis as a poet.

In those days, believe it or not, it was impossible to get a poem published if you did not have an "Anglo-Saxon" name, but I decided to stick to my name; that decision made me "Jewish." And since I had made the decision I wrote poems about Jewishness.

My name itself had no content whatever. Most Jews' names are more recent than the last names of Negroes. That is, most Jews got names when Napoleon broke the ghetto system in Europe and the Jews either were given the names of a German or Polish town or made up one. *Shapiro* comes from a German town named Spira, I am told. I couldn't care less. So it was not the name that held me, as you might hold on to *Vanderbilt* or *R. J. Reynolds*; it was the foreignness of the word. I hung onto that; I wanted to know why my name was a kind of curse.

Years later I published a book called *Poems of a Jew*. That was when I was finally decolonized. When I printed that book I was already American. I was as rootless as a Texas millionaire with Negro and Indian blood in his veins.

When our literature got under way, it began like a census to list our cultural deaths. There was the grand gesture of Whitman like a captain on the bridge waving goodbye to the Past. There was Captain Ahab hunting down the great white "blood consciousness" and sinking the ship of white civilization along with it. There was Huck Finn, who lit out for the wilderness, running for his life, like his author, from respectability. There followed that long recital of the failure of the American hero—the epitaphs of Spoon River and Winesburg, Ohio; the brutal caricatures of the American bourgeois: the salesman, the evangelist, the politician; the corruption of pioneer and settler by the rootless materialism of the New World. Hemingway assaults the virility of the American male; Faulkner's vast gallery of Southerners portrays the decline and fall of a world under a curse—he calls it rightly the curse of slavery. Of the heroes of the American novel, only the artist is left unscathed. He is Ishmael in the cultural desert.

It is the motif of rootlessness that gives our literature its greatness to the outside world. Whatever the value of literary prizes, consider the names of Americans who have been awarded the Nobel Prize for literature: Eugene O'Neill, Pearl Buck, Hemingway, Faulkner, Steinbeck, and Eliot. These writers deal mainly with modern man in the void. If they are part of what is called the Western Tradition, they lie at the very edge of it. Each phase of American literature marks a further step away from that Tradition. As each "colonial" group in America finds its literary voice, we are moved deeper into the void. Huckleberry Finn, Ahab, Joe Christmas, Herzog—it hardly matters who the hero is; he leads us on the search for his authenticity. It is the unauthentic American artist who reaches back to the Tradition.

The Martinique writer and psychiatrist Frantz Fanon says in his book *The Wretched of the Earth* that when the African native "begins to pull on his moorings, and to cause anxiety to the settler, he is handed over to well-meaning souls who in cultural congresses point out to him the specificity and wealth of Western values." And he adds: "But every time Western values are mentioned they produce in the native a sort of stiffening or muscular lockjaw."

The Culture Conference or Congress is a twentieth-century institution which has never been looked at squarely. I myself make it a point to avoid those conferences, but I have attended enough of them here and abroad to know that they represent a more or less official machine dedicated to the status quo. They seek to hold the line for traditional values. For this reason the Culture Conference is supported by government, by foundations, and by writers and artists who have a stake in the tradition. The Culture Conference is opposed to decolonization, at least the decolonization of culture. The hidden premise on which it operates is the superiority of European culture. It must therefore work hard to reconvert the "native" and bring him back to a sense of cultural inferiority. I once attended one of these conferences in Tokyo, where it was agreed beforehand that politics could not be discussed. Here were a multitude of writers from all over the world, among them some of the most famous and some of the most political, who voluntarily emasculated all discussion at the outset. Instead they talked about the art of translation.

A few years ago you could ask in all seriousness: Is a Negro literature possible in America? The question implied a negative. I am among those who felt that the Negro had nothing to gain by becoming literary, that he had nothing to say according to the tradition of letters as we know this tradition. He could only create a pseudo-literature, the novel and poem according to Uncle Tom. We had seen this happen with Paul Laurence Dunbar and the early slave poets. Between a transliterated Negro dialect (itself a phony dialect) and *Oxford Book* English there seemed no choice. If there were to be an authentic Negro medium, where would it come from? Obviously it could not come from the standard classics of American literature, poetry, or prose. Perhaps something could rise from the church spiritual, a form of poetry which worked upon secret levels of meaning, or more likely from the blues. But almost nothing of the sort appeared to be happening. A literature is not created in a vacuum; it is created out of love for its medium. Could and should the Negro love the Anglo-American language? Or was it possible that he had his own version of it, as the Jewish writer had his?

But a literature is more than a version of language; a novel or poem is more than a work of art. Literature is an accurate transcription of the quality of thought and feeling of the writer and his people. What audience would such a literature have, if any? Was there a Negro audience to read *Native Son* or *Invisible Man* or Tolson's *Libretto*? You suspected that there wasn't, that such works would be for a small white or "mixed" audience. The publication of *Native*

Son was a great shock to the white reader, not only because of what it said but because a Negro had written it. Negroes didn't produce works of that caliber, nor did they read them. Literature, so the mythos went, was white man's business.

Even the books by Richard Wright were in the white tradition; his audience was the traditional audience, as were the values implicit in the work. Ellison's *Invisible Man*, which I wrote about elsewhere as the Great American Novel, is a masterpiece, but again in the white tradition. Ellison might even be called a white Negro. Neither what he says nor how he says it is without precedent in the general literary consciousness. Like Wright he corroborates the white liberal's worst fears; like Wright he illuminates the guilt of the settler vis-à-vis the native. In fact, it seems to me there is more *negritude*, if I may use the word, in Faulkner than in either Wright or Ellison. Faulkner is better able to present the sensibility of the Negro, albeit the Mississippi Negro, because Faulkner's characters are not always at the point of dramatic crisis.

What Wright and Ellison proved was that the Negro can write a novel as good as a white novel, as good as anything in the Tradition. But this obviously was not enough. Especially as the Tradition was beginning to come apart at the seams. For a Negro literature to come into being, it had to start from the bottom, not from the top.

At some time in its career a people makes a decision to embrace the art of writing. It has no obligation to at any time. The Jews produced virtually no literature after the Old Testament except commentaries. The Jews were in a state of cultural withdrawal all during the diaspora. Scholars will disagree but cannot convince me that the Jews produced any literature or art or music worth mentioning until the great revolutions of the eighteenth and nineteenth centuries freed the Jew from cultured bondage. It is in our century that the Jew has suddenly begun to sing and paint and write, for this is the century of cultural liberation all over the world. Ours is one of the greatest periods of art in history, and it is great insofar as we have broken with the Tradition. To break with the Tradition does not mean to annihilate it; it means to place new values upon it. It means to pick up the pieces and maybe throw them down again. Malraux means this when he says about the greatness of modern art: The fragment is king.

The greatness as well as the horror of the twentieth century is that it is a last judgment. It is a time when every value is called into question everywhere and on every level of the human experience. It is the genius of our age to question.

The racial revolutions of our age are more effects than causes. They are the result of universal indignation over the failures of our culture. One country famed for its music and its philosophers tried to destroy a whole nation in its midst by murder. Another country famed for poetry discovered that it held a large part of the world in virtual slavery. Another country famed for its sense of liberty and its adoration of the arts suddenly collapsed from internal weakness and corruption. These were all European countries of great antiquity. In the East rose a superpolice state with a paranoid belief in its historical destiny. In America we assembled and exploded the ultimate weapon.

For many years I have been trying to loosen the hold of the academic or "colonial" mind over poetry. It encourages a poetry as well as an entire literature of reference, the kind that refers back in every case to prior commitments, historical, religious, or philosophical. In a sense it is a useless battle; attacking the Establishment only tends to strengthen it. It would be better to ignore the existence of the literature of reference and to create whatever we think valid than to go on tilting at windmills. This is what the Beat writers did; they were successful because they refused to take part in the academic dialogue. If someone asked one of the usual deathly questions, such as "What is the role of the artist in the modern world?" they would be likely to answer something like "Fried shoes." Refusal to "play the game" kept them safe. Refusal to play the game won freedom for India and is winning freedom for the American South. Refusal to play the game will turn the dehumanized "multiversity" back into a place of learning.

The importance of the Negro writer in the world today is far out of proportion to the number of books we have to go by. But the significance of Negro writing today is paramount because everywhere, not simply in America, the Negro is in the position to ask the questions. The "hyphenated" Jewish writer is no more. Time has solved that problem. The Jewish writer either is assimilated into the modern bourgeois world with all its neuroses or is a settler in the biblical land, carrying on skirmishes against the Philistines or the Egyptians as in the days of old. A few American Jews try to keep alive the mystique of the diaspora, but with little success. Most modern Jews themselves reject the myth of the dispersion for our time. They go to Israel and have a look and then hurry back to Detroit or Omaha. Today the American Negro faces the same dilemma; Wright, Ellison, Baldwin, Tolson know that Mother Africa is not for them. And the Africans know it too.

Everywhere decolonization is taking place we find the disappointment of the visitor who feels rejected from his dream. But this is part of the awakening, part of the process of freedom itself. If the African looks down on the American Negro, he has earned that right. If the Afro-American feels out of place in Nigeria or even Liberia, he knows at last the limits of his dream.

We can witness at the moment three phases of decolonization in our culture: *nostalgia, assimilation,* and *negritude. Nostalgia* is homesickness not for the good old days but for the bad old days. *Assimilation* means a cultural entente at the expense of any mystique. *Negritude* means assertion of the realities, historical and "mystical" as well.

The early literature of America, all of it, is nostalgic for the worst. It is as true of Anne Bradstreet as of Phillis Wheatley. And in fact the masses of people at any time fear the heavy responsibilities of freedom and pine for the bad old days when all choices were made for them. Not to have to choose is a freedom, the freedom of the slave. The Negro poets who cultivated a "slave" dialect were in fact in accord with their condition; they consented to the cultural authority of the white "prosody," as the white colonials acceded to the cultural authority of the Old World.

But assimilation too is nostalgic. It was often said of German Jews before Hitler that they were more German than the Germans. Which didn't stop Hitler from rooting them out. The nostalgia of the American-Jewish writer who is assimilated into American literature is curious. I was talking with a famous American writer who had made Jewishness the theme in his books. Speaking of the new Jews, the Israelis, he said: "But they aren't Jews any more!" I agreed. Those new Jews had lost their consciousness of the diaspora; they had fought their way back into the mythical homeland and were lost to the old Jewry. But cultural assimilation of Jews into American life was relatively easy and has all but been accomplished. A Jew does not have the problem of the Hindu, the Oriental, or the Negro; the Jew looks more or less "American" anywhere he goes; even his name is not held against him as it once was. But cultural assimilation also means national oblivion for the nation assimilated. You can only pretend to act like a Jew; the writer or artist can do this easily because that is his business. The American Jew of average sensibility, on the other hand, experiences the common cultural amnesia of Americans of any extraction. While the American-Jewish figure in fiction has a cultural nervous breakdown over American twentieth-century values, he longs for the bad old days when his father was a bootlegger or a peddler because he was suffering the crucifixion of the culturally underprivileged; the father would do anything to keep his family Jews, to turn them into doctors and lawyers or rich merchants. With economic freedom they could then be Jews. Only it didn't work that way, for Jewishness meant suffering, and an unsuffering Jew was an anomaly. An unsuffering Jew is a goy. Hence the nostalgia of the assimilated.

The Negro is luckier; he can never disappear from his condition in the Caucasian world any more than a Hindu or a Japanese. There he is, unassimilable and un-nostalgic, the biggest fact of life in the modern world.

Our century is very great because with us all the chickens have come home to roost, because great men of goodwill—statesmen, presidents, leaders of men, artists, and young people—have demanded the exaction of promises made to nations by visionaries and the spokesmen of freedom. This is happening under our eyes; we are all a party to it. Nostalgia is obsolete. Assimilation may well be. Neither is of vital importance. I prefer the idea of negritude. At least it is the first great idea or concept that can deal with the biggest fact of modern life without trying to water it down.

I will give three examples: Aimé Césaire, Léopold Senghor, and M. B. Tolson. Césaire is a Caribbean, Senghor is a Senegalese, and Tolson was born in Missouri. The first two use French for poetry; Tolson uses English or American. (My designation of Tolson's language is that he writes in Negro.)

Or rather, all three of these great poets write in Negro. That is what negritude means in literature. It does not mean accommodation to the standards of the settler or to his nostalgia for the mother or father country. It does not mean making peace through disappearance into the scene; nor, as Senghor has shown in his political writings, does it mean war. It means insistence on the pride of selfhood without hatred. No oppressed people in history has had less sense of revenge than the Negro. Retribution is not Negro.

Negritude is simply decolonization under the positive aspect. Senghor has no grudge against the Tradition (as I do) or against modern technology. On the contrary, he welcomes everything that will make possible greater harmony among men. This is the wisdom of the French in the decolonized man, the daring of the French to push an idea into action as far as it will go. There are, I believe, no African poets of the English language of his stature. The English are still the heirs of apartheid.

Césaire's discovery of negritude—he is pinned as the inventor of the name—is that of the disaffected assimilationist, the Parisian from the colonies who became a Marxist and by nomination a surrealist, even though surrealism is a luxury of the white civilization, a toy of people who can afford unconsciousness. It is also a desperate attempt to rejoin civilized brilliance with a *raison d'être*. Surrealism is an adrenaline shot in the heart under superb cultural conditions. It revives a culture which does not really want to live. Césaire, as I understand it, did not rise to the bait when André Breton elected him to the surrealist school. I am not criticizing surrealism, which is of fundamental value in all modern arts; I am pointing out the naiveté of the French in enlisting colonials in aesthetic causes which were far from the realities of the African or the American Negro.

Negritude in the famous poem *"Cahier d'un Retour au Pays Natale"* ("Memorandum on My Martinique" is one translation)—negritude is the realization of pity for the modern world with its great inventions and its great alibis. It shouts hurrah not for the "steel blue speed" of the modern but for those who have never invented anything:

> *Hurrah for those who never invented anything*
> *Hurrah for those who never explored anything*
> *Hurrah for those who never conquered anything*

I know of only one American poet who in genius and experience even approaches the concept—M. B. Tolson. And Tolson knows that the concept is different with us. In American culture, according to the ground rules, there can be no separatism even by race and color. What then? Is there a long road of assimilation and miscegenation ahead? Can there be an American negritude?

Tolson is an American who was also the Poet Laureate of

Liberia. He lived in Oklahoma in an all-Negro town where he was twice mayor. In various capacities as editor, I have published more poetry by him than anyone in America. He has a superb reputation among a few poets and critics but is unknown to students and to the general reading public. This is not because he is difficult to read (which he is), for difficulty of text is the stock-in-trade of the poetry-teaching profession. *Tolson is not read because he was a Negro.* A blind spot in the white literary eye will not recognize a great Negro poet.

To complicate matters, Tolson's *Libretto for the Republic of Liberia*, commissioned by the first African republic, has in its American publication an introduction by Allen Tate. He sees Tolson as an exception because "for the first time . . . a Negro poet has assimilated completely the poetic language of his time and, by implication, the language of the Anglo-American tradition." Tate is one of the canniest critics in the business, the American T. S. Eliot, as it were. But the crux of the matter is that Tate says: ". . . the distinguishing Negro quality is not in the language but in the subject matter . . . ," for subject matter can only deal with your suffering and contaminate the beauty of poetry.

I have tried to counter this statement in my own introduction to Tolson's recently published *Harlem Gallery*. Tate considers that the use of Negro subject matter in poetry, which he calls "the tragic aggressiveness of the modern poet," limits the Negro poet to a "provincial mediocrity." But in trying to assert that Tolson has been assimilated by the Anglo-American tradition, he puts Tolson in quarantine and destroys the value of the poem—possibly this critic's conscious intention. Thus it took a Southern intellectual and poet to introduce Tolson's *Libretto*. That was the only possible literary context for a great Negro poet ten or fifteen years ago: he must in that context be captured and returned to colonization, to that Tradition which had enslaved his ancestors and would continue to do so if it could manage it.

The refusal to see that Tolson's significance lies in his language, Negro, and that only that language can express the poetic sensibility of the Negro at the door of freedom, is a final desperate maneuver to contain the Negro within the traditional culture. And for that it is too late. The Tradition is already antebellum.

The falsification I speak of is that of trying to assimilate Tolson into the Tradition when he was doing the opposite. The fact that Tolson's *Libretto* is unknown by white traditionalists gives the lie to the critic's assertion that Tolson has risen above Negro experience to become an "artist." The facts are that Tolson is a dedicated revolutionist who revolutionizes modern poetry in a language of American negritude. The forms of the *Libretto* and of *Harlem Gallery*, far from being "traditional," are the Negro satire upon the poetic tradition of the Eliots of our age. The tradition cannot stand being satirized and lampooned and so tries to kick an authentic poet upstairs into the oblivion of acceptance. But the Negro artist won't stay in the attic any more than he stayed in the cellar.

Tolson says it better in his big poem:

> The Great White World
> and the Black Bourgeoisie
> have shoved the Negro artist into
> the white and not-white dichotomy,
> the Afroamerican dilemma in the Arts—

the dialectic of
to be or not to be
a Negro.

This essay stops at the threshold of the Black Revolution or the Black Recoil or whatever it is called. I prefer to think of it as a Black Apartheid, a deliberate withdrawal into racism for whatever gains it can produce. I doubt whether any non-black critic can deal with this phenomenon, not this early, at any rate.

Is Poetry an American Art?

As POET, EDITOR, essayist, anthologist and professor, I have been involved in American poetry all my life. And as poet, editor, essayist, anthologist, and professor, I have finally had to confront the question, Is poetry an American art? The question implies a negative. If we assume the question has any authenticity—that is, is more than the braying of an amateur critic—what are its implications for the American poet, editor, essayist, anthologist, and professor?

American poetry nowadays has the reputation for having accumulated a large and impressive body of works. In the English language we are said to be the present leader in the art. Numerically as well as qualitatively, we make the best showing. Nevertheless, I believe that American poetry is a European transplantation which has never really taken root with us and never will. Ours is a hothouse poetry, kept alive by artificial respiration and fluorescent light. Otherwise, it is a poetry of brickbats.

We've all heard this *ad nauseam*. Our poetry is either academic or vandalistic. And yet I think it is so.

I remember a remark by the British poet George Barker which used to offend us. Barker said: American poetry is a very easy subject to discuss for the simple reason that it does not exist. Today, the remark makes better sense to me. I recall T. S. Eliot's aside which used to rub me the wrong way. Speaking of Walt Whitman, Eliot said that he was a great *prose* writer. I did not really understand Eliot's condemnation until I found something like it in Whitman's own notes. Whitman wrote that the barriers between prose and poetry must be broken down once and for all. He said:

In my opinion the time has arrived to essentially break down the barriers of form between prose and poetry. I say the latter is henceforth to win and maintain its character regardless of rhyme, and the measurement rules of iambic, spondee, dactyl, etc., and that even if rhyme and those measurements continue to furnish the medium for inferior writing and themes (especially for persiflage and the comic, as there seems henceforward, to the perfect taste, something inevitably comic in rhyme, merely in itself, and anyhow), the truest and greatest poetry (while subtly and necessarily always rhythmic, and distinguishable easily enough), can never again, in the English language be expressed in arbitrary and rhyming meter, any more than the greatest eloquence, or the truest power and passion. While admitting that the venerable and heavenly forms of chiming versification have in their time play'd great and fitting parts—that the pensive complaint, the ballads, wars, amours, legends of Europe, etc., have, many of them, been inevitably render'd in rhyming verse—that there may have been very illustrious poets whose shapes the mantle of such verse has beautifully and appropriately envelopt—and though the mantle has fallen, with perhaps added beauty, on some of our own age—it is, notwithstanding, certain to me, that the day of such conventional rhyme is ended. In America, at any rate, and as a medium of highest aesthetic practical or spiritual expression, present or future, it palpably fails, and must fail, to serve. The Muse of the Prairies, of California, Canada, Texas, and of the peaks of Colorado, dismissing the literary, as well as social etiquette of over-sea feudalism and caste, joyfully enlarging, adapting itself to comprehend the size of the whole people, with the free play, emotions, pride, passions, experiences, that belong to them, body and soul—to the general globe, and all its relations in astronomy, as the savants portray them to us— to the modern, the busy Nineteenth century (as grandly poetic as any, only different) with steamships, railroads, factories, electric telegraphs, cylinder presses—to the thought of the solidarity of nations, the brotherhood and sisterhood of the entire earth—to the dignity and heroism of the practical labor of farms, factories, foundries, workshops, mines, or on shipboard, or on lakes and rivers—resumes that other medium of expression, more flexible, more eligible—soars to the freer, vast, diviner heaven of prose. . . .

That last sentence—Faulknerian or something—reduced to a beginning and end and avoiding the middle reads in effect: The Muse (of America) soars to the freer, vast, diviner heaven of prose. . . . In my limited knowledge Whitman is the first poet ever to speak of the *heaven of prose*, and I would like to nail that expression on the desk of every American poet.

Whitman is the one great poet we have produced, and by that loose term I mean simply a great world poet. He is also our one innovator. Yet, it was Whitman who demanded the obliteration of the art as it had been known.

We can, I believe, understand the character and importance of American poetry, so-called, when we perceive that the art is not native to us and that it can be produced only under laboratory conditions. And many corollary facts can be adduced from the same premise, for example, the fact that most of our poets are products and functionaries of the university. The fact that this poetry is almost completely literary, that is, that it depends on predigested cultural contents for its health. The fact that self-destruction is more of an occupational hazard among our poets than among any other writers. (This is not true of our novelists, for example.) The fact that there is not and never has been an audience for poetry in the United States. The fact that we have substituted scientific and critical analysis of poetry for the use of it, whatever that might be. The fact that poetry has failed to reach the drama qua poetry. And the fact that our most influential poets, such as Pound, Eliot, and Williams, all moved poetry as far in the direction of prose as they were able but without succeeding in bringing about a permanent *rapprochement* or fusion of the two.

I notice with some wonder that a similar process may be taking place in England. I have in mind the strange poem *The Anathemata* which David Jones published in this country roughly a decade ago.

This poem by Jones could hardly have been written without the example of the *Cantos*, to which it is greatly indebted in form. The poem itself, however, is a Christian poem, rich in the mythologies and liturgies of Britain. It is not inconsequential that Eliot and Auden have both given *The Anathemata* their highest praise. Jones has very possibly made the kind of breakthrough for English poetry which the other twentieth-century British poets failed to do. The true influence of Pound and Eliot may be felt in England in this way: the mythic form is broken, prosaic prosody may well be the salvation of English poetry, which has fallen on hard times, though this form I think insufficient for the needs of American poets. Mythography with us is artificial and all but meaningless; in England it retains its validity. The peculiar situation of American culture imposes upon us our cultural amnesia, our most salient and formidable characteristic. Even what we have left of the classical and religious forms, symbols, and ikons is blurred and vestigial, in conflict with the forms and ikons of our actual life. I can now understand and be more tolerant of W. H. Auden's return to the English Church. The American Void must have terrified him, as in fact it terrified Eliot. And Pound's wild-eyed quest for order led him to a more secular mythos of the Virtuous Banker and the Precise Definition. Much of Auden's best poetry, incidentally, is prose, but I doubt if European poetry can ever be as freewheeling as the American in this respect. It cannot be, in fact. American poetry must be *sui generis* if it is to progress. I would like to reintroduce the term *progress* into the literary consciousness, for our poetry has been standing still for generations.

Whitman had the greatest insight after all. This might account for his monumental unpopularity in America. For Whitman is unpopular not only with Americans at large—*nonexistent* would be a better word—but with poets. Whitman is dangerous to American poets, like a pesticide. Even a poet with the great gifts of Hart Crane could only view Whitman as the good gray poet or great pink mother. For despite his admiration of Whitman, Crane could never free himself from the most formal European poetics, a pseudo-Elizabethan rhetoric and the "iambic" line. Crane is one of our finest twentieth-century poets—and of the most self-destructive variety. And what are we to make of the paradox, for example, of Pound's dependence on Whitman's prosody while rejecting the sense of Whitman's poetry? And Hart Crane's identification with the sense of Whitman while rejecting the revolutionary forms?

In a footnote kind of way, I think also of Eliot's rejection of Milton during his free-verse years and his ultimate acceptance of Milton as Eliot drifted back into the traditional European forms. I beg the theological and psychological questions, not knowing how to deal with them. I'm inclined to judge a poet by his prosody, not his "philosophy." Unless I'm deluding myself, in prosody all the cards are laid on the table. Milton was as revolutionary as Eliot; rather, we might say, Milton is to English poetry what Whitman is to American prose. Both were "translating." Milton was "translating" the idea of the epic. Whitman was "translating" the mystique of American politics. Milton was improvising on pagan rhythms. Whitman was improvising on the Constitution and on the *Brooklyn Eagle*. Both in fact were drifting out of versification at different and appropriate rates of speed. To use a happy vulgarism, we can say both were in orbit. I admire *Paradise Lost* in the same way that I admire *Leaves of Grass*, and I recognize that both books are failures, that is, they are monuments, not living forces. They are the Stone Guests of Anglo-American poetry. They freeze us in our tracks.

American poetry, however, is polarized between Poe and Whitman, not Milton (until Eliot raised that ghost). The

Poe-Whitman syndrome is the clue to the failure of our poetry. Or perhaps we should say that because of Poe and Whitman we have great prose.

Poe is the death of our poetry; Whitman, the midwife of our prose. Let me fall back on D. H. Lawrence, who can do this better than I can.

Lawrence is excellent on this theme, and his own vacillations are very much to the point. Lawrence was quite American in his disdain for poetry. Poe horrified him because Poe was pathologically incestuous, tearing down the delicate barrier between brother and sister, male and female, past and present. But Whitman disgusted Lawrence also when Whitman spoke of *merging*. Whitman wanted all mankind to form a kind of daisy chain of love. Lawrence stamped his foot at that kind of cowardice. He ended by nominating Poe a ghoul and Whitman a Great Soul (whatever that is). But Lawrence had the scent: the purely destructive Poe, with his scientific detachment—the last thin disguise of ego; and Whitman, whirling us into the spiral nebulae—daddy pushing the cosmic swing, endless rocking. And Lawrence had the common sense to elicit Whitman, who would go beyond oneself instead of insisting on oneself.

But Poe had no self. Poe preferred to become potting soil, night soil, to borrow a beautiful Irish expression.

It is precisely this circumambience or space program of Whitman's which accounts for his unpopularity among our contemporaries. If we leave out the poem about the learned Astronomer, Whitman is all learned astronomy, geography, and television. I'm not the first critic to suspect that the collected poetry of T. S. Eliot and Ezra Pound is a redaction of *Leaves of Grass*, an attempt to hush up the joyous sense of vision in order to keep mankind's nose to the grindstone.

When Poe had successfully and scientifically disintegrated the psyche, he died and went to Paris. And there, as we know, he was made the patron saint of Symbolism. This bizarre form of literature is the foundation of modern poetry, with its belief in nuances, effects, spooks, and cultural memory. We find this Gallicized Poe working a great influence on the moderns, even though the *American* Poe is repudiated by Eliot and the other moderns. The *American* Poe in the United States is, of course, the man of postmortem effects which Lawrence had in mind. And curiously, it is this popular Poe—despised by the Literati—which bears the greatest resemblance to the literature of the absurd. "The Bells" or "Ulalume" or the whodunits are literature of such low caliber that they approximate the anti-literary. Intentionally or not, Poe is still one of the great destructive forces of literature. This explains T. S. Eliot's fear and contempt of Poe, for Eliot would like to salvage and revive literature. Eliot would like to retain the ratiocinative Poe without the romantic slag. And the disembodied, Gallicized Poe is pure in this respect. Poe is the author of the doctrine of the uncontaminated poem, which I refer to as the laboratory poem.

Whitman could not possibly affect Europe. Whitman is more or less on the wavelength of India, the cosmic wavelength, but in Europe it just sounds like a lot of United States static. Swinburne found Whitman attractive for a time but dropped him. Only a dissident European like Lawrence could stomach Walt. And similarly, very few Americans can stomach him either. Our own wavelength as far as poetry is concerned is still European: reason, form, continuity, fear of spontaneity and originality. This is why we can produce only a variant of English poetry and why we have no American poetry except for a few followers of Whitman who are mainly pseudo-Orientals. The pseudo-Orientalism of Whitman and our New England Transcendentalists is repeated by our contemporary Beat poets as Zen or Yoga.

The rational line of modern poetry, when it flirts with the East—the line of Eliot and Pound—is quietistic and orderly and is directed toward a controlled politics and a state church. We get Confucius in Pound, a variant of the eighteenth-century Jefferson, or we get a mysticism of surrender and passivity, as in Eliot.

The irrational line of modern poetry, when it flirts with the East, is anarchic in politics; it is apolitical and religiously egocentric. Such is the American variant of Zen, which sees this psychology rightly or wrongly as a technique of self-expression. Not as a way of making peace with nature or history, but as a way of thumbing one's nose at life and time. American Zen is about on the level of the American fascination with judo and the haiku; both are techniques of combat. With my minuscule knowledge of the Japanese, I yet think we have not understood them very well.

Nevertheless, the ambition to separate our art from Europe is a healthy ambition, and the drive to the East was inevitable. It was equally inevitable in the time of Whitman and in our time. We must appreciate this intellectual flight in Eliot's Vedism, Pound's Confucianism, and the Beat writer's Zen. What such writers share is an intolerance for American hedonism and violence, what is called The American Way of Life.

Modern American poets, for the rest, have held to an uneasy compromise with French poetics, in Cummings or Wallace Stevens, or to a mindless adherence to the standards of English literature. And this Anglo-American poetry, as I have suggested, is quite naturally the province of our "English Departments."

American poetry—what there is of it—has a powerful centrifugal force. It throws itself out of its country. I know of no other poetry which has done this. Think of the pride of the British poet for Britain, of the almost religious adoration of the French poet for France, even a Rimbaud or the poets of the Resistance. Then look at American poetry with its bitterness, disillusionment, its striking-back, its treason; it is even in Whitman. What does it mean? Why is there so little good American poetry which is not self-consciously anti-American?

Years ago I put together an anthology of American poetry for college students. The chronology ran from Anne Bradstreet to Allen Ginsberg. A secretary at the publishing house objected so violently to the latter item that she had a nervous breakdown and had to be led away. The Ginsberg poem was "Howl," and the publishers themselves were concerned about sales, especially in parochial schools. They included the poem nevertheless. In compiling this anthology I did my one and only piece of original research. I went back and read all the books of American poetry that had been called that. Little if any of it was. My scoreboard ended up something like this: seventeenth century, Anne Bradstreet and Edward Taylor (no Wigglesworth). Eighteenth century, nothing. Or rather, Philip Freneau, mostly because he had the good sense to ignore the Hartford Wits. He is probably our first American poet, but unfortunately he isn't much of a poet. Nineteenth century, Bryant, Emerson, Longfellow, Whittier, Poe, Holmes, Jones Very, Thoreau, Whitman, Melville (a perfectly awful poet), Bayard Taylor, Henry Timrod, Emily Dickinson, Lanier, and Father Tabb. The rest of the gallery, the bulk of it really, is given over to twentieth-century poets.

It is an extremely unimpressive record for a nation born and conceived to remake the world in its image. Taking a dismal view of the anthology, we might say with accuracy that we have given birth to only one poet before the present century, Walt Whitman. There are a few false starts, such as Poe and Emily Dickinson. The rest is padding.

As far as I can tell, Whitman was the first American writer to be conscious of the fact that the language of England no longer applied to us, though we speak it. It was a language dissolving. A curious linguistic process obtains with us: it is a destructive process and it is fascinating. It works this way. We admit, in greater or lesser numbers, immigrants from all over. We immediately destroy their language, simultaneously destroying our own. What we get rid of are the cultural vestiges and overtones. We cultivate what used to be called broken English. Now, no one seriously suggests that we have a new and separate language or even a derivative language, but everyone agrees tacitly that we have scarcely a language at all but only a medium of communication.

After the Civil War everyone was indoctrinated into the Northern mentality. This meant (aside from the love of the factory and the office, the industrialization of the farm, and the hatred of nature) the accelerated demolition of cultural vestiges. An Old Country language became a matter of shame; the very trace of an accent was distasteful. It has taken a mighty effort on the part of the present government to institute foreign-language programs, for unconsciously we resist them. We do not wish to come that close to the recent and ugly past. Next to the French, with whom we have so much in common, we are linguistically the most intolerant people in the world—and proud of it.

It cannot be said that Americans have a mother tongue. We have removed the singing organ of the nightingale. On the other hand, all the arts in this country *except poetry* are flourishing, as everyone is aware. Painting, sculpture, theater, music, the novel and short story, and much other prose—we are creating very lustily in every direction except that of the poem. Our poetry is still English, still written in the hieratic language which is to us about as meaningful as Etruscan. We speak a variant of English certainly. Yet we associate the language inevitably with its greatest form of expression, English poetry. Now what can English poetry mean to a third-generation Czechoslovakian used-car dealer in Nebraska whose children are my students? For my part, I am on the side of the student.

What is the rationale of visiting this poetry upon millions of central and southern Europeans, Scandinavians, Jews, Negroes, Japanese, or Navajo Indians? Classical Greek would make more sense—or Latin certainly. Yet most English professors in America can't read two words of Greek and only six of Latin. This has never ceased to amaze me. The great bulk of English literature was created by men saturated in the classical languages, men whose sensibilities were shaped by the endless discipline in those languages. How many English professors know Italian, and how can one be knowledgeable in English literature without knowing it? I am speaking as an outsider, an impostor really, for I have too much respect for the scholar's profession to think that I am any more than a guest in any university. But as a writer I know that English poetry was not conceived in a vacuum, that it is a part and only a part of European literature, and that American literature is perhaps the first original point of departure from that great culture.

There is little evidence that Americans have ever clutched poetry to their hearts. Jefferson was more interested in Italian and German music than in Shakespeare. Benjamin Franklin packed a copy of *Fanny Hill* in his luggage when he went abroad as an ambassador. Lincoln, a great writer, was no litterateur. Our great prose writers of the nineteenth century wrote execrable poetry, for example, Melville and Thoreau; Mark Twain was the opposite of poet (or, from my viewpoint, a great poet who wouldn't stoop to verses). All of our great writers ("poets" in quotes, if you like) are prose writers. William Carlos Williams made English poetry his chief target of abuse. Cummings tried to veer toward a divorce from English forms by cultivating the graphic atomic forms of Apollinaire. Stevens beat prosody to a new flatness. The only good poet in the *English* tradition we have produced in our time is Robert Frost. I myself have never been able to see anything in the slightest American about Frost. Oxford and Cambridge knew this. He was our last Colonial, the shining light of that group of British poets who called themselves the Georgians. It can scarcely be said that he lived in America. His habitat was that mythological New England which, since it does not exist, might as well be Old England. We know very well that Frost is not read in the United States; he is studied. I won't go into the question of Frost as our Establishmentarian poet or Virgil. Or why William Carlos Williams, our most American poet since Whitman, who was once supposed to serve as poetry consultant to the Library of Congress, was unseated before he could exercise that function. The government feels safer with a poet of the Tradition, European tradition, that is.

Frost, it goes without saying, is a master. But it is no accident that he had to go to England for recognition and that to the end, except for the great honor given him by President Kennedy, his audience was English.

I think also of the almost catatonic depression of E. A. Robinson, a poet displaced in America, or the bitter self-hatred of Robinson Jeffers, a Whitman without joy. Jeffers had hoped to spend his life in Ireland and escape this country forever. The fact that Jeffers wrote in Whitman's forms —traducing them, really—only reinforces the irony or paradox of the expression "American poet."

It would be tedious to rehearse the present situation in our poetry, this poetry so endlessly and cruelly satirized by our novelists, and rightly so. The poet in the academy, the Writers Conference or Writers Colony, the Fulbright poet, the poet-critic—these are what posterity shall know us by. I will not discuss this phase of the business but simply touch upon the types of poetry we get from this environment.

First of all, we have many, many poets, all highly trained and expert in the skill of writing poetry. I am not trying to be witty when I say that the average graduate student who works a little at it can write a poem as well as Yeats. My opinion of Yeats has suffered considerably from this discovery. Was Yeats a graduate student?

The huge majority of these poets of ours are nestled in or

around a college or university. The American university has taken on the responsibility for the care and feeding of poets. For a long time I admired this hospitality but after engaging in it for a number of years decided that it was a snare and delusion. A poet on an American campus, if he is not a bona fide professor, is no more than an exotic insect, a zoology specimen, a Live One. He exists entirely in the third person. He fled from the town where he had no identity. In the university he has so much identity that he might as well be under a microscope. Freshmen pull his wings off and deans wear him like a scarab. But I am off the subject.

Where are the poems themselves published? In university quarterlies, naturally; in secular monthlies, governed or influenced by university culture; and in magazines such as the *New Yorker*, which entertains a slightly gamy approach to literature. Or else in certain select little magazines far from any public view.

For me it is impossible to distinguish between one of these marvelous mechanical poems and another. They always seem to me to be written by the same person or Thing. I can't name five poets writing in the English or American language today who have enough individuality or style to be distinguished from one another. That some get ahead of others in reputation is purely a matter of chance. Or so I believe.

But there is also a poetry of revolt in the United States. This poetry of revolt is better, more engaging than the university poetry, but in the end, it too is Academic.

In a larger sense, of course, all our poetry has been a poetry of revolt or at least of complaint. This is the most significant fact of all. Such a poetry rejects the very basis of its existence. It rejects what I call the poetic situation, that which is characteristic or what Williams called the *local*. Our poetry is criticism, very nearly in a technical sense, as our criticism is very nearly philosophy. We have a poetry of violence and a poetry of wit. The violence may be inner or outer in direction. And I notice about my two favorite United States poets, Whitman and Williams, that they report upon the violent but do not themselves become violent. Perhaps it was because Whitman and Williams knew the street and not simply the writer's colony, the European salon, or the academy that they developed a sense of proportion about American life. Whereas the *poète maudit* is committed to cursing a society he does not know, the academic poet is committed to cursing the street. Or rather, he does not curse; he witticizes and versifies. Yet the poetry is good, well made, and made to last. It's for the "quality." And the violence is real and records true horror and frequently ends in blood. But I cannot be content with either poetry. Our poetry reflects only corners of the city; the poet flees from university to university like a pilgrim in the Dark Ages hurrying from one distant cathedral to the next. Our poor modern poet, full of self-pity, booze and pot, his pockets stuffed with stanzas and passports. Or else he flows from the Left Bank of the Seine to the Left Bank of the Ganges miraculously, being a mendicant. I have no quarrel with any of that except to ask him once in a while: Where are you from? Why don't you sit down and take a load off your feet?

American poetry in our time has been a brilliant form of introspective photography. But the famous photograph album of the modern anthology is only to leaf through in some unborn dentist's office, a momentary and mindless

239

distraction before the consolation of the novocaine. In different ways our opposite poets, the Academes and the Bohemes, are both anesthetized. Isn't this because they are trying to write poetry, on the one hand, and *be poets*, on the other? To *be* a poet in America—what is this like? To write poems in America—isn't that turning back the clock?

Some young poet recently wrote an article in which he was saying about me and others: Leave us alone. Shut up about Whitman and Williams and prose and let us write our poems in peace. Maybe he is right. An overnight collapse of the stanza might be as dangerous as the abolition of the army. Poets still need close-order drill and the barracks mentality. It's too bad that they do. Novelists don't, nor does any other kind of artist I know of. But poets are still the hostages of convention.

What would an American poetry be like should we have one? Certainly it would not be recognizable as such. It would be nonsensical, hilarious, and obscene like us. Absurd like us. It would be marked, as we are, by cultural forgetfulness and lack of principle. It would be void of values and ideals, sensual, joyous, bitter, curious, gossipy, knowledgeable to the last minute detail, ungrammatical, endlessly celebrating the facts, objects, neuroses, murders, love affairs, and vulgarities of America. Certainly it would develop favorite forms, but these would be soluble in prose. It would be comical and slack and full of junk; impure, generous, bookish, and cheap. It would be mystical, savage, drab, and as hateful as Joyce Kilmer's "Trees." As sloppy as Whitman and—well, it would be like the great American novel which every American poet ends up writing as a tribute to "the diviner heaven" of prose.

For poetry is—let us admit it—a minor art of America,

like pottery. Our poetry becomes more and more ceramic as the decades roll by. And outside the pot shop the boys with their hammers and rocks peer in at the window. The novelists of this country pay their respects to poetry out of courtesy and professional *esprit*, but they know, as we know, that the jig is up. Poetry has long since become a pastime, a way of puttering around. Henry Miller wrote me once that he had been puzzled all his life by his suspicions about so much famous poetry and that usually in his reading he sought great poetry in prose. He admired certain German, French, and Oriental poets and Whitman in this country. But on the whole, he drew back from the sacred object called the poem. I had helped him understand this, he said, for which I felt pleased. And for myself, I also seek poetry in prose and in foreign poets. Notice the tremendous pull toward translation in our time. Our poets, the best of them, have turned translation not into an art but into a new poetic medium. What does this point to except a failure of our own medium? Doesn't it mean that our poetry can no longer digest the contents of our life? For this kind of translation is not scholarly or even culture-tradition translation; it is a lifeline or a feeding tube from afar, a temporary supply of life to revive our sickly poetry. We will translate Cavafy one day, Catullus the next, Evtushenko, Lorca, or Gottfried Benn. We do this as if to reassure ourselves that poetry is possible in the old manner. But at bottom we don't believe it. We don't believe the spatter of questions at the close of "The Waste Land" or the beautiful gleaming lines of Homer and Ovid and Cavalcanti in *The Cantos*. *Dove sta memoria*. But we have no memory. Memory is a luxury Americans cannot afford.

Everything in our literature tends toward the dissolution

of what people usually call poetry. We happen to have great literature—the political works, the strange and wonderful novels and tales, the polemics, sermons, speeches, asides, criticism, even journalism and reports—and a few unexpected flashes of poetry. But poetry itself we do not have, except that poetry which flowers under the light of prose. How typical it is of our poetry, even a century back, that it is tortured into existence. Emily Dickinson's heartbreaking style or Emerson's the same, repeated in our time in the exquisite timidities of Marianne Moore and the stylized elegance of our university wits. I suffered through Cummings' struggle against the great monuments of the Tradition and his momentary honeymoon in France, Jeffers' gigantic bitterness, Sandburg's hiding in the shawl of Lincoln, and Roethke's roving back and forth between Yeats, the *New Yorker*, and *Leaves of Grass*. Trying to write poetry in the old manner is murder for us. All of which sounds like the lengthy obituary which Rexroth did when Dylan Thomas died.

We have tried so hard—and failed—to produce a poetry of sensibility. Let us give it up. We have experimented with every extreme to no avail. The art of poetry is foreign to us. To some this is a bitter pill to swallow, but we'd better take our medicine. I think I understand finally the flight of our great exiles, the lonely achievement of Whitman, and the triumph of other arts of language in this country except ours. "The heaven of prose"—that is a corny expression to conjure with and to nail on the walls of Yaddo or the MacDowell Colony. But it makes sense. For if some Tibetan or Amazonian were to ask me to name the great poems of this country I would name a couple of poets and add something as preposterous as the works of Thomas Jefferson and Thoreau, *The Rosy Crucifixion, Huckleberry Finn, Henderson the Rain King,* etc., etc. The poetry might well be placed in the archives of Washington, not even in a library. Nobody reads it except students, who have no choice, and the teachers who think it necessary to talk about. Nobody loves it. Nobody wants it. It's mostly a great stack of Confederate money which you can hold sorrowfully in your hand and wonder: Did people ever really think you could spend it?

As a summing up, I would like to share the responsibility for what I have said. I am in earnest when I argue that American poetry is yet to be born and that what we have optimistically called our poetry is only a garden of chemical flowers. I share the responsibility with Whitman, who laid it on the line when he denied the possibility of a formal poetics in America. I elicit the support of Eliot, who shrewdly named Whitman a great prose writer. Pound, who demonstrated how the Old World forms might be broken. Williams, who struggled so long to locate in language the rhythm of American life at its worst.

I have been trying in my small way for years to help devalue the false currency of our poetry. We need a poetic stock market crash. Yet, we have had it; we had it really at the Boston Tea Party; we have it in every generation which rebels against the Old World cultures. The saying goes: Every nation gets the poetry it deserves. Is this what we deserve? Why don't we turn the question around to ask: Do we deserve a poetry at all? Our history shows very little inclination toward the art. The one brief upsurge of poetry we have had was during the 1920's: Sandburg, Fletcher, Lindsay, easy poets who wanted American listeners. The Americans listened more or less politely and then went about their business. Fletcher killed himself. Lindsay killed himself. Sandburg became a famous historian. It was almost as if the muse of America had muttered: Give them enough rope. . . . Exile or monasticism became the only method of survival for the poet: abroad or behind the campus wall, anywhere, elsewhere, even Skid Row. The Southern poets exiled themselves to the North.

For years I've battled publishers to print more poets, sometimes succeeding in getting some new man's work in print. Now I don't know but that the publishers weren't right. For generally the publisher is only shamed into printing poetry. The Old World is drilled in the superstition that poetry is the highest form of art. If so, it is certainly not the highest in this country.

Perhaps we should teach our children that once upon a time there was a thing called poetry, that it was very beautiful, and that people tried to bring it to our shores in boats but it died. And a few people couldn't live without it, so they went back to the Old World to see it. And others built elaborate greenhouses, called English Departments, where they kept it breathing. And they watered it with the most expensive electricity, but it didn't like it here and died anyhow. And some fractious students lost their tempers and began to smash the greenhouse windows. And then everybody started reading and writing prose.

The True Artificer

THE MYSTERY OF art is the presence of form. The poet arrives at a knowledge of its own kind, a knowledge which we can share, we are led to believe, without form. Herein lie all the disagreements philosophers and critics have ever had about the nature of poetry. For this knowledge cannot be shared, cannot come into being, until it is formed. The world is always on the verge of thinking art trivial because the reasoning mind cannot take form seriously. Form, says the reasoning mind, is bound to be play, and some philosophers at their wits ends throw up their hands and declare that art is only a higher kind of amusement. Why it should be "higher" than bullfighting or quoits then becomes the second hard question. The reasoning mind cannot imagine how serious utterances can really be serious unless they are put directly, that is, in prose.

This attitude about the triviality of form is puzzling because it does not seem to apply to anything except works of art; for all knowledge of any kind is formal, and not simply poetic knowledge. The formality of philosophy resides in logic and dialectic. The formality of natural science resides in the selection and organization of data; mathematicians even go so far as to talk about the formal *beauty* of an equation, thus leading some people to think that mathematicians are as unbalanced as poets. The formality of supernatural knowledge resides in rite, sacrament, and the repetition of formulas. Why, then, is it preposterous for the artist to express himself in form?

Perhaps the answer resides in the paradox that artistic material is made of human experience. Human experience itself is formless, chaotic; at any rate we cannot comprehend the "form" of human experience satisfactorily. Human experience is chaotic, but human experience in art is orderly. The poet discovers an order for his own experience; the expression of this discovery is by definition formal. How can it be otherwise? For he has entered into ties with the world where apparently no ties existed. He has not "sought" form nor "achieved" form nor "invented" form: he has experienced it. He has entered its presence and it exists by virtue of his presence. And when it comes into existence it shows certain characteristics, which are these.

Beauty: a work of art is beautiful. Symmetry and harmony: beauty is symmetrical or partakes of symmetry, and is harmonious or partakes of harmony. Wholeness: beauty must be whole, not fragmentary. Symmetry plus harmony plus wholeness equal formal beauty: that is our equation. And poetic artifice consists of finding the symmetrical, harmonious whole for a given poetic (personal) situation. The natural difficulties of finding such a solution for experience in all its actuality and economy and authenticity make the poet an artisan and the labor of his days painstaking, niggling, and seemingly unworthy of one who is known as a voyant, prophet, singer, idealist, and heaven knows what.

Once we accept the equation of symmetry and harmony and wholeness for art we can proceed rapidly to those uses of symmetry and harmony which are peculiar to each kind of art: in poetry, repetition and melody and rhythmic plot. The rhythm of poetry has to do not only with meters but with melodies (alliteration and rhyme and sound-development) and with the rhythm of ideas and the rhythm of images; more than that, with the rhythm of feeling.

Rhythm is the most obvious and the most profound quality of art. To understand the role of rhythm in art is to understand the very nature of art. To regard rhythm as a secondary characteristic of art is to fall into the hands of the rationalists of art and the people who talk about form and content.

Poetic rhythm can be reduced to meter, and meter can be analyzed minutely (though it seldom is) for its bearing on other elements of symmetry and harmony in the poem. Meter also bears a direct relationship to the language it represents. Eventually any particular language decides on a rhythmic norm—a certain number of syllables to the typical line and a certain distribution of rhythmic values within the line. Seemingly, this is the height of convention and inelasticity, and yet the poet is never at a loss for new ways to vary the formula. The reason is that meter in the abstract has no applicability, while applied meter is as various as the words which make up the line.

Meter in the abstract bears a relation to the language it

uses, but meter in the particular bears a relation to and an identity with the sense of the words. Where this is not the case we feel a dislocation of form, and suspicion sets in that something has gone wrong with the poem. The meter in any particular case gives the exact linguistic emphasis the poet is after: thus we do not feel meter separately from meaning; we feel the double weight of the right thing said with the right pressure and the right speed. And this form must also correspond with the poet's own peculiarities of speech, his own vocabulary and grammatical needs. It seems impossible to accomplish all these acrobatics at once, but there is plenty of evidence to prove that it can be done.

The meter of poetry gives it its obvious and visible symmetry, but to think of meter as anything except the symmetry of the sense is to fall at once into the form-content delusion. Meter exists because of the laws of symmetry, harmony and wholeness. The poet is bound to these laws and has no respite from them.

This is the barest possible statement about poetic symmetry. I wish now to touch on the simplest point of harmony, which in poetry is alliteration.

If someone in conversation uses an alliteration, he is likely to be laughed at. This laughter expresses uneasiness, the suspicion of affectation and even of insincerity. The presence of as simple a form as an alliteration indicates art-making, artifice. Perfection in common discourse would make anybody think the speaker had rehearsed his lines: we would wonder what he had up his sleeve. There is also the fact that an alliteration creates a point of tension when it occurs, or a reflection that throws the hearer back to a prior place.

On the other hand, a poet comes upon the idea that

everything everywhere is falling through space. No matter where he got the idea, from a Greek philosopher or a Princeton mathematician; he is brought to this idea in his own life by seeing leaves falling from the trees in autumn. The dying season reminds him of human death, the slow death of the world, the universe, etc. Of course, the poet is saddened by so much impending disaster and he is going to try to act this out in the poem. This he does all the way through his work, and I shall take the little line of climax which says—this being a German poem—*Wir alle fallen.* There are two points of harmony here, both alliterative. One comes with the repeat of the *all* sound (which, by the way, runs through the whole poem). Repetition of the same sound is itself an expression of tension and denotes a pitch of emotion. Again it should be said that if one used two such sounds together in prose he would run the risk of ridicule, while in poetry he is obliged to create such harmonies.

The other point of repetition is the lettering, the repeat of the *f* sound. Anyone who thinks alliteration is trivial thinks poetry itself is trivial. Alliteration works in several ways at once: it adds a rhythm to the other rhythms of meter and sense; it heightens feeling in the reader's mind; and more important, it gives finality to the idea by setting it off as a separate figure. In a sense it traps the idea so that it can never again escape. Perhaps this is what people mean when they say that good poetry is memorable. I prefer to say that, in a case like this, the poet has proved what he thought and felt.

All poetry is rhythmic but not all poetry is metered. When it is not metered the poet usually has to supply some other regulating artifice to create symmetry and harmony.

Often a non-metrical poetry is highly imagistic, the images bearing the weight of the whole form. In some cases image-making is almost the primary business of the poet and there are poets who can get by almost completely with images. As I mentioned earlier, image-making and imagination are two different things and sometimes opposites. The child who makes a bush of a bear is not making an image; he is making a mistake of imagination. The poet making images does not seek hallucinations but realities, as when Lawrence speaks of the Bavarian gentians "giving off darkness, blue darkness." This "reality," I should add, is not a matter of objective observation but of poetic involvement. It is produced by emotional contact, like the expression we create in someone's eyes by looking into them.

Poetic imagery is not simply picture-making and picture language. Imagery works through all the senses, sometimes separately, sometimes together. But the eye and the ear are the senses most affected, although the sense of touch is probably more at work in poetic imagery than we usually suppose. The poet produces image sensations in very devious ways, and with the aim of breaking through dull usage and exposing the naked sensory quality of his statement. This act in itself comes as close to a description of the poet's artifice as we can get, for the ability to make images out of words presupposes everything else about the poet: his personal involvement with language and with his desire to turn experience into language. It can be said of the poet that he feels in language, and that sometimes feeling does not come alive in him until it has been verbalized. It is difficult for other people to believe in the poet's sense of the physical reality of words; critics try to understand poetry with a more limited sense of language, and this relative insensitivity makes the critic bestow magical powers on the poet. The image-making sense in the poet is really not as futuristic, as "creative," as critics think: it is more the desire to get it right, to say the thing accurately, to find the true value of the locution for each case. Imagery affects everything in a poem except perhaps meter. Indeed, if there is any dichotomy in the whole work of art, it is not form and content, or image and idea, or feeling and statement, but image and meter. Image includes every verbal function in poetry, and meter, of course, is not verbal but temporal. It may be that it is the time element of poetry which, in fact, takes the poem out of flowing chronological time and puts it into a time-world all its own.

The most important class of image is metaphor. This is the boldest of language figures and is even a synonym for image. Metaphor takes to itself the properties of all words and is concerned with those properties. Metaphor can assign new properties to words but not with license. In fact, it is the business of metaphor to find out the sensory and ideational possibilities of words which are inherent in them and which they acquire through use and abuse. Only in this way can metaphor bring about the metamorphosis in poetry which the poet needs.

A good image is a good picture, a proper likeness, a physical truth, and a symbolic truth. When the poet calls England a precious stone we get a vision of something small and precious; we get a feeling of indissoluble hardness which resists ages of change; and we get a sense of eminence also, that which is the center of something. The poet then speaks of the sea in contrast. The sea is soft, less precious, fluid, the element in which we find the precious stone. The line reads, "This precious stone set in the silver sea." In metaphorical terms the meaning "beautiful, safe, beloved England" becomes "this land, the king's which he wears forever in his crown."

The difference between a poetic and a rational statement about England is that the latter is more abstract. The historian would say "the power of England." The poet images this power by talking about England as a jewel of the sea. And the artifice of metaphor here consists in finding the symbolic particular for the abstraction.

There is one other element of poetic artifice I wish to mention, this one the most difficult to say anything sensible about. That is the music of poetry. The chief sensory quality of language is music, but the music of language cannot be coded and reduced to scales and harmonic tables. Still there is no question that the sound of words in poetry does most of the work of producing images and sensory meaning. Every language has a melodic system of its own and every poet within his language has a melodic system of his own. And this sound system is based on inherent sensory meanings and inherent verbal meanings.

There are some people who say that no word has inherent meaning, only given meaning. I have even heard of one of these men telling his children that on Monday they would call meat *bread* and bread *meat*. On Tuesday they would call meat *wood*, and on Wednesday *ice*. By Saturday, I imagine, the children would be ready to burn all the family poetry books in the fireplace. On the other hand, a poet like Paul Claudel believes so deeply in the inherent meaning of words that he even argues for the graphic extension of meaning; a word to him even looks like what it means. But let that go. George Saintsbury, a nineteenth-century critic, used to say that inherent meanings in sound do not exist: he was a semanticist of sorts. Saintsbury said that there was nothing somber or lugubrious about the sound of *gloom* or *doom*, as poets contended, for if that were so, how could you account for the word *bloom*?

The rationalist of language believes in the story of the Tower of Babel, namely that more than one language is a curse. Semanticists are always trying to take the curse off words by reducing all languages to one, and one so useful that with it the Hottentot could converse with the biphysicist about the House of Lords. The poet believes in the endless multiplicity of language and dialects and personal styles: he glories in every change the language makes, and he knows that each change comes from a deep necessity in the language and that the language will reject every change which is not a true change. There is a natural French Academy in language which holds court over every nuance and innovation: it may be that this is the assembly in which the poet is the unacknowledged legislator.

Every word in every language is intrinsically and extrinsically meaningful. Every word that comes into existence has the esthetic and moral approval of the people who made it and used it. When we have two words which are supposed to mean the same thing, we may be sure that they mean different things. Is there no difference between *flower, flos, fleur, blossom, blume, bloom*? Is it an accident that the word *bloom* may refer to a lump of wrought-iron? Or that the word *love* has residual meanings of pleasure and belief?

The highest compliment we can pay the poet is to say he has "ear." Ear is the ability, the genius, for feeling simultaneously the harmony of the whole poem and the sense of the sound for each particular word. The function of ear is not musical purely and simply: it is the ability to know the musical sense of the line. We can understand this on the elementary plane of onomatopoeia, where sound imitates meaning.

With ear the poet can do almost anything, yet he can never depart from the sound possibilities inherent in a word-form. If a word with a loud sound has a "soft" meaning (for instance, *bough*) the uses of the word in poetry will be quite restricted. The fact that there is always wind where there is a bough increases the loudness of meaning slightly. The quality of the word is limited by this internal sensory conflict. The word *bloom*, because of its heavy sensuous sound, will always cast something of a shadow over the line in which it appears. If the word *bloom* were more important than the word *flower* in English, we would be a different kind of people with perhaps a more tragic, more melodramatic view of nature.

There is a simple proof of the ruling power of sound in poetry, namely, translation. Everyone is familiar with the terrible loss that occurs when a poem is taken out of one language and put into another. Indeed, the loss is practically total. But what is lost is not merely a pleasing and harmonious series of sounds of the original: what is lost is the very meaning of the original poem. A Chinese proverb says that translation is the reverse side of the brocade. Needless to say, the reverse side of the brocade is useless. Translation is practically as useless; we see only a rough design and a maze of horrid knots and loose ends on a dull field. The sound may be no more than color in one sense: in a deeper sense it is everything that creates the meaning of the poem. This does not mean that the sound *corresponds* to the meaning. It means that the sound produces the imagery, that the inherent sensory meanings of the words are revealed by the choice of the word for its context. The poet knows that there can be only one choice for every particular case. After he has turned over hundreds of candidates in his mind, he comes upon the one and only choice. And what can the translator do but recreate the whole poem from the bottom up?

II

To speak of poetic artifice is always risky because the very mention of artifice assumes that it involves a separate and distinct creative act. But no reference can be made to artifice without pointing to particular cases. Artifice does not come into action until poetic knowledge is born. To speak of one without the other is meaningless. For this reason I wish to retrace what I have just said about rhythm, meter, image, metaphor, and ear, this time in terms of what we can call sincerity.

The poet has a dual obligation to sincerity, one to himself and one to the poem. This is a far different matter from the form-content equation. Sincerity to self in art means the power of accepting the reality of one's milieu in terms of oneself. This sounds the simplest and most commonplace of requirements, but it is the most difficult, and in fact the all-but-impossible human requirement. It is this attribute which we associate with saintliness and the utmost wisdom. It is the essence of humility before actuality. But acceptance of the milieu does not mean resignation, surrender, or blind praise. It means belief in existence. It means a break with every other situation, the recognition of the inescapability from the unique situation. It means a divorce from the historical function and a marriage with the poetic-creative function. This attitude is neither revolutionary nor traditionalist; it is impossible for the poet to generalize his condition so far in either direction. Yet in sincerity he breaks through to new land, a symbolically disruptive act which is recognized by conventional minds as dangerous. The true poet makes this breakthrough without ill intention and without malice: the "experimental" poet does it with evil intent. Since the time of Baudelaire the notion that poetry is malicious has become so widespread that poetry boasts of its destructive powers. Modern poetry represents official sincerity, or the myth of sincerity (called integrity), but little modern poetry is sincere except in relation to its myth. That is, modern poetry says that this is a bad world and we will not say anything about it except that it is bad. Anyone who says it is good desecrates the myth. Thus, the approach to the myth of language must be that in this world the language is debased—etcetera, etcetera.

Acceptance of the situation for the poet is the sign of sincerity to self. This acceptance implies less rather than more involvement in the outside situation. The scene is where he is. He does not seek out the scene. Of the poet who goes out into the scene we always ask the question: Is he sincere? The great nationalist poets, the great rhetoricians, the makers and users of systems convince us, if at all, in spite of their giantism. These poets substitute will for sincerity and they carry with them our suspicion that their real aim is to dominate the scene, and not necessarily to know it.

Sincerity to the poem follows naturally from acceptance of the scene. Sincerity to the poem is the expression of the other deeper sincerity. The old aphorism "style is the man" strikes close to what I am saying. It is not that the poet achieves style as a highjumper achieves height, as much as it is that he achieves selfhood and personality. When we say *style* we are apt to think of surfaces, but it is our duty as readers to distinguish between style which is only a mask and style which is the outer form of inner reality. The poet of masks does not fool anyone for long. The true poet is incapable of imitation. We do not think Shakespeare was unoriginal because he used Plutarch and Holinshed. The story is always there, always in existence: it is what the poet experiences from it that is his theme. The leaves are always falling, the ladies are always fickle, the soldiers always dying, the poor always suffering. Some of this sinks into the poet's soul and cheers him or hurts him, and changes his life. And being changed he changes how to say it.

The poet's artifice consists in making his lines conform to the degree of change he has experienced. The alterations he makes time and time again in a single phrase or a single word are not for "effects"; they are a search for the exact degree of change which he has lived and which is part of him. This is sincerity to the situation. But the search for the right word is carried out also in the other direction, in terms of the possibilities of the language. This is sincerity to the poem. Thus it is that all authentic or sincere poetry is new and surprising and all insincere poetry trite. The trite is bound to be untrue because the degree of the situation has not been taken. The trite can only be "universal"; it can have only general statistical truth, not human poetic truth. The term *trite* is also coupled with the term *sentimentality*: both imply half-truth.

Sincerity in terms of rhythm means finding the rhythm of the language itself and finding the personal expression of this collective rhythm. The rhythm of poetry differs radically from language to language, but in one language it never goes very far from a norm. Even in extreme cases in English rhythm—for instance Hopkins, Whitman, and Eliot, who all tried to escape the norm—the basic meter is present. What is astonishing is the infinite variety that exists within the norm of our simple English line. American poets today are making the mightiest effort to turn the wheel of rhythm, and may succeed—but so far we have no proof that a new era has been reached for English rhythm. The most widely used new rhythm is modelled on a tri-syllabic rather than a di-syllabic meter; in Pound it takes an abbreviated form of the classic hexameter:

Surrounded by herds and by cohorts looked on Mt. Taishan

The rhythm is sincere in terms of modern English and it is sincere in terms of the classical aims of the poet. But the form is limiting because it can be sustained in English only by an elaborate use of conjunctions and other connectives:

And the flute lay there by her thigh
. . . .
And then went down to the ship

The whole form spreads because of the meters, requiring the largest possible canvas for work. Modern metrics in general show more tendency to compromise than this.

The poet cannot know what to say until his ear has heard it. Up to that point, experience is still in the realm of sensation, locked in. But by being doubly aware of his situation and the condition of the language, the poet does something for the poem and for the language. Language itself seeks form. There is a kind of poetic soul in language which everyone contributes to and takes from. The poet immerses himself in this language-consciousness; he is at home in this element above all. But his task only begins at this juncture.

Meter is the frame of poetry. It frames not only the whole with symmetry but it frames each part within the larger frame. Without meter, as we know from free verse poets, there is no principle of selection, unless the poet supplies one. Meter drives rhythm into pattern: it does the same with imagery and sound. The lines of force in a poem can be traced through meter: without it everything else is in danger of dislocation. Sincere meter permits natural word order, natural to the language, natural to the poet's language, and natural to the particular poem. Sincere meter permits the flow of feeling through imagery and the sounds of the lines.

A poem must do what it says. This dictum can well sum up the responsibilities of the poet to his craft. If the poem says *I love you* the words must act out this conviction and feeling in such a way as to convince a reader that the act of love is beyond question real. Most poems that fail merely say; they do not do. But the good poet goes to infinite pains to re-create the scene and mood and quality of what he says. Each word is exploited for its image content, and here the poet must concern himself with the sensory possibilities of the words in terms of their truth to the situation and to himself. The situation can be made real only if he finds it in himself to be capable of the experience he is writing about. He searches for meanings in terms of the senses. The intelligence of art is sensory intelligence, the meaning of art is sensory meaning: unless the poet can argue through language colors, language shapes, language sounds, and through the natural image-making genius of language, he fails as a poet.

Through ear we can trace the poet's total sense of harmony, as through meter we can trace the invisible field of force which holds the poem's body in shape. Ear, specifically, is the ability to find the sensuous correspondences of meaning: ear makes physical what is only implicit in meaning. Ear is harmony itself, from one point of view: it is also the guide to sincerity to the poem and sincerity to self. Ear is the critical faculty of the creative mind, but ear cannot function unless the poet is wholly involved in the situation and the situation wholly involved in him. It is an active, not a passive faculty, and it is this which distinguishes it from the faculty of judgment or the faculty of observation. As soon as one speaks of ear he becomes involved in the presentation of the total poem, the wholeness of which is its meaning. Ear, from the poet's point of view, is equivalent to his own total experience of the finished poem: a vision of it. Ear, to the reader, is his acceptance of the poem because it is good.

The artifice of poetry is without science, without philosophy, without religion. You cannot write or understand a poem philosophically, you cannot write or understand a poem religiously, you cannot write or understand a poem scientifically. The uniqueness of a work of art is its primary characteristic. Outside the work of art there is no rationale which can shed light on it. The poet therefore has no obligation to "explain" his poem in other terms, for there is nothing to explain unless something has gone wrong.

Criticism which usually tries to view poetry in the light

of other knowledge thus has the double meaning of explanation and negation. But the attempt to make poetry "mean" more than it does is a sign of desperation about other things. Esthetics, I daresay, flourishes in a time of pessimism. Art flourishes at any time when the individual spirit is left free. True poetry does not require explanation, in any case, because of the law of beauty which demands immediate response to the whole work. Good poets never play with meaning: on the contrary they make meaning foolproof. There is no such thing as a good unintelligible work of art. And there is no such thing as a good work of art which is not immediately apprehensible in the senses. This dictum can be tested against Homer and Dante and Shakespeare and a handful of contemporaries: there is always the handle by which the cup is held, be it plot or logic of circumstance, or something else.

The artifice of poetry is essentially dramatic, and no drama is effective without immediate response. The poet is a playwright who dramatizes his experience; he is the actor who acts it out. Most poets, even when their poems fail in immediacy, defend their work by claiming that their poems leap the gap from poet to reader, even when they don't. But there are some poets who believe that the difficulties of understanding are natural to poetry. Such poets are usually amateur philosophers or theologians. Poetic knowledge is at its best profound and manifold, but poetic artifice demands that this knowledge be made to transform the poem into an immediate perceptible whole.

Modern metaphor is sometimes spoken of as a form in which the literal term is buried: the reader has the job of picking the lock. Supposedly, the poetry gains from this extrusion of meaning and the senses are set free to deal with the secondary results of the meanings. But it is quite obvious that the poem loses more than it gains by this method. In any case, such a method throws into jeopardy the entire basis of art. Nearly all contemporary art that goes bad does so as much because of the "suppression of the missing term" as because of lack of talent. To take away from the artist the primary obligation of immediacy is to leave him a prey to intuition and every license of the imagination. Also it permits the theory, used not only by poets but by critics of poetry, that a poem can mean more than it says, and that it can mean several things. A poet who talks about the four, six, eight or ten "levels" of meaning either has his tongue in his cheek or is trying to impress the police. Any such theory is an invitation to bedlam. Every artist by instinct should fight against the principle of multiplicity of meaning: when for some reason he finds it impossible to form his work any other way, he should admit this as failure in himself, and not try to blame the state of civilization, the collapse of culture, the rise of "mass language," and other circumstances which are not properly his business. It is the poet's job to discover the way to integrity of meaning, not his job to destroy integrity of meaning. Poetry that defends fragmentation borders on apocalyptic knowledge and insane knowledge. Poetry that defends the derangement of the senses, synesthesia, associationalism and the like, drifts rapidly towards a religious state of mind in which poetry itself becomes a religion and an art of prophecy. The good poet is known for the limitations he puts upon his material as well as for the wholeness he creates out of it. It is for this reason that the best artists frequently seem to be doing the same thing over and over again. The inferior artist, who abhors limits, becomes napoleonic and thinks all he has to do is turn his face like a bright light on any scene, and the scene will become illuminated.

Poetry creates a total scene only by implication. The scene within the work is whole but it does not signify a system. This kind of knowledge is the opposite of philosophical knowledge, which seeks a whole order. It is the opposite of scientific knowledge, which seeks a whole order of a different kind. It is the opposite of religious knowledge, which seeks a total order in its own way. Poetry lies eternally outside any order of things which seeks or finds a self-contained system of ideas or beliefs. The current of poetry continually crosses these other currents in a counter-direction. Yet the limited personal truth of poetry and art gives the only permanent evidence of human reality we have. This is why philosophers and politicians and even scientists quote poetry: there is nothing else in human knowledge to prove what they are saying. The accurate quotation of poetry is equivalent to a point of evidence.

Artifice itself is proof. It proves to the poet that what happened could happen. The poem brings into physical existence the always dying reality of experience and the bright or blurred sensations of memory. And artifice brings into existence for the reader the reality of the poet's vision. Let us not abuse the word vision: it is an ocular term, not a fortune teller's. It is not the vulgar conception of poetry as ideal knowledge or future knowledge or transcendental knowledge or pure knowledge or any of the things we read about in books of poetics.

The twentieth century has made the discovery, among so many others, that poetry must be written. This discovery has not yet led to a revision of poetics: so far it has led only to a mechanistic view of art. We have given up the notion of oracular poetry, poetry of the depths, trance poetry, and so on, but we have swung over to the extreme on the other side. Nowadays critics talk about structure, tenor, function, texture, using the language of mechanics. They approach poetry through the language of psychology, whereas the vocabulary of emotion among them is considered primitive and even obscene. If a critic pronounces a poem beautiful, everyone hangs his head in shame. Nevertheless, we are better off than the critics who used to talk about inspiration and imagination, and it is even possible that we are coming close to a civilized poetics. The obstacle at present is the existence and even growth of a mythopoeia which would raise poetry to an even higher status than government, ethics or religion. The public has instinctively fought off this religion of poetry, but most of the literary public has been weakened or disaffected by the pretenses of mythos. Myth is easily changed into culture propaganda, as was the case in Russia and also in countries where the artist changed to the seer. It makes no difference whether the poetry is supposed to be for the peasants or for the aristocracy: as soon as poetry becomes *for* something or somebody, it is doomed. A poetry that distills values or sets standards or projects myths is at once official poetry. It is tragic for poets and for everyone else that poetry in our time cannot be taken seriously unless it poses as *something like* philosophy or *something like* religion or *something like* science.

And yet the discovery that poetry has to be written is a good sign. This could only have happened in America, where there was no poetry until a century ago and people set about (as Americans will) to find out how it is done. We even started schools for this purpose, to the vast amusement of Europeans. The discovery that poetry must be written has unfortunately helped those zealous people who believe in something called Communication. Both historic poets and mythic poets believe that poetry is a kind of higher Morse Code which can be translated into ordinary language if one knows the signals. But poetry does not communicate in this way at all. The poet does not communicate to the poem; nor does the poem communicate to the reader. The very term "communicate" is a propaganda word which expresses a false reality. A poem is a perfectly intelligible thing in itself: it is coherent; it is whole; it is beautiful; but it is not winking at anybody. This is why the poet has a choice about publication itself: it would not necessarily change his poetry if he locked it all in a strongbox. Most poets probably release their work because of a variety of psychological reasons and not because the poem is *for* someone else. Even the common experience of viewing a particular work is, in a sense, fortuitous, for the creator has no obligation to anything but his creation: he knows, of course, that a given work should have a predictable effect on an audience, but he cannot be sure. I do not think the good poet intentionally hides his work, nor does he shout it from the rooftops. He gives it because he is proud to have made it, but it is given to no one. The giving in art consists in the making—when the poet has finished the poem and it lies on the table before him, he has done his supreme act of charity. It would be wicked, if knowing it to be good, he then destroyed it, but the poem says only: This is what I am. When the poet writes a poem "to" his mistress, the dedication can only be an afterthought. The poet has experienced the lady's beauty and his love for her (which is colored by her love for him) but the work of the poem takes place quite apart from this maze of feelings. The poet at the point of creation sits down with the question: What happened to me? Where was I when it happened? His spirit then gives witness of injury or exultation, his memory remakes the scene, he begins the search for words to tell the story. And the *time when* he does these things determines whether they will be done at all. Shelley's glorious image of inspiration as a fading coal tells what happens to the poet who waits. Waiting is death to art. Almost anyone can recover from experience: only the artist can arrest the quality of experience.

At the bottom of every poem lies the personal history of poetic artifice, the ceaseless engagement of the poet with the quality of experience itself, the efforts to reach the poem without violating his own truth or without violating its verbal possibilities. This can only be done by finding the wholeness of the situation itself. Wholeness is achieved through the virtues of symmetry and harmony. And symmetry and harmony in a related and complete work result in a thing of beauty. *Beauty is a quality of poetry and not its aim.* Its aim is to give finality to the particular personal human truth.

There is a legend about the end of the world which pictures a poet standing in the doorway of his lonely cottage, watching the approach of a pestilent cloud. He knows he is the last living man and he knows that death will come to him in a few hours. What does he do? How does he prepare for his own death and the death of the world? He does not sink down in thought or prayer; he does not attempt to record his final hours; he does not seek an escape from the inevitable destiny. He turns back into the house and goes to his writing table; he takes up the poem he is writing and studies it again. He begins the new corrections.

This is the legend of the true artificer.

The Death of Randall Jarrell

THIS IS NOT a eulogy, not a memorial, not one of those exercises in the objective perception of value for which the age of criticism is justly infamous. Randall Jarrell was not my friend, nor was he my enemy. But he was the poet whose poetry I admired and looked up to most after William Carlos Williams. This I said many times in many ways in my criticism. I praised his poetry more and more whole-heartedly than any other of his contemporaries. My praise, it may be, did not sit comfortably with him, for he spotted me as an outsider, or one who was constantly battling to get on the outside. Jarrell was very much an insider. There was a terrible conflict in his soul between his instinct for freedom and his desire for cultural asylum. This conflict gave him his style, his literary style, his lifestyle. It is a style deceptively free. His bookplate might be the question mark. The most common and significant expression he uses at crucial points in his poetry and in his prose is *and yet.* . . . I thought of naming this essay "Randall Jarrell—And Yet," but I decided to be more ambitious. I shall try to situate Randall Jarrell among his fellows rather than doing his portrait. I think there is a message in his death, for me and for his generation.

Let me dispose of a little personal data first, a few observations which will perhaps illumine my not too extensive relationship with him. When I was editing *Poetry* magazine, and after I had published hundreds—could it have been thousands?—of poets, I noted that the manuscripts of Randall Jarrell, whether poems or prose, were the only perfect manuscripts I ever saw. I mean that they were letter-perfect. There was no question of a typo or any other kind of graphical error. He was my only scrupulous poet, for most poets write the way they dress and their manuscripts look like somebody else's laundry. And this minor perfection of Jarrell's was reflected in the precision of thought, especially in his prose, which all the same sometimes took on a slightly euphuistic contour. I think euphuistic is the word; *baroque* describes certain of his stylistic processes, a style of inlay in which quotation it so exquisitely handled that everything Jarrell quotes sounds as if he wrote it. He was a great, you might say a dangerous, listener. And yet his style of reportage is comic, for he fears loftiness and bombast like the plague. One looks forward to the publication of his letters. We can be sure that the voice of the poet and of the culture gossip is there. Charm is overwhelming in all his writing; *wit* is too platitudinous a word for his work, and the sharply outlined involutions of his thought deserve a better word than *wisdom.*

He gave a marvelous summation of contemporary poetry

in a lecture once. I asked him if I could publish it in the *Prairie Schooner*, which I then edited. His reply was: "I'd be delighted for you to print the lecture in the *Prairie Schooner*. You've always been my favorite editor because you're not like an editor at all." I put the best construction on this remark that I could, especially as I knew it to be true, more than true, a complimentary reprimand of *my* style of life and letters. Except for an early merciless review of one of my books, he was always understanding about me—and acidulous. We were of the same group, so to speak, and had fought all the same wars, and he had a right to cry *Whoa!* when I came galloping by.

All the poets sat on the edge of their seats while Jarrell, who everybody had to admit had earned the right to do so, put together the jigsaw puzzle of modern poetry in front of our eyes. When I was finally fitted into place, with a splash of color, I felt a relief that I *fitted* and a regret that that puzzle had been solved. I will repeat what he said of me because it is germane to my evaluation of Jarrell: "Karl Shapiro's poems are fresh and young and rash and live; their hard clear outlines, their flat bold colors create a world like that of a knowing and skillful neo-primitive painting, without any of the confusion or profundity of atmosphere, of aerial perspective, but with notable visual and satiric force." He then goes on to mention my influences, Auden, Rilke, Whitman, and he does not need to say that these are also his influences, more his than mine, because Jarrell assimilated his Auden and Rilke and Whitman, along with his Corbière and Grimm and even Robert Frost. I assimilated nothing but was only influenced by. I rejected Influence out of hand and waged a one-man children's crusade against the Past, the Graeco-Judaeo-Christian thingamajig, so that Jarrell could say of me with amused amazement: "Both in verse and in prose Shapiro loves, partly out of indignation and partly out of sheer mischievousness, to tell the naked truths or half-truths or quarter-truths that will make anybody's hair stand on end; he is always crying: 'But he hasn't any clothes on!' about an emperor who is half the time surprisingly well dressed." There is a slight concession here: Jarrell admits that the emperor is dressed like an emperor only *half* the time, while I contend that he is badly dressed even when he is naked.

I will be done with this "interrelationship" in a moment, but I am leading up to something important, a whole or half- or quarter-truth which I am bound to utter. I will read a poem I wrote about Jarrell; it is a prose-poem, as prosodists say when they run out of verbiage, and is in my last book. I don't remember Jarrell's reaction to the poem, but I aimed to please him when I wrote it.

Randall, I like your poetry terribly, yet I'm afraid to say so. Not that my praise keeps you awake—though I'm afraid it does. I can't help liking them. I even like the whine, the make-believe whiplash with the actual wire in it. Once when you reviewed me badly (you must) I wrote you: "I felt as if I had been run over but not hurt." That made you laugh. I was happy. It wasn't much of a triumph but it worked. When people ask about you I am inclined to say: He's an assassin (a word I never use). I'm inclined to say: Why are you always yourself? Your love of Rilke—if it's love—your intimacy with German and God knows what all, your tenderness and terrorization, your prose sentences—like Bernini graves, staggeringly expensive, Italianate, warm, sentences once-and-for-all. All the verses you leave half-finished in mid-air—I once knew a woman who never finished a sentence. Your mind is always at its best, your craft the finest craft "money can buy," you would say with a barb. I'm afraid of you. Who wouldn't be? But I rush to read you, whatever you print. That's news.

And this is also news. I am quoting from the News Notes section of *Poetry* magazine soon after Jarrell died. "There was a public ceremony at Yale on February 28th to honor the memory of Randall Jarrell, who was killed last autumn in an automobile accident. John Berryman, Richard Eberhart, John Hollander, Stanley Kunitz, Robert Lowell, William Meredith, Adrienne Rich, Robert Penn Warren, Richard Wilbur, and Peter Taylor came together at Yale to participate in the tribute, for which the chairman was Norman Holmes Pearson. Mary Jarrell, widow of the poet, read 'the last recently written poem that truly pleased him,' 'The Player Piano,' as yet unpublished. The Yale *Daily News* reports that she 'received an impassioned standing ovation as she walked to the lectern.' Elizabeth Bishop, Cleanth Brooks, Robert Fitzgerald, Marianne Moore, John Crowe Ransom, and Allen Tate, who could not attend, sent testimonials which Professor Pearson read. . . ."

When I read this little notice in *Poetry* I was dismayed at my conspicuous absence from the list. Had Jarrell left it in his will to keep me off the Yale campus? Impossible. I had a blood-boiling moment of suspicion or paranoia that the Bollingen Committee or Professor Pearson or Robert Lowell had blackballed me from the club. My anti-cultural-committee activities span many years, and I have tried to sabotage organized culture whenever possible—not always successfully, of course. When the National Institute of Arts and Letters elected me as a member, I declined. But when their officers called me and said nobody had had that much cheek since Sinclair Lewis declined, and who the hell did I think I was, I chickened out and let them enroll me. When I went to watch the President sign the Arts and Humanities bill, some writers said: What are you doing here? Spying, was all I could say. And now Randall had been organized in death by some cultural subcommittee and all I could think was: Now he knows what it feels like to turn over in his grave.

Between the instinct for freedom and the desire for cultural asylum others can make a choice, and always do. Culture Committees love funerals. There is, even in one's fellow poets, a touch of the vulture; when the poet lies on the roof of the Tower of Silence you can hear the shuddering of ragged wings.

I remember once that Robert Lowell and Randall Jarrell were playing a game. The game was Who's First and it was Lowell's game. The idea is to grade the poets until the downgrading wipes most of the competition off the board. Two or three remaining contenders then engage in a death struggle. Jarrell played this game with a will, but his winning instinct was no match for Lowell.

In Jarrell's bibliography published in 1958 there is a good introduction which contains this sentence: "Most critics predicted the emerging greatness of a Robert Lowell or a Karl Shapiro, but few guessed that Jarrell would outstrip them, especially in so short a time." This judgment is sound as far as I am concerned and certainly as far as Lowell is concerned. I'm not playing Who's First, I hope, because I don't think the game is worth my time or anyone else's. Comparisons of Lowell and Jarrell are irrelevant anyhow. Lowell is primarily a figurehead which he himself personally carved out of solid rock. The effort was immense,

Churchillian in blood, sweat, and tears. But one feels that Lowell writes poetry to *get even*, while Jarrell became a poet because he couldn't help it.

Some years ago I volunteered to write an article for the *Evergreen Review* about Lowell. I said I would call it "Robert Lowell *as* T. S. Eliot." A while later I said I would change the title to "Robert Lowell as Cassius Clay." I finished up by not writing the article at all. It was not Lowell I was after but the *maître d'hôtel* psychology of literature which Lowell espouses.

In the Jarrell lecture which I published in the *Prairie Schooner*, Jarrell says this of Lowell (I am paraphrasing): Robert Lowell is the poet of shock. His style manages to make even quotations and historical facts a personal possession. "Make it grotesque" could be Lowell's motto. (In the context Jarrell is contrasting Lowell with Richard Wilbur, a poet who makes poems out of the things of life rather than out of life itself.) Jarrell thought that Lowell possessed and wrote out of a life, yet he knew that this life was at least as unreal as Wilbur's life-by-virtue-of-the-things-of-life. Here is a direct quote: "Lowell has always had an astonishing ambition, a willingness to learn what past poetry was and to compete with it on its own terms." My comment is what Jarrell politely implies, that competition is the sole inspiration of such a poet. Jarrell says in a parenthesis that Lowell bullied his early work, but his own vulnerable humanity has been forced in on him (a statement of tremendous humanity and pardon) with a shadow of fear above. Of Lowell's poems he mentions their stubborn toughness, their senseless originality (an expression to conjure with), and their contingency. Some of the poems justify the harshness and violence and what Jarrell calls their barbarous immediacy; he ends by complimenting Lowell, without having convinced us why, for his largeness and grandeur, and throws him a fish in this sentence: "You feel before reading any new poem of his the uneasy expectation of perhaps encountering a masterpiece." In an earlier treatment of Lowell in *Poetry and the Age*, Jarrell wrote: "Cocteau said to poets: *Learn what you can do and then don't do it*; and this is so. . . . As a poet Mr. Lowell sometimes doesn't have enough trust in God and tries to do everything himself; . . . But probably the reader will want to say to me . . . what Lincoln said about the drunkard Grant: 'If I knew his brand I would order my other generals a barrel.' "

Our generation—the generation of Jarrell, Wilbur, myself, Roethke, Lowell, Schwartz, Bishop, Ciardi, Berryman, Kunitz, Nemerov, Whittemore—one is almost inclined to add Merrill, Lynch, Pearce, Fenner, and Smith—our generation lived through more history than most or maybe any. We lived through more history even than Stendhal, who fell, as he says, with Napoleon. We were reared as intellectuals and fought the Second World War before it happened and then again when it did happen. We witnessed the god that failed and helped trip him up. We predicted the Alexandrianism of the age and like everybody else we throve on it. We drove our foreign cars to class to teach. And we bit the hand that fed us, but not very hard, not hard enough. The hand went on signing papers. Once upon a time we were all revolutionaries of one stripe or another, but when we got married and settled down, with tenure, we talked technique instead of overthrow. Half of us stopped rebelling and not because of middle age. The age made it so easy to be a poet, or to

survive on lobster, the age gave in so sweetly to our imprecations, the age so needed us to help it hate itself, this
spineless age ended by softening the backbone of poetry.

Dylan Thomas was the anti-symbol of our group, that
Dylan who died after he saw the faces of mice in the Bris-
tol crystal. It was Thomas who taught poetry to stop thinking, and we resented that! Though we were not all drunks
and suicides, we had our goodly share. But all of us felt the
rot of institutionalism in our bones. Jarrell got it down in a
novel, the kind of novel the age demanded, the exposé of
sensibility. Jarrell's novel *Pictures from an Institution* is so
brilliant that it defeats itself as a fiction; it becomes a horn-
book of avant-gardism, sophisticated to the point of philistinism. Jarrell is misleadingly philistine, say, about Modern
Art of all varieties. It is because he is impatient with failure
or imperfection or goofing around with the Muse. But this
impatience of Jarrell's is also a veritable lust for perfection;
and both the impatience and the philistinism are what you
might call Texan. *And yet*, what Jarrell does to Gertrude,
his anti-heroine in the novel, is almost beyond belief. Can
anyone be that worthy of hatred? One wonders what Gertrude thought when she read her portrait. Gertrude is one
of those savage Southern female novelists who leaves the
world in terror of the art of fiction.

The setting of the novel is Benton, a very expensive
higher education academy only six versts from Sarah Lawrence or Bennington. Benton's President Robbins doesn't
fare any better than the loathed Gertrude, and the only
lovable character in the book is a German-Jewish composer-
in-residence named Rosenbaum. Jarrell attacks avant-garde
institutionalism and everything it implies by immolating
President Robbins and all his kinfolk in the way Gertrude

might. He attacks dehumanized letters in his lip-smacking crucifixion of Gertrude. True humanity, true culture, true wisdom are preserved in the broken-English Rosenbaums. Jarrell's love of the Good German led him deep into the Black Forest, deep into German childhood. I shared with him his love for *Der Rosenkavalier*, for Elisabeth Schwarzkopf (who was not a very kosher German), and even for Mahler. Germany is the preconscious of Europe, almost all, no, all her geniuses are maniacs, Germany itself is a maniac, the bright dangerous offspring of the Western soul. "Must you learn from your makers how to die?" Jarrell asks the war spirits in one of so many of his Germany-inspired poems. In a note to the poem "A Game at Salzburg" he says that there is a game that Austrians and Germans play with very young children. The child says to the grownup, *Here I am*, and the grownup answers, *There you are. Hier bin i': Da bist du*. Then Jarrell says: "It seems to me that if there could be a conversation between the world and God, this would be it." There is an almost unbearable sorrow in this colloquy, a German-Jewish sorrow, so to speak. Jarrell lets Dr. Rosenbaum say: "The people in Hell . . . say nothing but *What?*" To which Jarrell adds: "Americans in Hell tell each other how to make martinis."

I am not reviewing the novel, but I give it a central place in Jarrell's work as a kind of negative plate of the poetry. The empty intellectualism of America is pinpointed at Benton: the author says, "Nowadays Benton picked and chose: girls who had read Wittgenstein as high school baby-sitters were rejected because the school's quota of abnormally intelligent students had already been filled that year." Jarrell, not quite a Des Esseintes, suffers from a disillusionment of America which all our best artists share, suffers from the disappointment at the failure of the healing-powers of poetry in this nation. Benton—American higher education—is only a rarer kind of custom-built Cadillac. One can almost begin to see the coat of arms emerging on the enameled door. One is already afraid of who is inside. He says, lapsing into what he thinks: "Is an institution always a man's shadow shortened in the sun, the lowest common denominator of everybody in it?" It is bitter to answer yes, but so it is in the modern Institution. In his anthology of short Russian novels, Jarrell quotes Turgenev on Tolstoy. Tolstoy "never believed in people's sincerity. Every spiritual movement seemed to him false, and with his extraordinarily penetrating eyes he used to pierce those on whom his suspicion fell." The early Jarrell published the beginning of a massive attack on Auden, the most conspicuous idealist of the age. Later he forgave Auden, ideals and all.

Jarrell's generation, my generation, inherited the question of Culture, Mass Culture versus True Culture. It is our *pons asinorum* and we all had to cross it. Jarrell worried the problem more than most of us because he could not take for granted the purely elite esthetic of Eliot, the motto of which is High Culture Only: No Foreigners Allowed. Those of us who grew up with the *Partisan Review* on our kitchen tables and who wrote for it with great pride had a slightly altered version of High Culture. With us it was High Culture plus social revolution. We won the Second World War but lost the social revolution. We lost it to what Jarrell called the Medium, the Medium being a kind of symbol for Mass Culture. In the backwash of power and prosperity that engulfed America after our victory, the writers fled to those island citadels called Institutions. Whether it was Benton or Harvard or Berkeley, each of these Mont St. Michels harbored its refugees from the world, from Mass Culture, from the Medium. Jarrell said the acceptably righteous things about Mass Culture, that it either corrupts or isolates the writer, that "true works of art are more and more produced away from or in opposition to society." And yet he knew the writer's need for contact with the mass and qualified his rejections of the Medium. Part of the artist, he said (I am quoting from *A Sad Heart at the Super-Market*): part of the artist "wants to be like his kind, is like his kind; longs to be loved and admired and successful." Part of Jarrell longed to be accepted by the Medium, but the thought of that depressed him. He asked, "Is the influence of what I have called the Medium likely to lead us to any good life? to make us love and try to attain any real excellence, beauty, magninimity? . . ." The answer has to be no. The middle-aged woman in the supermarket who buys All and Cheer and Joy for her gleaming washing machines sees only the image of death staring at her in her rear-view mirror. Let me read this poem, which in my mind is already a famous poem.

NEXT DAY

Moving from Cheer to Joy, from Joy to All,
I take a box
And add it to my wild rice, my Cornish game hens.
The slacked or shorted, basketed, identical
Food-gathering flocks

Are selves I overlook. Wisdom, said William James,
Is learning what to overlook. And I am wise
If that is wisdom;
Yet somehow, as I buy All from these shelves
And the boy takes it to my station wagon,

What I've become
Troubles me even if I shut my eyes.

When I was young and miserable and pretty
And poor, I'd wish
What all girls wish: to have a husband,
A house and children. Now that I'm old, my wish
Is womanish:
That the boy putting groceries in my car

See me. It bewilders me he doesn't see me.
For so many years
I was good enough to eat: the world looked at me
And its mouth watered. How often they have
        undressed me,
The eyes of strangers!
And, holding their flesh within my flesh, their vile

Imaginings within my imagining,
I too have taken
The chance of life. Now the boy pats my dog
And we start home. Now I am good.
The last mistaken,
Ecstatic, accidental bliss, the blind

Happiness that, bursting, leaves upon the palm
Some soap and water—
It was so long ago, back in some Gay
Twenties, Nineties, I don't know . . . Today I miss
My lovely daughter
Away at school, my sons away at school,

My husband away at work—I wish for them.
The dog, the maid,
And I go through the sure unvarying days
At home in them. As I look at my life,

I am afraid
Only that it will change, as I am changing:

I am afraid, this morning, of my face.
It looks at me
From the rear-view mirror, with the eyes I hate,
The smile I hate. It's plain, lined look
Of gray discovery
Repeats to me: "You're old." That's all, I'm old.

And yet I'm afraid, as I was at the funeral
I went to yesterday.
My friend's cold made-up face, granite among its
    flowers,
Her undressed, operated-on, dressed body
Were my face and body.
As I think of her I hear her telling me

How young I seem, I *am* exceptional,
I think of all I have.
But really no one is exceptional,
No one has anything, I'm anybody,
I stand beside my grave
Confused with my life, that is commonplace and
    solitary.

So in that life which is our Way, there is no excellence. But one wonders, to use Jarrell's pun on the great word *All*, if that is really all. When the prophets of High Culture (I called it Hi-Cult in one of my own essays) all died out, leaving only Dwight Macdonald to rave against the Medium and Kitsch and Camp and all those once-fashionable diseases of the age; when Eliot fell in love and died, and Pound discovered silence—in short, when the Twenties and Thirties ended, it was already the Sixties, and it had become hard to say where the Medium ended and the iso-late poet began. How could a specialized study of the intel-lectual, say, *Herzog*, be a best-seller? What mass audience was it that picked that up? Even the woman in the super-market quotes William James. The question with us, with Jarrell, was the probability of accepting the supermarket and its brightly packaged values. Or must one be an Allen Ginsberg and situate Walt Whitman in the supermarket, only to say: "See, I told you so! America has to start over from scratch."

In *Poetry and the Age*, one of the best handbooks of anti-criticism criticism we have, there is an essay on the ob-scurity of the poet. My edition of the book is dated 1955, a fatal year for pronunciamentos about the Audience, the year when some giant beast slouching toward the City Lights Bookshop gave birth to "Howl." "Tomorrow morn-ing," Jarrell was saying, "some poet may, like Byron, wake up to find himself famous—for having written a novel, for having killed his wife; it will not be for having written a poem." Jarrell was wrong; the whole generation was wrong about the Audience and the Poet; "Howl" gave us the lie. For myself, I was delighted and immediately sent in my resignation to my generation. They accepted it gingerly but with inquisitorial silence. In the same essay Jarrell had said, "The general public . . . has set up a criterion of its own, one by which every form of contemporary art is con-demned." This statement too, which had for so long been so widely accepted, was already obsolete. A decade after "Howl"—and I see that poem as a symptom rather than as a cause—the general public itself became the contem-porary art audience. There are very few places in our geog-raphy any more which resemble a Nebraska of the spirit;

and in any case, philistinism today is no longer spontaneous but organized, political. Condemnation of the artist today is no longer mere provincialism; it is, to use a not very old-fashioned term, a form of fascism. And the general public, whatever that is, is choosing up sides. The Medium still dominates the sensory experience of the masses of people, but the Medium itself has become an initiate of Hi-Cult. The Medium has also had courses in modern poetry and electronic music.

The Berkeley or California Rebellion, like the Whiskey Rebellion, was a protest against a central culture. The California Rebellion struck out at every form of institutionalism it could clap eyes on. This too was a generational revolt and continues to be world-wide; it is, as most writers about it have noticed, more a sociological upheaval than a new motion in the arts. There is no innovation in Beat arts; the poetry stems from traditional rebel poets, Rimbaud, Pound, Whitman, Artaud. And the counterrevolt against Revolt stems from what was left over from the old-guard elite and also from members of Jarrell's generation. Jarrell would not, I believe, commit himself to the new barbarians, as some writers call them. He could not; he was too urbane, too civilized, too much a lover of the perfect. I cannot imagine him favoring for any reason the later phase of revolt art and all those electric guitarists who carry their echo chambers with them wherever they go, portable Aeolian winds, and whose motto seems to be Death By Drugs. Perhaps finally Jarrell recognized how much of an institution *our* generation had become, how much an institution he had become. I was in more of a position to face the music, the music of the electric guitar, because of my resignation. It was no surprise to me when I published a collection of essays called *In Defense of Ignorance* to receive a letter from a prominent member of our generation that complimented me highly on the book and said how much it was needed, a letter which ended, "but I would appreciate it if you didn't tell anybody." It was of course not Jarrell who penned this.

Jarrell's beautiful fable called *The Bat Poet* is, like all true fables, open to various readings. A child can read it as well as a philosopher as well as a poet, each with the same comprehension. A little light-brown bat leaves the pack to go out into the world of daylight to "hang there and think." The real bats don't understand the poet bat, who uses such things as colors in his poems, for the bat poet is a poet. Busy work-a-night bats don't care for color and have no truck with poems. After trying out his poems on such creatures as the mockingbird, who criticizes the bat poet's prosody and complains how hard it is to be a mockingbird; after failing to write a poem about the cardinal, who is perhaps too beautiful even for a poem; after bargaining with the chipmunk, who is the bat poet's most sympathetic critic (although naturally a poem about the owl gives the chipmunk the primordial Angst), the bat poet writes his best poem about, of all things, a mother bat zigzagging through the night with her baby clinging to her body. The chipmunk decides that everything the bat does is upside down. At last the bat poet decides to go and read his bat poem to the bats themselves, but when he gets to the barn where the bats collect, he has curiously forgotten his most important poem and just hangs upside down and goes to sleep like all the other bats.

Whether to be a bat or a poet: that is the question. Maybe the poets of Jarrell's and my generation were all hybrid bat-poets, going back to the institutional barn and then lighting off in broad sunlight to write poems about the righteous and dyspeptic mockingbird, the rich-bitch cardinal, the kindly and existential chipmunk, the Owl who gets us all indiscriminately in his claws. When I got my first copy of *The Bat Poet* I couldn't read it. The title and the drawing bothered me. It was the only thing of Jarrell's I didn't leap to read, and I gave my copy to a student. When I went to find a copy I found that my library at the university had never heard of it, that no bookstore in my part of the world had ever heard of it, that nobody I knew within hailing distance had ever heard of it, except that there was a mint copy in the state capitol building, which I obtained.

The basic assumption, the basic critical theorem of our generation was that poetry didn't really *go* in this age, that the age demanded everything of the artist except his art, and that the poet was still declassed. Insofar as there was any truth in the assumption it was a minor truth. When Jarrell defended Robert Frost in calling attention to "the other Frost" he was reminding his intellectual contemporaries that even a popular poet could make the grade. But Jarrell was really saying about Frost that he was a poet whose popularity was perhaps accidental. Conversely, Dylan Thomas, whom Jarrell thought correctly one of the most obscure poets of the age, was popular by default. It might be truer to say that Frost and Thomas were not only creative but also performing artists, not only performing artists but artists in action. Frost and Thomas lived their poetry, on stage and off; they were one with it, while our generation tended to hide or to collect in small conspiratorial groups. We barely learned to *read* poetry, because, as we said a little wearily, we *wrote* it. And because we wrote poetry that we were not necessarily committed to read, because we held to the cold North American delivery, we could seldom muster more than a token audience. Even Robert Frost, finally one of our great readers, insisted on the verb *say* for his recitations. Jarrell's bat poet picks up the idiom: he says he is going to *say* a poem to the mockingbird, and so forth. The opposite of *to say* is *to sing*, and even tone-deaf Yeats chanted his works. Pound revived a chant for the *Cantos*: it was one of the qualities that attracted him to the Beats. But the classroom voice and the High Church voice were dominant in the generation of Jarrell. And yet, what else were we to do in America, we argued, in a language which is inflected only in moments of violence? We shift between the nasal monotone and the double spondee. Jarrell is the one poet of my generation who made an art of American speech as it is, who advanced beyond Frost in using not only a contemporary idiom (although in Frost it is necessarily fictitious) but the actual rhythms of our speech. Here Jarrell is unique and technically radical. No other poet of our time has embalmed the common dialogue of Americans with such mastery. And because he caught our bourgeois speech he caught our meaning. Here is part of the marvelous essay-poem about, of all uncapturable things, Woman.

WOMAN

"All things become thee, being thine," I think
    sometimes
As I think of you. I think: "How many faults
In thee have seemed a virtue!" While your taste is on
    my tongue
The years return, blessings innumerable

As the breaths that you have quickened, gild my
    flesh.
Lie there in majesty!

              When, like Disraeli, I murmur
That you are more like a mistress than a wife,
More like an angel than a mistress; when, like Satan,
I hiss in your ear some vile suggestion,
Some delectable abomination,
You smile at me indulgently: "Men, men!"

You smile at mankind, recognizing in it
The absurd occasion of your fall.
For men—as your soap operas, as your *Home
    Journals*,
As your heart's whisper—men are only children.
And you believe them. Truly, you are children.

Should I love you so dearly if you weren't?
If I weren't?

              O morning star,
Each morning my dull heart goes out to you
And rises with the sun, but with the sun
Sets not, but all the long night nests within your
    eyes.
Men's share of grace, of all that can make bearable,
Lovable almost, the apparition, Man,
Has fallen to you. Erect, extraordinary
As a polar bear on roller skates, he passes
On into the Eternal . . .

            From your pedestal, you watch
Admiringly, when you remember to.

Let us form, as Freud has said, "a group of two."
You are the best thing that this world can offer—
He said so. Or I remember that he said so;
If I am mistaken it's a Freudian error,

An error nothing but a man would make.
Women can't bear women. Cunningly engraved
On many an old wife's dead heart is "Women,
Beware women!" And yet it was a man
Sick of too much sweetness—of a life
Rich with a mother, wife, three daughters, a wife's
    sister,
An abyss of analysands—who wrote: "I cannot
Escape the notion (though I hesitate
To give it expression) that for women
The level of what is ethically normal
Is different from what it is in men.
Their superego"—he goes on without hesitation—
"Is never so inexorable, so impersonal,
So independent of its emotional
Origins as we require it in a man."

(It is a long deep poem of a couple of hundred lines such as)

You call to me, "Come"; and when I come say, "Go,"
Smiling your soft contrary smile . . .

two lines packed with as much meaning as "The Death of the Ball-Turret Gunner."

An age's poetry does not purify the dialect, or any of that nonsense which aesthetic moralists believe, but an age's poetry fixes the age for those who care to gaze upon it in another age. Most of the poets of Jarrell's generation, when they were not simply describing, setting up the landscape of the city dump or suburbia or attacking the gleaming machinery of our brilliant kitchens, most of our poets dealt in minor points of ideology, lives of the saints or of boxers, or the symbolism of automobiles. Our technique was irony and nothing but irony, more kinds of irony than the Arabs have words for *camel*. But Jarrell, for all his indirection, spoke directly to the theme and in the direct idiom of our semiliterate educated classes. He listened like a novelist—I have already alluded to his ear—he heard the worst of us as well as the best. Things like iambic pentameter hypnotized him not. He used it as one sits in a Victorian chair in a friend's house, but how well he knew a Victorian chair when he saw one.

No one has ever caught a French writer or a German writer or an English or Irish or Scotch writer asking what a French, German, English, Irish, or Scotch writer is. But American writers ask practically nothing but What is an American writer? Meaning. What is an American?

Jarrell is almost as pro-American as Whitman himself. He applauds Marianne Moore's sayings about America. He praises her Americanness and makes more famous the famed line about our language: "grassless / linksless, languageless country in which letters are written / not in Spanish, not in Greek, not in Latin, not in shorthand, / but in plain American which cats and dogs can read!"

For *Paterson Book I* Jarrell reserved greater praise, predicting, because it was the most American poem ever, that it might become the "best very long poem that any American has written." *Paterson* didn't pan out that way, for Jarrell or for anyone else, but Williams did. Williams revealed America, New York on its horizon, "a pillar of smoke by day," says Jarrell, "a pillar of fire by night." Williams and Jarrell play with the remark of Henry James that America has no ruins; America is full of ruins, says Jarrell, the ruins of hopes.

M. B. Tolson, the great and practically unsung Negro

poet—he too is dead—says somewhere in *Harlem Gallery*
that the dilemma of the Negro between the white and the
black bourgeoisie is: To be or not to be—a Negro. The
Negro has a choice, is what Tolson argues, and he (and I)
would rather the Negro become a Negro. But this dilemma
does not exist for the paleface American: there is no choice
of to be or not to be an American. Once an American, once
an American poet, one can only ask: I am an American (or
an American writer); is there anything I can do about it?
American poets, even as late as Jarrell's generation, tried to
do something about it by remaining only as American as
their passports demanded. A few of us, following Williams,
wore the stars and stripes in secret, like The Man Without
a Country. Jarrell and I are two of these. The generation of
our fathers wore the flag with the cross of St. George or the
flag of the stars and bars, and some of them sported the
ribbon of the Legion of Honor and one or two the Red,
White, and Black. None of my generation sported the Iron
Cross, which one sees nowadays in dime stores in America
for little boys to play Nazi. But almost all of the generation
of Jarrell at one time or another played Red or Pink.

The value and the quality of poetry, unfortunately or
fortunately, have nothing to do with moral or political contents. *The Divine Comedy* is banned in Pakistan or used to
be, for religious reasons; modern art and poetry are or used
to be banned in Red Russia, also for religious reasons. Sad
to say, many poets are political or moral idiots, even among
the great. In our own time we have to fight the tendencies
which threaten what is dear to our own lives and ideologies. But in Jarrell's generation we were almost to a man
humane humanists, and, unlike our predecessors, were
democratic in politics, agnostic in religion, and baroque in

literature. Among us only Robert Lowell and myself could be described as extremists, and our extremism had different derivations and opposite goals.

Jarrell suffered deeply through the Stalinist-Francoist-Mussolini-Hitler years, hoping against hope for a betterment in the human condition. His first book was called *Blood for a Stranger* and was printed in 1942, a war book. He retained only a few of these poems when thirteen years later he published his selected poems, but the themes of war and fascism—war as fascism—were always in his mind. Jarrell has written more good poems about the wars and about Jews and Germany, the good Germany perhaps, than anyone else. He has written also the most famous and the best war poem of anyone in the twentieth century, in five lines.

The volume called *Little Friend, Little Friend*, though it has some of his best-made single poems, is a thematic book, a war book in which the poet is personally absent. The title page carries the penetrating explanation of the poem, the pathos of modern war in the code language of flyers: ". . . Then I heard the bomber call me in: 'Little Friend, Little Friend, I got two engines on fire. Can you see me, Little Friend?' I said 'I'm crossing right over you. Let's go home.' "

The anguish of the soldier is shown less in his anonymity, his exile from the human race, than in his emotional, sentimental desperation. The chief symbols—though Jarrell did not write to manipulate symbols qua symbols—are the mother and the cat. It is no Baudelairean cat (woman the destroyer), no T. S. Eliot cat (a kindly figure from the bestiary); Jarrell's cat is the object of love, if not a love-object, a cat who listens. The mother is pure mother who "thinks heavily: My son is grown." That's all; he's grown, therefore he is a soldier. The pilot falling from his plane sees the smoking carrier and its guns as children's toys. For it is true that in the elemental iconography of war everything is stripped down to a child's arithmetic: mother, soldier, cat, gun. There is a salient difference between our war poetry such as Jarrell's and that first great war poetry written in our fathers' war by Wilfred Owen and Sassoon and Rosenberg and Blunden and so on. The British war poets who showed everyone how to write anti-war poetry were themselves all outstanding warriors and heroes. They cried out against war but were as conversant with blood as Lawrence of Arabia. None of my generation were war heroes, that I remember, nor even outstanding soldiers. It says in a note in one of Jarrell's books that he "washed out" as a combat pilot and became a celestial navigator, a much more suitable classification for a poet. In a sense we waited out the war in uniform. Jarrell's ball-turret gunner is also washed out—of the turret with a hose. Unlike the war poets of the First World War, who never recovered from the experience, our generation did. We inherited a historical perspective which was denied our fathers. We foresaw and witnessed the whole world turning into the State. The war was of secondary importance to us even while we were part of it. When we came home there was grass growing on all the highways of the forty-eight states, but not for long. Our army went from demobilization to college or to television school; our poets became the university poets. But the tragedy of our generation—and I believe it is the tragedy— was that our army never melted away. It remained, it grew bigger, it was more and more all over the world. It became the way of life, the state; if not the garrison state itself, then something resembling it mightily. The war never came to a stop; only the protocols of armistice were suspended. Our poetry from the Forties on records the helplessness we felt in the face of the impersonal organism of the age—the Impersonal itself which is always death to poetry.

There is a literary commonplace that American literature is essentially a child literature. That *Moby Dick* is a boy's book—I was given a copy when I was seven—that every American hero is Huckleberry Finn in disguise, that poets are really little girls in mufti, that the artist has to prove his masculinity, and so on. A culture without mythos is forced into ideology. Whitman is an ideologue; his negation of mythology is 100 per cent American. Our poets when they deal in the myths do as Jarrell did, following Rilke and other modern artists, analyze and psychologize Orestes or Orpheus. We understand without belief. This is the opposite of using comparative mythology in order to revive and enforce belief, as Eliot did. Our poetry studies behavior and leads us back to the child. With Jarrell too the child becomes the critic and the center of value. Our mythology is the First Impression, the earliest consciousness; all the big people are giants out of Grimm, and most of them are bad. When a little girl is moving to a new house she thinks:

> The broody hen
> Squawks upside down—her eggs are boiled;
> The cat is dragged from the limb.

She thinks:

> We are going to live in a new pumpkin
> Under a gold star.

Theodore Roethke was a modern kind of nature poet, a biology poet with the eyes of a microscope. Jarrell was the poet of the *Kinder* and the earliest games of the mind and heart. All those wounded soldiers and shot-down men turn back into children, for a wounded man is again a child. In the poem called "The State" the child says:

> When they killed my mother it made me nervous;
> I thought to myself, It was *right:*
> Of course she was crazy, and how she ate!
> And she died, after all, in her way, for the State.
> But I minded: how queer it was to stare
> At one of them not sitting there.

In his earliest collected work, one of those five-sided anthologies which New Directions invented to launch young poets, Jarrell worried the bone of Romanticism, trying to find a rationale for his departure from what he called Modernism. The crux of the problem of our generation was the Modernism which Eliot and Pound and Joyce represented and which Jarrell said did not apply to him or to us. He pretended that Modernism was dead but knew how well it would flourish in the academies. He catalogues the faults of Modernist poetry as well as has been done: the emphasis on connotation, texture, extreme intensity, forced emotion, violence, obscurity, emphasis on sensation, perceptual nuances, emphasis on the part rather than on the whole, and much more. He even enumerates the Modernist poet's attitudes: anti-scientific (Jarrell was one of the few poets of our age who was not anti-scientific and who understood that Science was not necessarily the intruder in the house); anti-commonsense, and anti-public. He ends this essay, which is very early and very fine, with a touch of the style to come.

He has his hypothetical reader ask him a question: ". . . the reader may have thought curiously, 'Does he really suppose he writes the sort of poetry that replaces modernism?' " And he replies with an ambiguous, a diplomatic yes.

It was, say, Eliot, who is yet the most convenient target of attack for new poets, because Eliot erected targets wherever his mind led him; it was Eliot who invented Modernism and had it patented. And it was Auden who first shot at the target and missed. Jarrell took care of Modernism in practice better than in theory, as later he took care of Auden. It became necessary for everyone my age to attack Auden, as sculptors must attack Mount Rushmore. Nevertheless, Auden and Mount Rushmore still stand and probably always will. Jarrell, I think, failed to help establish our generation as a separate force and simply, not so simply, went his way to write some of the most quietly agonizing poetry of our time. His overestimation of Lowell represented a kind of fear that, generationally speaking, we did not exist. He half-feared being ingested by the Lowells. But I am a child, said Jarrell, I am the bat-poet; let me go and I will send you many much juicier poets. I will send you my mother and father and a fat girl in the library and even my cat. When John Ciardi put together an anthology of our generation with self-introductions, Lowell was too busy to write his (as I was too) and Jarrell reprinted his encomium about Lowell for Lowell's introduction. The roster of the generation in that version of it reads: Richard Wilbur, Peter Viereck, Muriel Rukeyser, Theodore Roethke, Karl Shapiro, Winfield Townley Scott, John Frederick Nims, E. L. Mayo, Robert Lowell, Randall Jarrell, John Holmes, Richard Eberhart, John Ciardi, Elizabeth Bishop, and Delmore Schwartz. It is an impressive list, in my view, a loose confederation of states which had no president. I must say something about Schwartz. Dwight Macdonald wrote a memorial about him in the *New York Review of Books*. In it he said all the things an editor of the *Partisan Review* should say, all the hi-cult clichés which the *Partisan Review* takes as gospel. It is strange, to say the least, that this great publication, one of the great intellectual quarterlies of our century, should always have been so obtuse about poetry, as if (which I believe was the trouble) they didn't understand it. They took a Stalinist view of poetry, which is that poetry should go back where it came from, and then modified that view with Trotsky's rather nineteenth-century bohemian view of poetry, which reminds one touchingly of perhaps Verlaine. They could swallow the *Four Quartets* hook, line, and sinker and turn on the Beat poets like the OGPU. Macdonald, politically brilliant, a jaded libertarian with the old Marxist leadership principle in his heart, Macdonald says that Schwartz was killed by America, a statement that wouldn't stand up five minutes in a provincial psychiatrist's office, any more than that same college cheer that went: America killed Dylan. Macdonald says: "Poetry is a dangerous occupation in this country, as the biographers of too many of our best twentieth-century poets show, from Ezra Pound on, including the recent deaths of Randall Jarrell and Theodore Roethke. This is not a new thing . . ." And then Macdonald launches into Baudelaire on Poe. ("For Poe the United States was nothing more than a vast prison . . ." and so forth.) This dismal, sociologically oriented view of poetry (now being taught in junior high) was shared neither by Schwartz nor Jarrell nor myself nor by any of the poets I know of. Whether poetry is a more dangerous occupation in America than tree surgery or insurance salesmanship is hard to say. Macdonald points to Delmore Schwartz's tremendous urge toward self-destruction but contents himself with the easy out that America got Delmore. It is one of those facile aesthetic lies which lead to the formation of poetry committees.

There is this about Schwartz as about Jarrell: both refused that lie, and both were tormented by the strategy of escaping from the elite committees which survive by virtue of the lie. Macdonald, discussing his friendship for Schwartz, cites the Jewish-Gentile difference between them, as if this were an area of misunderstanding for an editor of the *Partisan Review* or even *McCall's*. Jarrell, unlike Schwartz, did not become a part of *PR*, although he edited poetry and did the poetry reviews for the *Nation*, a magazine which is intellectually unidentifiable. The *Nation* in our time was more congenial to poetry than the great quarterlies, which always subordinated the poem to the ideology of the magazine. Jarrell wrote some of his best critiques for the *Nation*, in that kindly intellectual morass where one was allowed to Become rather than Be. In the quarterlies one must have already arrived.

So, after all, Jarrell was hung up, as we all were, by the sense of common sense, Thomas Paine's or Henry Ford's or the Scientist's. And after all, Macdonald has a truth in his craw, that poetry (he meant, I think, *being* a poet) is dangerous. *In danger* would be a better phrase, as children are in danger. It comes to the sadness about us that poets are not loved or are loved in the wrong way for the right reasons or—whatever that saying is. It comes to the fact that America the Mother wants to love her children but is much more successful at killing them off, or just making them successful. Jarrell had a brilliant, sure, and subtle mind, and would have been the greatest poet since whoever the last great poet was, had he not lacked the sense of power. He lacked it, to his disaster. It is what you might call a psychological factor, *the* psychological factor. He came of a generation that could not hate Mother America but which was afraid of her and for her. There is no one of our generation who betrayed her or who tried to topple the Victorian Statue of Liberty into the drink. Jarrell was the least anti-American of all of us, and the most. He recoiled from the boredom and the horror and the glory of the day-to-day life. But what he did in his poetry, which had never really been done before, was to face the modern scene and to—what more is there to say—to face it. He faced the music of the American Way of Life. But the subject wasn't anything that Dwight Macdonald would know about, because the elites never stoop to the observation of the actual. It wasn't anything that the power-mad poets would ever see, because they are so busy climbing Mount Everest that they don't know what millennium they are in. Jarrell tried to do the impossible: to observe and make poetry of a chaos, without being either inside or outside of it. He did it better than anyone else, better than it can be done. He did it passionately and with superb control. He did it with lies and subterfuge and great prose. He did it by hiding and spying, reporting and keening. I would imagine that he wept himself to death, out of frustration for the Kafka-like manias of our time, including those of the intelligentsia; out of the ambition which he denied himself because he was more intelligent than any of us; out of the love of the natural which denies the political. He died, you might say, because his heart was in the right place and his heart was even stronger than his intellect. Jarrell was split between his heart and mind. He was modern, which means hating being modern. He was born after Humpty-Dumpty fell off the wall, and he knew that T. S. Eliot Scotch Tape couldn't put anything back together again.

The Career of the Poem

A DELICIOUS obliquity one sometimes hears at literary conferences and such places is the question: Are you a writer or a poet? The question, of course, is a high compliment, if one happens to be a poet. It bestows on the poet the keys to the kingdom; it takes him out of the realm of mere literature and installs him in the empyrean; it frees him from any of the normal ties to the world with which other men are bound; it makes him a kind of god.

There is a part of the world which wants to sanctify the poet and make him an object of worship. For is not the poet incorruptible? Is not his integrity beyond reproach? Is he not a man of wizardly insight and towering intelligence? Is not his learning instinctively deep even when it is not broad? Is he not the sole symbol of freedom in a regimented universe? Is he not impervious to the lust for money, power and position? Is he not also that Tiresias who sees into the future, who descends to hell and flies up to heaven?

These are hard questions to say no to, but let us say no, for the sake of truth, and then see what there is, if anything, that makes the poet a superior being. For certainly the poet is as corruptible as anybody else, and more times than not displays the manners of a corporal and the morals of a bellboy. His integrity, although he wears it on his sleeve, is very much to be doubted. His insights into anything but poetry—and very often poetry itself—are apt to be as wrong as anyone else's: we have only to think of the political writings of poets. His intelligence varies as much as that of other men and bears only an indirect relationship to his talent. His learning is always suspect. His love of physical freedom is another superstition: many poets would be perfectly happy in jail if they didn't have to work. As for freedom from money-lust, power or position, one has only to read the lives of the poets to be disabused of this fantasy. A history of literary politics would read like a combined version of the more lurid pages of Gibbon and the Marquis de Sade.

Poetic fame, poetic honor, or what you will, is part of the iconography of history. The fame of Byron on the Continent had nothing to do with his poetic stature and everything to do with his role of hero. Being a poet helped his heroics; the heroics did not always improve his poetry. History seizes on the heroic element in the artist and hugs it for dear life. And sometimes the artist himself adopts this quixotic pose, and he then becomes a party to a literary conspiracy and begins to confuse poetry with history, logic, science, system-making and God.

Nevertheless, the world wants the poet for what he is not, and the foolish poet goes to the world. This liaison results in the two false uses of art which we have been discussing: the one that makes the poet a man of the people, or a man who leads people, or a man who makes the whole world kin, or a man who states universal truths. This is the idea of the historic poet. And the other that makes the poet a purveyor of myths, an oracle, a seer, an almost-philosopher, an aristocrat of the spirit, a being who perceives transcendental relationships. This is the idea of the mythic poet.

Literature of this kind always produces doctrines and fiats and manifestoes. After a time it becomes anathema for the historic poet to write anything which is not a folksong, a patriotic ballad, a rhetorical screed, an epic, or a Methodist hymn. In the other camp it becomes anathema to write anything which does not add to a symbolic system of ideas, or which does not code or decode the mythos of culture. Perceiving this strife, the readers of poems, if there are any left, decide that it is a fight between pessimists and optimists, intellectuals and emotionalists, romantics and classicists, or some other misleading dualism.

Now and then we get a really consistent poet who will align his politics, his religion, his science, and his philosophy so that they all work together. We then have what is called a Great poet. Even if in the nature of his system this poet must decide to eliminate people themselves, he is still called Great. The term refers to a kind of military genius. On the other side, we have the poet who perpetuates myths of the ideal world or the dream world, and this one is called a Major poet. Yeats is Major but not Great. Pound is Great but not Major. A minor poet, incidentally, is one who has no master plan of strategy either for the world or for the cosmos. Rilke, who is probably the best modern poet, is neither major nor minor nor great and is something of an embarrassment to critics. He is both emotional and "intellectual," both obscure and simple, both metaphysical and symbolist, both formalist and anti-traditional: in short, he is himself, like any poet who abdicates from theory and literary politics.

Both historic and mythic poets regard themselves as official poets. They acquire aides-de-camp among the estheticians and the press, and conduct their affairs along the lines of any other business or political enterprise.

The desire of these official poets to provide answers to all questions is indicative of the intellectual temper of the times we live in, and is not confined to artists, by any means. A man who makes a discovery about the mind develops a psychology to explain all human behavior. A historian will explain all history by means of a theory of cycles. An economist will retell the story of man from the point of view of physical want. One man will explain everything about the human race from the dogma of the Fall of Man. A later prophet will see all history as a noble struggle to improve—the dogma of the Rise of Man.

Literature is contaminated by systems. The libertarian poet, the religious poet who plies the dogma of his church, even the "scientific" metaphysical poet: these look for an absolute doctrine of life on which to build. In a healthy world this slavery to ideas does not exist and the members of my quadrivium do not contaminate each other. Philosophy pursues the absolute and calls itself the love of knowledge. Science pursues demonstrable knowledge and calls itself the love of natural law. Religion pursues goodness and calls itself the love of God. And poetry pursues human personal knowledge and calls itself the love of beauty. With poetry, as with other forms of knowledge, there is no crossing the line, no violation of the nature of the thing, without contamination. All art that does so is marked by insincerity, whether intellectual insincerity (the poet who takes a system of ideas to his bosom and writes verses to hang upon his Tree of Life) or emotional insincerity (the artist who tries to experience history).

What claim, then, has the poet to any knowledge except the personal knowledge of truth or beauty? Absolutely none. What claim has he to be a specialist in culture, morals, politics, religion, philosophy, science or even esthetics? Absolutely none. But if that is the case, what claim has the poet to any fame at all? Is there then no basis for poetic reputation, no reason for exalting poetry among the works of man?

Certainly there is. The seeker after truth and the seeker of truth through beauty are necessary to the world. But they are not rulers of the world or leaders of the world. The idea of the sacred poet is one of the most unsavory and dangerous ideas in our civilization. How and when the sacred poet was born I do not know, but in our own age this superstition has grown steadily for a century and a half. In Mozart's time the composer and performer were seated at table with the valet and the cook. This strikes us as cruel and degrading, but our exaltation of the artist is just as shameful. Perhaps it was when kings began to topple that the artist began the march up the table. This is one of the points of contamination I have been talking about.

Those poets who staked out claims on the frontiers of time are the ones I call mythic and historic poets. Their descendants set themselves up as arbiters of history, or of morals, or of standards of taste—practices which have nothing fundamentally to do with poetry. Mythic poetry and historic poetry are both corrupt forms of art, and both are corrupted by power.

A civilization in equilibrium does not make the poet a sacred cow, which when it barges into a citizen's house is hung with garlands of flowers. A civilization in equilibrium needs the poet as much as it needs the priest, the scientist, the scholar and the abstract thinker; he is never made a superior symbol of authority in any way. A civilization without poets is a moribund civilization: it has no love of its way of life. But a civilization in which the artist is worshipped is on the point of suicide. The artist should be treated as the equal of all other people who contribute to the sum total of knowledge, but no more, except within his own guild, when he deserves their honor.

There is no such thing as a subject for poetry; that subject is a matter between the poet and his poem. But if this is so, why rule out myths and the diatribes of historic poets? One reason is that such poetry is false knowledge: the poet cannot possibly have the experience of the whole of the race or nation, any more than anyone else. But another reason is that such poetry is supposed to be sacred, hieratic poetry, and this I consider evil. We should strip the poet of his false honors, false titles and false powers. Of course, if someone were to draw up an *index expurgatorius* of all the mythic and historic poems in history, the world's anthology would weigh a good deal less. But matters are not as bad as all that. Most poets write true poems in spite of their divine mission to purify something or other. Most of Whitman's poems stand among the masterpieces of literature: his pseudo-philosophical-political ramblings we can forgive. Yeats was one of the finest poetic talents of our time, but being caught up in an all-explaining magic, he turned to Madam Blavatsky's metaphysical cookbooks. Even so, he wrote magnificently to his dying day. But why should we allow this license of intelligence to Yeats any more than we would allow it to Millikan or Whitehead? There is no answer.

Poetry springs from the love of personal truth and it results in a thing of beauty. Beauty is a condition of art, an absolute condition, and an instrument of the kind of truth which we are here concerned with. But the worship of beauty is a form of idolatry which is little better than worship of the golden calf. People went to churches during the Renaissance, not to worship the pictures, as we do now, but to worship God; yet we do not question their love of art. Mozart was made a papal knight but he was not canonized. Yet in our time a French scholar has proved the existence of a religion built around the adolescent poet Rimbaud.

There is always the tendency to find some more noble use of art than the mere search for the personal truth of life—as if that were not sufficient. Art must lead others, art must improve others, art must even cure others. Yes, art leads us to perceive truth in beauty. But art is not medicine; art is not pedagogy; art is not jurisprudence; art is not the decalogue. The true poet does not fall into these attitudes of doctor and teacher and priest. He is detached from such quarrels. Other poets in their pride accept the world's challenge and purvey all sorts of real and quack remedies for readers who ask for them.

The apologist for knowledge, and not only poetic knowledge, always takes it on himself to explain how he is really
king of the cats. Poetic apologists are plentiful and I will
cite only two typical credos. The first was written over a
century ago.

> Poetry is indeed something divine. It is at once the centre
> and circumference of knowledge; it is that which compre-
> hends all science, and that to which all science must be
> referred. It is at the same time the root and blossom of all
> other systems of thought . . . what were our aspirations . . .
> if poetry did not ascend to bring light and fire from those
> eternal regions where the owl-winged faculty of calculation
> dare not ever soar? . . .

These wild sayings need no comment except this: Shelley
redeems them, and all but refutes them, in the same essay.
And yet it is precisely the hysteria of apologists which we
must guard against. I quote next from an essay written in
our time by a man whose object is to justify to the world
the ways of modern poets. This is typically the contemporary position about the value of poetry.

> It seems likely that one reason there has been so little
> great literature is that at most times so little has been re-
> quired of it: how often has a Virgil felt obligated to create
> the myth of imperial culture? . . . how often has a Dante
> turned up to put into actual order all that had been running
> into the disorder of the rigid intellect and the arbitary will?
> Ordinarily, past times have required little of literature in the
> way either of creating or ordering a culture. The artist's task
> was principally to express the continuity of his culture and
> the turbulence that underlay it. . . . Those who seem to be
> the chief writers of our time have found their subjects in
> attempting to dramatize at once both the culture and the

turbulence it was meant to control, and in doing so they have had practically to create . . . the terms, the very symbolic substance, of the culture as they went along. . . .

It is not easy to understand this excerpt from Mr. Blackmur, chiefly because it is so loaded with pseudo-scientific jargon, but in essence it does not differ from Shelley. Or rather, it is Shelley with the interposition of modern science midway and Matthew Arnold three quarters of the way. And it is a retreat from Shelley in that it concedes the abdication of the poet-king: the king of knowledge is now in a university library brooding over the usurpation.

The true poet is a constant prey to the world and its leaders because of his inability to accept knowledge he has not tested for himself. This almost scientific intransigence makes him both untouchable and desirable. He is fair game for the world's rulers and is as subject to kidnaping as those physicists who end up in a closed city built for the dreams of science. Hence the poet sometimes becomes the tool of the objective thinkers of the world and betrays his nature and purpose by trying to make his truth available to others. That, in fact, is the antinomy in poetic knowledge; that the artist is restricted to his own world and cannot universalize what he knows. He can do no more than find the form of what he knows and relive himself through creativity. Thus poetry is neither historic nor prophetic but occupies a separate world of time and value. The implication that the poet is a spiritual brother of God, both being members of the same profession, is intolerable. The poet cannot even enjoy as much spiritual intimacy with God as the mystic or the saint, nor can his knowledge of God be as intelligible as that of the metaphysician. The poet's spiritual rapport with

God is relatively crude and is like that of the magician and the psychologist rather than that of the mystic. For the poet, the unitive experience is forever blocked by the nature of creative work, art being an embodiment of personality and not a surrender of personality to the larger Being.

But poetry is not solipsistic knowledge, nor is it knowledge of the infinite, nor even of the distant. Poetry is knowledge of the self only, but there is no self without a world, and no embodiment of self without art. To extend the poet's meaning beyond this point is to render him and his work meaningless. This is what usually happens when we touch art with the wand of doctrine.

History is a precious and noble fiction. Without it we would be living in a temporal chaos. Only saints can live without history. History indeed is the vital core of civilization: it gives us the symbology of our lives. History might even be called the world's poem, the poem by all hands, because history does for the world what the poet does for himself: it creates its image. But the poet himself, the true poet, must live outside history like the saint. This is self-evident: if he accepts history he will be silent to the truth in himself.

The fate of works of art is always a matter of chance. The history of art is a history of chance. The historian of art, to be convincing, must be as much artist as historian, for history, like all other knowledge, must be formal and exclusive. The hierarchy of values is also a fiction, and is always being upset by new turns of history and by the advent of new works of art. For this reason, no good historian attempts to write history while it is happening, any more than a poet tries to write a poem while he is making love.

The French symbolists attempted to evaluate poetry by evolving a sempiternal time-formula for the work of art. The poet was conceived as body, the poem as soul. It was indeed a perversion of the old Manichaeist theory in which the world was considered evil. The symbolist was a potential suicide who spent his holidays in the cemetery; he was the author of the clever and infamous doctrine that the poem begins to live when the poet is lain in the tomb. And it was this flattering unction that gave the blessing to all future "purists" in art.

Poetic reputation, like the career of a work of art, cannot be understood in terms of value. Poetic reputation has to do with the fact that value is attributed to a particular piece of work. There are so many examples of this in the history of art that it is difficult to find the exceptions. It pleases our historical sense to say that Hopkins was "in advance of" the Victorians and had to wait for the understanding of a later generation. But the *Rubaiyat* had the same career as *The Wreck of the Deutschland*; someone had to pin the label of greatness on it. In one sense, the history of poetry is no more than the history of opinion.

The non-historicity of art is one of its most significant characteristics. For the poet there is no progress, no evolution: for poetry there is no progress, no evolution. There is only the eternal problem of rebirth. Literary historians know this well. A man at the height of his powers may produce his worst work. In art there is a refinement of skill, as in any other trade, but no assurance of success. This fact is true because the poet enters a new and different world with each poem. The other worlds are lost to him and he can re-enter them only like any other reader. This constant re-entry into the world of new relationships makes of the poet neither messiah nor explorer but only a man fully alive in spirit and in body to existence itself.

Poetry intersects with the fiction of history, as it does with philosophy and science and religion. But all this is accidental and unpredictable. True poetry memorializes the scene, the time and place, and the world takes this as tribute. But the poet did not set out to memorialize anything. It is only as a by-product of art that art brings the past to life. There are "periods" of art, no doubt, but they tell us nothing about the individual work or the individual artist. Period does little more than point to the poet's vocabulary. Poetry helps create history: it helps rewrite it. This also is a by-product of the creative act. The history of literature is filled with men who attracted no attention in their lifetime and who did attract it later. It is filled with men who attracted attention in their lifetime and did not attract it after they died. And it is filled with men who attracted attention both during and after their lives, but never steadily, never eternally.

Even the great mythological characters come and go like the lost Pleiad. There is really only one way to perpetuate myth: that is by turning it into belief. But this form of contamination (which exists actively in our period) needs no further comment. The "universality" of a particular myth does no service to art; on the contrary it deadens art. The lively medieval myth of Tristan and Yseult was originally a tale of the triumph of love. In our period it became weakened to a tale of the triumph of death. Which is the right version? Both are "right." But there is a dangerous didacticism in the 19th-century version, with its awful wallowing in the sty and its dark message that love and death are one. The original tale is rich with authenticity and credibility: the latter-day version is obviously more concerned with a formula—and a deadly one—directed to history. It is interesting to note that the symbolists worshipped the art of Richard Wagner and saw him as a priest and the opera house as a church. It is equally interesting to note that Wagner himself was a political writer who was one of the advance founders of the Super-Germanic racial myth. The conjunction of myth and history occurs in actuality in Wagner and by implication in the theorists of the symbol.

There is no rationale to success in works of art: anyone who has read the life of one poet knows this. On the other hand, there are certain works which are taken as touchstones of the age in which they appear. Such poems or works of art color the very atmosphere of life for a time. I suppose there are many examples: *Hernani*, *The Raven*, the painting *The Night Watch*, even Whistler's *"Mother."* But these works are not necessarily the best works of the period nor the best works of the author. I am inclined to think that these symbolic works, so-called, are really the brain-children of History. In any case, they are carried about as standards for a time and are then entered into the chronicles of the age.

There is nevertheless a true fame for the work of art, one which the poet himself values, one which the world values as well. This fame has nothing to do with the esotericism of myth or the power of public appeal. It has to do with authenticity. In art we refer to truth in terms of authenticity: that is the only way we have to get at it. How this authenticity is established by the poet and how it is recognized by the reader is another question. But suffice it to say that if this quality did not exist we would be living in a chaos in which every work of art would be the equal of every other work of art. This truth is personal truth. It is not universal truth nor is it merely what is called a point of view. It is a truth which the writer does not doubt and which the reader is convinced of in spite of himself; and the means of persuasion is beauty. Probably it is this relationship which makes some writers think of beauty and truth as interchangeable. In any case, in a work of art we as readers can vouch for the beauty. The truth we take on faith. If we doubt its beauty we doubt its truth. One of the worst criticisms we can make about a work of art is to say that it is unconvincing.

The personal truth of works of beauty cannot be equated with mythic truth or universal truth. We do not pretend to believe or not to believe what the poet says in order to follow, appreciate, or love the poem. All we have to believe is that the poet is sincere. Let one shadow of a doubt fall across our minds and the poem disintegrates. But the term *belief* is somewhat misleading; for poetry is more an act of passion than act of thought. Poetry occurs because a "belief" has been kindled by passion and made incandescent. There cannot be a cold poem. And the belief is more often than not a matter of emotion; that is, a belief which pulls the emotions into it. The creator of beauty is engaged in a constant struggle with the reality of his own emotions. Emotions do not exist in a vacuum; they are produced by contact with the world. The poet never moves out of this world of struggle in which his emotions ("beliefs") lock with experience. His recollections of these struggles are the subjects of his poems.

But how does this affect someone else? What is my poem to you? It is an embodiment of myself or part of myself, which would otherwise be lost, as most men's lives are lost to others, except in memory. It is the rescue of my passion from disintegration. The poet wrests from the world the revelation of his personal reality. I need not point out that this is one of the most common themes of poets of all ages. When the sonneteer cries that his poem will make the lady's beauty live forever, he means that her beauty has become part of him; that part which creates his poem. Thus the poet triumphs over formlessness, the formlessness of his own life and of all life, the design of which is hidden from us. For many people, reality does not come into existence except through art. Through art we see with another's eyes, but we see no more than one truth. This truth may be the affirmation of our own reality. Indeed, that would be a lofty enough reason in itself for the high position of art.

The love of beauty, like the love of knowledge and the love of God, may be the metaphysical affirmation of man's divinity. At least, it is deeply satisfying to think so. Personal experience plus obedience to the laws of beauty—those strange laws which every artist discovers for himself—this is the equation for the creative act. And obedience to the laws of beauty implies a belief in the harmony of all things.

The poet's fame and honor are based on his love and knowledge of beauty: he does not love religion, science, or philosophy more, or as much. And it is love of beauty which other men sometimes interpret as love itself. The poet is a man of love. But he differs from others in that he is so fired with the love of beauty that he must create beauty itself. Beauty feeds him with the desire to create beauty. No good poet departs from the obsession

with beauty for a second. The moment he does he is lost—
off on the journey to historic life or mythhood. If the poet
must play priest, philosopher, or politician, he takes care
to watch that his poem is not crushed by the burden of
preaching, philosophy, or politics.

Looking back on the 20th century, readers will have a
difficult time explaining the prevalent attitude of hatred
among our artists. But once they separate the conventional
myths and attitudes from the poetry, they will find that
modern poets behaved in much the way that other poets
have. And they will discard the poetry of stereotyped emotions and official intellectual strategies. Culture poetry will
find its way to the encyclopedias. The other poetry will
remain, more or less, barring the accidents of time.

The poet leaves an actual record of his passion in the
presence of world reality. He creates the image of himself,
sometimes only a part of himself, sometimes his full self.
With Shakespeare we have the whole image; with Baudelaire we have a stylized and fragmentary image. But whole
or fragmentary, the image is not always pretty. Yet when it
is a good likeness, we recognize it and appreciate its handi-
work. And the creation of this image takes place, like any
other creation, through love. What the poet loves helps
create his poetry and himself.

Let us give up the old pedagogical idea that the effect of
poetry on the world is salutary. To believe that men are
bettered by poetry is as narrow as to believe that they are
worsened by it. Let us think of it another way. Let us think
of creation in art as the vocation, and only the vocation of a
certain kind of man. Let us then give it the honor of any
vocation for knowledge. But let us admit also that the sum
total of the creation of an artist can equal only himself.

Such knowledge would seem useless to most men and, in fact, the usual view of poetry is precisely that. What poetry does is to ennoble the man who writes it by developing in him an almost habitual love of beauty. This may be the basis for supposing that poets are better than other people. Perhaps the vocation for art and the occupation with beauty do purify the writer; but this purification can take strange and exotic forms.

The fame due to poetry should not be exaggerated. A poet creates out of the necessity for seeking truth through the medium of beauty. The thing of beauty sets out on a career in the world. Sometimes it becomes legendary: sometimes it fades quickly from the face of the earth. But where it remains it leaves an image of its maker. Seeing it, other men have the sense of one man's affirmation of life, whoever he was, wherever, whenever he lived. Then we recognize, if we can read these works, the intelligence, the talent, the acts of a man who placed love of truth above all things and who could not find truth except in beauty. Thus tragedy and death itself turn beautiful in art.

It may be that everything reaches toward its absolute, the condition in which form can live harmoniously with freedom. The absolute of the poet is not abstract knowledge, not phenomenal knowledge, not knowledge of God, but knowledge of life. Life is the absolute he reaches for. And insofar as he creates himself he has fulfilled his purpose.

The fame of art rises from the world's dream of freedom of spirit. The poet is not the buoyant and volatile singer of visions; on the contrary, he is more the Doubting Thomas who finds it hard to believe in the accepted abstractions, and who must prove them all over again for himself. One might say that the poet's freedom really consists of scepticism. The world admires the poet the more when the world begins to distrust its own laws of conduct. It is in times of disbelief that art is taken most seriously, because then the artist appears to others to be a veritable rock of personality. In such times also the poet is inclined to accept the position of superiority to his fellows.

There is reason enough to exalt poetry. The artist is the only person whose work immortalizes life itself—his life and the lives of those who happen into the picture. It is this work which gives us a true knowledge of the maker, the poet, and of his world. It is knowledge of doubtful value, perhaps, but it is nonetheless true knowledge. One can learn nothing from art, really, except a kind of curious wisdom—the wisdom of love.

I have tried to avoid using specific illustrations and even quotations in these remarks, but I want to point up what I have been saying by citing one poet whose career embodies many of the pitfalls and perplexities I have mentioned. The poet I have in mind has already become legendary in modern literature, and he is generally regarded as a martyr of modern society. I refer to Hart Crane. Crane in the generations since his suicide has become a leading poetic symbol for American poets. He has all the qualifications for the hero of modern culture. Crane came from the Middle West, he was poorly educated, he became "urbanized" and an exile from his own world; subsequently he was a drunkard and a masochist. But what is of greater significance, he combined the aspirations of the mythic and the historic poet in one flesh. Crane had neither the background nor the personal stability nor the humility to resist history and myth. As soon as he discovered mythic poetry he made the leap to the world of symbols and its attendant dreams of transcendental knowledge. But he was also a young American who wished to celebrate his nation, and he was pulled as strongly in the other direction, toward history. These were the two forces that tore him apart. What his actual talent was we shall never know, because it is obscured by theory-ridden symbolism, on the one hand, and by quixotic yearnings for the future, on the other. In Crane, myth meets history, and we witness the inevitable collapse of personality which is so characteristic of modern poetry.

What causes this dissolution and violent destruction of personality in modern art, this nihilism which the poet sometimes directs against himself and sometimes against the world? What turns the man of love into a thing of bitterness? Why does almost every title of a modern book of poems contain a negative? What is the significance of our official acceptance of the artist's drunkenness, perversion, crime, insanity and suicide?

I do not know the answers to these terrible questions, but I have tried to suggest one: slavery to doctrines of culture under the guise of history and myth; a slavery to which the young poet is offered no alternative.

The just honor of poetry comes from the admiration of mankind for the creation of one personality or one facet of personality. It is not unlike the honor we pay to the athlete or to the man who achieves wealth or success in his affairs. Our pride in him is the pride of created identity. But there is this difference: the poet who creates out of his life has done so because he was part of a particular place and time, part of a particular milieu and nation, and part of a particular age. The truer, the more authentic his work, the longer will last the soil from which he sprang and the clearer the character of his nation will appear to others. The treason comes with those artists who set out to become a touchstone of their time and place; the treason comes with those minions of culture who try to produce the poet who will represent them before the world. Culture says: We must have Art; let us set about having it. And the mythic poets and the historic poets flock to the banners. Meanwhile there is the true poet who has perhaps never published a line, who lives in a town from which no poet has ever come before, and whose greatest peril lies in his indoctrination with the false mythos of culture heroism.

This mythos inculcates in him the vices of exile as against participation in life; specialization as against wholeness of personality; anxiety and despair as against acceptonce of the scene; analysis as against creation. Powerful fanaticisms converge on the newborn poet: one is the fanaticism of symbolism which betrays the poet into thinking that he reaches the absolute and returns to the world to sing about it. A second is the fanaticism of world-creation which deludes the poet into thinking that he, the poet, is the maker of all things. These are the two major causes of false poetry which I have discussed. But there is a third fanaticism which tends to come into existence when the other two have been banished: this is the fanaticism of ego which has as its slogan, "All things are nothing to me." Indeed, it is this attitude of the absurdity of things which is today most likely to subvert the new poet and turn him toward some form of philosophical indifference and egotism.

Is it not because of the poet's commitment to total knowledge or his egotistical rejection of all knowledge that there is so little authentic poetry in our world? The artist cannot live by art alone, nor can he live by any of the absolutes of knowledge. He must live among *all* absolutes, however; he must recognize the laws of contradiction; and he must believe in the human imperative of sympathy and the poetic law of *Einfühlung*. Only then will true creation be permitted him. Our poets today are sent out into the world by their writing masters into what they believe to be an enemy civilization and a hostile universe. Little wonder that they behave ever after like soldiers on their first patrol. Little wonder that they all mouth the same stereotypes about our dying world and our dying way of life. Little wonder that the poetry of cultural anthropology and cultural history make up the bulk of the twentieth-century anthology.

It is hard to imagine how the next true poet will escape all the masters lying in wait to receive him, but that is uniquely and eternally the problem of the young true poet. Nor do I imagine for a moment that he will spring into being filled with love of country and sweetness of mind. We have not yet drunk all the hemlock of the age. And yet I believe the way can be prepared for the next poet by encouraging in him neutrality of mind and charity of feeling; by leading him to those works of art which are the beneficent products of personality, as well as those which are not. And not only to works of art but to works of science and philosophy and mysticism. This job of preparation, almost impossible in an atmosphere of cultural fanaticism, can nevertheless be accomplished if we draw volunteers from the belligerents themselves, and from the long-since dispersed audience. The first step must be to destroy the religion of specialization which relieves scholars and intellectuals of their obligation to evaluate contem-

porary works of art. Every teacher of literature, every professor of science, should take it on himself to pass judgment
on new works of poetry; every serious user of words should
do the same. We should respect also the man who is not
interested in poetry; he is a man for all that. This reading
of new works should be done with good subjective gusto,
not with a manual of criticism in hand. It should be done in
the first flush of feeling, when the mind is still warm with
the pleasure or displeasure of the work. The mortuary
gloom which fills most poetry lecture halls resembles nothing so much as a students' operating theatre: the clinical,
almost morbid curiosity of the listeners, the attitude of
strain, even the applause for the cautery of the bleeding
poem, all emphasize the life-and-death grimness of the affair. This is the opposite of a joyous occasion.

The ruling vice in literature today is an absolutism based
on one of many doctrines of cultural acceptability, all of
which are intent on the unconditional surrender of all others. We should not let the historic poet or critic tell us that
he is the defender of social values; we should not let the
mythic poet or critic tell us that he is the defender of the
Tradition and the true works of the spirit. Instead, we
should judge their works, bringing to them all the sympathy and intelligence and training at our command. But as
long as we fail to observe our final and supreme obligation
as readers, which is to pronounce upon the particular work
with our own personal opinions, we give our sanction to the
rule of Culture over art. The new poet is always the one
who outwits the guardians of the prevalent systems—and
mostly because he is not even aware of their existence.

Whatever the value of the poem *sub specie aeternitatis,*

it should be given as a fresh, complete, instantaneous thing; for these are the qualities which make for long life in works of art, and even for what we fondly call the immortality of poems. The career of the poem exists only in those moments when the poem is being given and being received.

American Poet?

For about a quarter of a century I have been putting together lectures and talks about poetry, criticism, modern literature, politics, religion, and culture. Most of these have ended up in journals or books. I have always written these pieces with gusto and sassiness, with the delight of an amateur filling in. I do not think of myself as a critic or a litterateur or a "spokesman" but merely as someone who responds to an invitation. I rise to the bait.

Now, for the first time, I have been stumped. Roy Basler asked me to speak here, following Ralph Ellison, on what would appear to be the easiest subject of all—myself. All at once I was tonguetied. I hardly ever write about anything else and seldom conceal the fact, yet a head-on confrontation with myself threw me out of gear. Perhaps I had never written about myself after all. I began to have the anxieties of a man who hears himself on a tape recorder or watches himself on television for the first time and thinks—My God, am I that phony!

The suggestion, of course, was not to regale you with my autobiography but to discuss my writing in relation to my milieu. But my writing *is* my milieu, and insofar as I am I, this is the only I, I know. A student said to me the other day, "I enjoy the way you deliberately mispronounce French." I was flabbergasted. And once a woman came up to me before a lecture I was about to give on anarchism and said, "I don't believe a word you are going to say, and I don't think you do either." I am a prey to rudenesses like this, but having an easy disposition, I blame myself for these intimacies. I wrote a glowing panegyric about Henry Miller a few years ago and have been asked a million times how much of it I meant to be taken seriously. People who disagree with me tend to consider me a liar. High-powered critics consider me a clown. A religious magazine once called me the Mort Sahl of criticism. I took this as flattery though it surely wasn't meant that way. I am a member of a sect sometimes called anticritics and I cannot in good faith expect to be treated with the dignity accorded to an Aristotle or a T. S. Eliot. It is part of the program of my sect to laugh criticism out of business, to play practical jokes, and in general to harass and demoralize the enemy. It is serious play.

I began this lecture about six months ago and have worked on it steadily and with an increasing feeling of failure. I filled three medium-sized notebooks with small script and typed about a hundred pages trying to develop my ideas. Only a minute quantity of this matter remains. It is more or less what I go through in writing a poem. I will write a poem many times and one day throw it all away and write a completely different one. But the "different" one could not have been written without the wrong ones. This is the process of getting at oneself. Only, in this case, I am not sure I succeeded.

Now, it is absolutely of no interest to you how much time and waste of time go into a man's poem or essay and I think it is ill-mannered for a writer to brag about his herculean efforts, but on this particular occasion I think the subject calls for it. For the subject here is that I do not know what the subject is. I have never asked myself what I am in relation to my poems. I am afraid to. The answer might turn out to be—nothing. What if I am no more than the sum of poems? What if the poems are not worthy?

Eventually I made a pattern of my notes and found I was trying to get at myself from several directions. One was "racial" (I debated about whether to put that word in quotes, and finally did). Another was autobiographical. A third had to do with my withdrawal from the Serious World into poetry. A fourth was an account of how I returned to the Serious World after having gained a reputation. To me this return signified the surrender of the prodigal wandering of my mind. And finally my present direction, which I am not sure about.

These are the things I am going to talk about, personally and in the abstract. I will apologize for "that frightful quantity of I's and me's" later.

Let me get the race business out of the way first. Anthropologically I would describe myself as an American Russian-Jewish Southerner. I think I have the items in the correct order. The word *Jew* in the Western World is certain to make anyone's skin twitch, including a Jew's. Some years ago I collected all the poems I had written having to do with this word and called the volume *Poems of a Jew.* The title aroused indignation from Jews and Gentiles alike. My chief reason for the book was to make people and myself say the word without any feedback. It would be a word like any other.

Now, when Ralph Ellison and I received the invitation to speak in the Whittall series we both had a slight attack of anxiety. I think we both experienced a fleeting fear that we were about to revive the minstrel show, with a Negro novelist and a Jewish poet as the end men. A perfectly innocent and gracious come-on can produce a severe attack of shyness.

I read *Invisible Man* again. It is not only the best novel about the American Negro, it is probably the Great American Novel itself. Ellison has got it all down. The Negro is invisible and that is his grief. He is not a single separate person but only a member of a category. The applicable expression, the significant folk prejudice about other races, goes: They all look alike to me. One refuses to recognize the other race except as a phylum. The individual is not to materialize, under any circumstances. I have an aunt who as a child walked from the white side of a Virginia town to the black side to hear Booker T. Washington speak from the back of a train. She was the only white person in the crowd. Her father, my grandfather, was a Russian Jew. Somewhere in this incident was a recognition of a visible Negro. For this I am proud.

But as visibility goes, the Jew is the opposite of the Negro. The Jew is always and only the individual and is so recognized. Jewish culture in modern history, as well as in the mythology, is the triumph of the visibility of the one self. In the West, only the Germans evidently have persisted in seeing the Jew as a collectivity. This might account for the fact that Germany could produce super-Jews such as Marx, Freud, and Einstein, while the Jewish mass was fated for obliteration. The German technique of non-recognition by obliteration is only the logical development of the technique which white people in Europe and America have carried out for centuries against people whom they do not wish to see.

It is practically impossible for a white person to understand the training a Negro must undergo to conceal his individuality. The Negro who made himself distinct, much less distinguished, was asking for the rope. For years I puzzled over the absence of Negro poetry in this country. The Negro had created jazz and jazz poetry, which had revolutionized music the world over. But he had no poetry with a capital P. What Negro would so assert himself or debase himself to write the Poem, that white and sacred object which sanctifies the white book? All we had was the Negro spiritual, the weakest example of Negro art—Uncle Tom on Sunday.

But with me visibility was a curse. I was raised as a middle-class Jew and underwent the formal training of a bar mitzvah, after which I lost all interest in what I had learned. My family was observant but only sporadically and without fanaticism. Fundamentally, religion was for old people and Europeans. As we know from American-Jewish novels, a generation ago the children of immigrants were pulled away from the old culture by the breathless and somewhat mindless opportunism of the New World. The new acculturation had to wait for a third generation, my generation. The formula has been stated often and applies to me. All of my uncles and my father are business people. Almost all my cousins are professional people. And my children and their contemporaries have a strong leaning toward the arts, perhaps even by encouragement. What will happen to the fifth generation I don't know. According to writers like Philip Roth, there is a strong possibility of character degeneration as a result of too much material or professional success.

Anyone writing about himself who says, "I became a writer because," and then enumerates causes, is guessing. But I guess about myself that I became a writer for some of the following reasons: a lack of interest in study (I went to three high schools and two universities and am without a degree); a hypersensitivity to my Jewishness, aggravated by complex social distinctions in the South and in Baltimore; a sense of inadequacy to face the street; boredom; self-pity; eroticism; lack of seriousness; bad memory; fear of lightning and dogs; love of impressions and hallucinations; a tendency to speak in analogies (which perhaps led to a love of rhyme); a love of the obscure and esoteric; and a desire to impress by being witty or profane or irreverent. I have said nothing about a love of poetry, for such a thing could hardly be more than a sum of a great many causes. All I know is that by the age of seventeen I spent most of my time and all of my money in secondhand bookstores. The poetry shelves were the ones I searched most closely. I stole a rhyming dictionary from my high school in Baltimore and also a beautiful edition of the *Odes* of Anacreon in Greek (which I could not read).

In my family's circle of friends there was no literary atmosphere, yet my father encouraged my older brother to write and perhaps even to become a writer. My brother won a literary reputation while still in high school. A poem of his won a state contest in Virginia, and he read it at the University in Charlottesville, where he later distinguished himself in every field of study he undertook. I tried to impress him once by showing him a book I was reading. It was a psychopathic study of Poe—that was perhaps the subtitle—and was my first introduction to the pathology of poets.

Yiddish, a rich Chaucerian language, was not taught to us, although my parents spoke it sometimes as a private language or with elders. I was not aware of a Yiddish literature until long after I had become a poet. The cultural attitude among our class of people was generally that of middle-class people everywhere—that culture belongs to the leisure class. As far as culture for Jews went, that belonged to the German Jews, who were somehow culture aristocrats. Culture in my mind was vaguely associated with Germany and in its negative connotations still is.

These few facts and observations scarcely add up to a vita. I am at present attempting to write a kind of novel in which I will be able to deal with realities regardless of the facts. Unimportant details are often the most significant for our understanding of a man's life and work, and I think that a novel itself is some such construction; whereas the autobiography of a writer is liable to be lusterless and wooden, when not full of misinformation. What poets have written well about themselves? Yeats' friends complained about his *Autobiographies*. Yeats himself in one of them catches himself in a lie and then asks, "Why did I tell that lie?" Yeats is not the best example, however, with his psychology of the mask, his ritualistic posing, and his sad love life. I suggest that poets cannot write well about themselves because what they consider important in themselves, the Serious World considers trivial. Furthermore, poets have difficulty distinguishing between reality and fantasy. This sometimes, rather frequently in fact, makes the poet a clinical case. I have never quite believed that rigamarole of Coleridge's about Kubla Khan, but it is as good a "truth" as any about the poem.

Saul Bellow, speaking here last year, quoted the well-known line from Stendhal's autobiography: "that frightful quantity of I's and me's!" In a new book of poems I have coming out I use three quotes from this book, the one mentioned and also: "How many precautions are necessary to keep oneself from lying!" And a third: "What! is it nothing but that?" Stendhal was always being surprised by his disappointment in experience. He says about his love affairs and about the Battle of Waterloo—"What! is it nothing but that?"

Stendhal's real name was Henri Beyle, but in writing his autobiography he didn't call himself either Beyle or Stendhal but Henri Brulard. It is the typical act of the artist, who knows less than his neighbors who he is. The world is about to celebrate the birthday of Shakespeare, yet after four hundred years the world still does not know who he was.

It is a social convention of immemorial standing that only certain people are permitted to speak of themselves in public. Artists fall in this class, as do comedians, criminals, and alcoholics. But on the whole, society and the guild of artists are content to leave this area of expression to a very few Augustines, Rousseaus, Gandhis, Cellinis, and now and then a Stendhal. Moreover, there is a strong tendency in literature today toward the "veridical"—the novel that tells all and the poem that expresses sentiment. But no one is any wiser about Henry Miller or Allen Ginsberg for having read their books. I think it was Keats who said that the poet is without character. It is even something of a platitude that the artist is a man in search of himself. For that reason, I am always suspicious of the poet who has found himself and who has delineated himself clearly and unmistakably to the world. Yeats, Eliot, and Baudelaire are such poets. Sartre felt the need to write a "pathography" of Baudelaire, which he calls an existential biography. He completes Baudelaire's personality, a necessary service in the case of a poet who invented the man called Baudelaire. Sartre coldly ferrets out the mother love of Baudelaire, his fetishism, and his inability to surrender to any experience except the peripheral. It is a study of the poet as onanist. We do not need a biography of Shakespeare, even if all the facts were laid before us. We definitely need one or many about the self-invented poet.

The writer's apprenticeship is a long and lonely affair from which he emerges cured of his loneliness, if he is fortunate. But in that case he may be cured of his writing as well. The density and unintelligibility of much youthful poetry is caused not so much by lack of skill as by the fear of communicating. The theory of poetic hurt has always been with us since ancient times—the lame foot and the cherished wound. "Mad Ireland hurt you into poetry," says Auden in his elegy for Yeats. And something or other does hurt the poet always "into" his poem. The youthful poet may withdraw first from the vision of ugliness which he sees everywhere around him; he would and does remake this world that wrongs the image of beauty. This is the

typical withdrawal of the poet and is the world's explanation of what he is. This same hurt poet may later become a
passionate public poet, a man of ringing ideals or a revolutionary. A good example is Swinburne, who graduated from
Our Lady of Pain to the Statue of Liberty. Byron is the
most celebrated poet of this kind.

I am talking about the poet, not about poetry. Modern
criticism has made it a taboo to talk about the poet and has
taken the poem out of context so completely that little or
nothing remains of it but its sensibility. It is perhaps the
triumph of the wound theory of art. And modern society
being what it supposedly is, the enemy of the individual,
the poet and all other artists inherit the wound. Sometimes
I think we should call them the poets of the Purple Heart.

But an ancient distinction was made also between the
poet with a happy gift of nature and the poet hurt into
madness. Of the poets with a happy gift of nature we have
few. We are not ready for that. Poetry as celebration we
have little of. Our joys are carefully disguised, so as not to
offend the canon.

I went through all the ritual stages of anger and denial
and enjoyed a long and lonely apprenticeship during the
Depression. The Depression was a fine time for me; it sub-
stantiated my anger and prevented me from getting a job.
My family was not poor. It was the time for young Communists but I was saved from them in several ways. I de-
tested meetings, I hated majority opinion (and so pretended to be a Trotskyite), and I carried on a private
flirtation with Catholicism. In those days of political involvement I studied piano and had myself tutored in Latin.

But the only activity I pursued in good faith was writing
poetry, or trying to. When I was twenty-one, I published a

book of my poems. Like most such volumes the less said about it the better, yet it served the purpose of getting me a scholarship to a university. That was not the intention of the book but was the only form of recognition it received. The poems were imitations of William Carlos Williams and William Shakespeare. The Shakespeare ones were terrible, the Williams pieces much better. Over the years, Williams has superseded Shakespeare in my taste. I don't mean that he is the greater poet but that he speaks to me still. I was attracted by Williams' simplicity and his obscurity, the way he would let a piece of a poem stand for a poem, and the way he loved typography. But it was many years before I understood his theory of the object. The New Critics were beginning to take hold in the journals and I was infuriated by the theorizing without understanding it. I hated to think that Williams had a theory. No one was more opinionated or more given to generalizations than I, yet I could not bear the opinions of others who were more entitled to have them. I still think I am right in this denial of the equal rights of criticism. It has always seemed to me that good poetry is obviously good and the discussion of it qua poetry is a waste of time. The career of a poem, on the other hand, has always intrigued me—how far it goes in the world.

In the midthirties, Auden and Spender began to be printed in this country, and it was through them that I learned what I needed to know about writing my own poems. I could imitate Williams but not proceed beyond his style. The big Pound-Williams influence later helped form the generation of Beat poets, but I have always failed to be Beat, no matter how hard I tried. I went on a trip to Tahiti and took with me Spender's 1934 *Poems*. They were

333

the hardest, clearest, loftiest, and most hurt lines I had ever seen in modern English. For me they were a textbook I had been looking for. While I was in Tahiti, the Spanish Civil War broke out. I returned home, not to join the Abraham Lincoln Brigade but to sun myself on the beaches of Atlantic City and write.

Auden, as every poetry professor knows, remade the whole fabric of diction for poets. He did the necessary and the seemingly impossible job of bringing poetic language up to date. Because of him poets today can use the language of technology and the theoretical sciences at will and without the self-conscious overtones of a word like *gramophone* or *motorcar* in Eliot. A line like "Here is the cosmopolitan cooking,/The light alloys and the glass" had the same impact on me as "For God's sake hold your tongue and let me love" had once had. Auden presented modern English to poetry.

When he came to this country in 1939, I wrote him a long letter explaining carefully that New England is not a part of the United States. I forget what this was about. He replied with a beautifully written postcard that said succinctly, "Thank you."

I continued my retreat, which ended with two years of undergraduate study in Baltimore. Ostensibly I was to enter graduate study in English, though in the back of my head was a plan to study classics. I never got to that stage of the game but was drafted into the Army about a year before Pearl Harbor. There was a one-year conscription law, my name was drawn from a hat, and there was no deferment. But by that time, A.D. 1940, I was beginning to publish poetry in national magazines and could carry this vice with me to the barracks.

The Army was a kind of echo of my Depression years. In the Army one is totally isolated as a person. Soldiers can only lead fantasy lives, with a few brutal hours or days of freedom in between the shouting and the ritual of training. The din is so great and so incessant that it acts as a silence. One can write because everyone writes in the Army. People who have never put pen to paper spend hours composing letters. I found I was in a Writers' Colony. And because I was in Virginia, in a strange way I felt I was home. By the time I went overseas, I had had published my first large group of poems in a volume of new poets. It was well reviewed by well-known reviewers and I felt my first gratification for my years of effort. Just then my orders came through to be shipped to Australia; I was almost insane with fury.

During the space of three years in the Pacific, I published four books, which must be some kind of record for a foot soldier. That term doesn't sound quite right. I was a company clerk in the Medical Corps and something of an adept at goofing off to write poems. It had long since become expected of me in my outfit, and I do not recall ever having suffered any abuse because of my "hobby," as it was thought to be. Until the time I reached home I received very heady praise from the critics. The tide began to turn when F. O. Matthiessen praised one of my books written in New Guinea as perhaps the most important literary achievement to come out of the war. The review was on the front page of the *New York Times Book Review*, and a large Signal Corps photograph showed me sitting on the wooden steps of a tropical tent reading one of my own works. I would like to say a word about this book, which was widely resented by poets and critics alike, perhaps because Matthiessen attached such great importance to it.

My outfit was one day informed that we would be de-activated for ninety days preparatory to going to the Dutch Indies. I sat down and sketched out a critique of poetry which I wanted to write in verse. I would write about thirty lines a day (which I did) and at the end of three months have what I wanted, a kind of 20th-century neoclassical treatise on the art of poetry. The book was divided into three parts called The Confusion in Prosody, The Confusion in Language, and The Confusion in Belief. Everything was going to be straightened out. As the subject was contemporary poetry, I had to use contemporary poets for my examples. The foreword opened with a salvo against criticism in general. It then announced that 20th-century poetry is a kind of zoo. The whole work was two thousand and seventy lines long; I numbered the lines to make them look incontrovertible. It was my initial anti-intellectual essay, one of a long series to come, and I neither remember why I wrote it nor why Matthiessen, who had written one of the definitive books on T. S. Eliot, praised it. William Carlos Williams has an essay about it in which he is generously ambiguous. But to most of the poets my age, I had announced myself as a Philistine.

The fact is that I had never had any ideas about poetry but only overpowering predilections and prejudices. My antipathy for criticism was almost constitutional, though I did not begin to read it seriously until I became a professor several years after the war. My last retreat occurred in this library. The books I read here when I was poetry consultant were esoteric and mystical books, the Kabala, theosophy, Jung, Ouspensky, Plotinus, and so forth. Orthodox philosophy did not attract me.

I taught modern poetry for three years at Hopkins, awk-
wardly, for I had never taught. I wrote out vast dull lectures on Francis Thompson and AE and the Georgians,
thinking I would work my way up to the interesting stuff
but somehow never quite got there. I fiddled around with
prosody a lot. At the first opportunity, I left the University
and went to Chicago to edit *Poetry*. I have taught in universities off and on for twelve years but have never felt at
home in what cultural symposiums call the academic atmosphere. Like most writers of today, I have written my
share of criticism about the Academy and its literary produce, but I doubt if I have contributed any solution to the
argument about the effect of teaching on writing and writing on teaching.

In any case, I breathed a sigh of relief when I gave up
my professorial role and sat down in Harriet Monroe's old
chair. *Poetry* magazine was going on forty years old when I
got there and was about as formidable a literary institution
as any in the country. More than that, one had the feeling
that if it collapsed, the entire city of Chicago would crumble into dust. That was the impression I got from the
mighty personages of the town who guarded over it spiri-
tually, while keeping it on a starvation diet. I have never
understood the marriage of wealth and culture, but I soon
discovered that my real job was not editor but money-raiser.
I am about as good a money-raiser as I was a soldier.
Once I passed Tony Accardo on the street, and the thought
flashed through my mind that perhaps the Syndicate would
help support *Poetry*. I didn't follow that up, but in the end
we founded a drinking club on the premises and that prom-
ised a solution until the whole thing unaccountably blew
up, the *Poetry* offices were banished to the attics of the

Newberry Library, and I went West. I once again became a professor and am likely to remain so.

So much for literary adventure.

Randall Jarrell gave a very courageous talk here a little over a year ago in front of the largest collection of live poets I have ever seen. In this talk he played the schoolmaster and gave all the American poets of the modern anthology a name or a grade. When he got to me he said I was neoprimitivist. Or rather he said my poems were like neoprimitive paintings. I must say I was pleased. I paint, not on Sunday, but whenever I find paint lying around. And in my paintings, which I find always make people laugh, I am ashamed to use shadow or perspective. I feel there is something dishonest about shadows and distances, but then I have never learned to draw. Nor do I wish to learn.

In poetry, I dislike shadows—"without any confusion or profundity of atmosphere," as Jarrell put it. Over a long period of time I have been charging quixotically at a huge shape called Culture without ever knowing whether I have scored against the leviathan. These tilts have taken various forms: against mythic form, symbolism, the Tradition, and so on. It is a kind of guerrilla warfare in which I am not the only assailant. Still, the battle against the Tradition and the continuity of culture and the presentness of the past, and so on, has become tedious. In the long run, criticism can't change anything. Only new works of art can do that.

American poetry is in a unique situation. At least I know of no other poetry which has its particular problems. I am referring to the English language. We have the language of England more or less by accident, for we might, giving and taking a battle here and there, be French- or Spanish-speaking people. Be that as it may, we have the language of England without the culture of England. The culture of this country is so multiplex that it is indescribable. In my state, for instance, there are dialects of German spoken which no longer exist in Germany. But the question is deeper than dialects. It is one of contents. There is also the fact that most Americans are descendants of uneducated populations and that whatever cultural aristocracy existed here in the 18th century has long since been swamped by wave after wave of subcultures. As poetry goes, we are precultured.

A century ago one man tried to create an American poetry with his bare hands. He did not succeed in that, but he did succeed in writing our greatest poems or some of them. The great literary works of America are predominantly prose, political works, fiction, even criticism. And in a sense the same thing holds in the 20th century. The attempt to impose the European mythos on our poetry has in part determined the character of what we call modern poetry, but this had to be done by missionaries, such as Pound and Eliot. And it had to be done through the agency of the American university. Pound's criticism consists of innumerable epistles directed to what he calls the Beaneries, our institutions of higher learning. Eliot's essays, the most formidable body of criticism in modern literature, helped set in motion a practical school of criticism which revolutionized the literary sensibility in our universities. (Eliot disclaims too great an influence here, though he is commonly thought of as the originator of the New Criticism.) And in turn this criticism affected not only the pedagogy of poetry but poetry itself. Many people, myself included, nowadays speak of university poetry. The battles, or rather skirmishes, between university poets and street poets have occupied our attention in the past few years.

All of this is related to something like a class conception of the art. The missionaries or exiles were addressing a newly arrived educated class, not a small elite but a vast army of Ph.D.'s or graduate students in literature. And these people by and large are themselves critics, instead of scholars, and frequently poets or people who want to write poems. And they have developed an expertise in the techniques which makes it sometimes impossible to tell who is a real poet and who is a technician.

I won't annoy you by trying to define Real Poet. Everybody has his own criteria. And I see no reason why there can't be poets, actual live ones, in the university or in the nightclub or on the assembly line. But I think that the poet is always nostalgic for the street, since he has become so urbanized that that is his only alternative to the university.

The most recent lecture I've given was called "Is Poetry an American Art?" The answer was: probably not. Some people asked why *American* poet; why can't one just be a poet? The answer is that you can't. A poetry is part of the character of the place. The place is inherent in the language. All of which is stated in the philosophy of Dr. Williams, who fought against the European influence on our poetry all his life and who said that *The Waste Land* was to modern poetry what the atom bomb was to mankind. (It was a necessary exaggeration.)

There is a legend that Apollinaire once stole the *Mona Lisa* from the Louvre. And there is the artist who decorated her with a moustache. They were trying to pry this criterion off the wall. It had become an idol, practically in the religious sense, though it is the opposite of a Madonna.

Masterpiece or not, this picture had acquired the power to judge all other pictures.

I sympathize with the thief of the *Mona Lisa* and with the artist who added to her charms. The motto of such poets is: let the past take care of itself. Everything is new.

It appears to me that American poets have begun to admit that the English influence is dead and that it never really obtained in this country as poetry. As an English professor, I foresee as a side effect to this discovery the withering away of the English department. The fact that English departments are at present the largest in most universities indicates some kind of sickness.) More and more poets, even of the educated variety, have begun to drop the mannerisms of the conventional poem and to play with the more intricate rhythms and tonalities of prose and speech. In a way, we are back to where we were when the new poetry began in the second decade of our century, back to the image, the cadence, and the statement without embellishment. And we have discovered the new poetry of the Old World and not simply the classics and the metaphysical poets. We are closing the gap between prose and poetry.

To allow standards to take root in this country, we have had to devalue the standards of the past. Someone or other is everlastingly trying to impose a literature a thousand or two thousand years old on a nation that is less than two hundred. Thus most of our poetry has been as rigid and unoriginal as the architecture of banks. But we find poets now arguing in favor of "bad" poetry. I am one. Bad is in quotation marks. Bad means good. It means not great or major or monumental or mythic or epic. Poets in my situation, poets who have withdrawn from the high culture, are more interested in the art of children, the untrained, the hallucinated, even the psychopathic and the criminal. I think this is true of most artists today except the poets of—if I may use the well-worn word—the Establishment. And if one works himself clean through the poem and comes out on the other side, into empty space, and finds himself poem-less, what then? I sometimes think I have done this.

It has been about five years since I wrote what I used to think was the best kind of poem I could write. That was the poem with a beginning, a middle, and an end. It was a poem that used literary allusion and rhythmic structuring and intellectual argument and the works. I had written for years for a famous New York magazine which one sees on cocktail tables the world over (I don't know why I am being coy about it, but at one point I was practically the poet laureate of that publication). One day I shook myself and said, "No more." I think it was because I started to collect those poems for a book and found too many I didn't want to see in a book.

So I began to backpedal. I worked for several years trying to break the style I had become habituated to. Eventually I came up with something more free which I could use. I had always been a fan of those D. H. Lawrence epigrams called *Nettles* and *Pansies* and especially those glowing bunches of poetry called *Birds, Beasts and Flowers*. My new rhythm, however, sounded too much like Lawrence and I knew I had not gone far enough back. Then I started reading French prose poems, Baudelaire, Rimbaud, and the *Éloges* of St. John Perse. While I was at this library Perse had once seen a prose poem or two of mine and hinted that that was the technique that mattered. But I had only written one or two such poems and waited a long time before I was ready to tackle the thing in earnest. This sounds as if I am about to present the great American prose poem, but all I mean to say is that I finally felt at ease in the form. What I was searching for was a medium in which I could say anything I wanted—which for poets is something like finding the philosophers' stone or the elixir vitae. For one thing, I wanted to be able to use the ridiculous, for another the nonsensical, for another the "obscene." I wanted to be as personal as I liked, as autobiographical when I felt like it, editorializing or pompous, in short, to be able to drop into any intensity of language I liked at any time. None of this was particularly original, but it was new to me. I wrote a huge stack of these poems, the form of which was governed by the size of a sheet of paper in the typewriter. When the publisher saw the manuscript he commented dryly that the only limits to the book seemed to be physiological. And not wanting to violate the fashion of slenderness for volumes of poems, we cut it down to about twice the size of the usual seed catalog.

It is as important to learn how to use one's skills as to acquire them in art, and just as difficult. The kind of poem I am talking about may be indistinguishable from that of the high school composition or the worst polyphonic prose of Amy Lowell, but that is inevitable. The writer must learn from his underlings as the painter learns from the billboard or the composer from the trombonist blowing the blues. This is what I think has been deficient in so much modern poetry—a fear of coming to grips with the raw material. That and too much attention to stock intellectual attitudes. The modern artist and sculptor are fascinated and delighted with the industrial world, but the poet has not yet heard of it.

On the last day of a Creative Writing class of mine last

week—I have taught myself to say Creative Writing without wincing; nobody would ever think of saying Creative Painting or Creative Music—after we had gone through the last purple stack of mimeographed student poems and had once again demolished the split-level house, bombed the second car, the streamlined church, and the powder room; Freud having been buried with the air conditioner and the last corybantic prose poem in praise of sex or LSD analyzed, I gave a valedictory. It was a little talk about the *Oxford Book of English Verse, 1250–1900*, and I contrasted it with the modern anthology. I hadn't thought of the *Oxford Book* or looked at it for many years, but it all at once crossed my mind that this book had been my bible when I was the age of my students and that in all probability they had never heard of it or anything like it.

It is true that this famous anthology is the product of Victorian taste, yet it would be difficult to imagine a much different version of the seven hundred years of English poetry. The Quiller-Couch *Oxford Book* (He did many of the Oxford anthologies) begins with the fresh and beautiful "Sumer is icumen in," dated around 1250, and ends with a muggy religious poem or hymn called "Dominus Illuminatio Mea." This final poem is anonymous, and one senses the editorial hand in this concluding work or benediction.

But in between the "Sumer is icumen in" and the "Dominus" poem there are seven centuries of the greatest poetry of the European culture, even with the omission of the great plays, narratives, and epics. And in all that poetry there is scarcely ever more than a suggestion of philosophical despair. It would be a tour de force to compile a minority report of the centuries, gleaning a darker side of the English creative spirit, opposing Rochester's ode "Upon

344

Nothing" to Milton's faith in order and Providence, or paying more attention to the satanic Swinburne than to Tennyson or Alice Meynell. But such an anthology would tell nothing, for until the magic year 1900, English poetry as we know it is essentially joyous. It is true that the Oxford editor would not even include "Dover Beach" and could see nothing better in Whitman than "O Captain, My Captain"; nevertheless the book is triumphantly representative and great.

By now there are several generations of students, at least, who began the study of poetry with the 20th century, that is, with the proclamations of failure, the failure of love, the failure of history, the prophecies of imminent darkness. *The Waste Land* is probably the first classic that impinges on their minds; however it was intended or has since been reinterpreted, it embodies the modern poet's code of the banality of modern existence and the evil of 20th-century man. And if not this poem, then one of a dozen others. The 20th-century reader of poetry must regard any poetry before our time as something as far away as the poetry of classical Greece.

I am not expressing a preference for the Oxford collection or suggesting a compromise. I am merely making the observation that the 20th-century anthology has closed the *Oxford Book*, perhaps forever. In this country, at least, we have broken the circuit between the poetic past and the poetic present. And I do not see how it can be otherwise with us.

What does this do to us as poets and to our poetry? American literature in a quite real sense is a boy's literature. From Fenimore Cooper to Salinger, it is a literature of youth. I was given a complete copy of *Moby Dick* as a child because it was a boy's book, and I read it as a boy's book, though it had some tough passages. And poetry was always something far away and long ago; Americans couldn't write poetry. There was one American poet, Edgar Allen Poe; one didn't press the point too far. I do not recall the name of Whitman from public school, though my memory may trick me. I think I discovered Whitman on my own.

The American poet has from the beginning been faced with a choice, whether to accept or to reject the *Oxford Book*, using that term as an oversimplified symbol. And in modern poetry the choices have been made. Of our four greatest 20th-century poets, Pound, Eliot, Frost, and Williams, two went abroad to repair the fences of the Tradition and to create, intentionally or not, a criticism which became a pedagogy which became a poetics. Frost refused to believe that the fences needed mending and quietly amassed a wealth of poems which all but proved that English poetry was still solvent. Williams nearly lost his mind watching these antics.

American binary psychology lends itself to poetry as to politics. We have in our century created two poetry parties called whatever anyone wants to call them, Paleface and Redskin, Academic and Beat, Classic and Romantic, or Republican and Democrat. And it is unfortunately true that the Redskins are pink with rage and the Palefaces blue with indignation. And it is also true that these two literary parties end up in the same anthologies—in one big unhappy family of poetry.

So many times have the characteristics of these parties been described, at least to those who read the literary journals, that there is nothing more to say about them descriptively. But there is much to say otherwise. I will stick to the usual nomenclature of Academic and Beat to avoid confusion.

The Beat professes Innocence, with or without a capital I. The Academic professes Guilt with a capital G. The Innocence of the Beat of course identifies him with American literature, even though the Beat chants hymns to Castro. The Beat extracts the quality of rebellion and revolution from American literature and then sits back and waits for the police to prove his point.

The Academic gaily assumes a metaphysical guilt, possibly a Christian guilt; in any case a kind of mandarin Hollywood guilt which presumes the nature of literary violence and destruction on the part of the Beat. The Academic forgives and protects the Beat. The Beat is overwhelmed by the failure of success.

This kind of nonsense seesaws back and forth. But modern poetry never seems to escape this biparty system, this wrangle over precedent and originality. In reality, both parties are literature-centered (to invent a typical vulgarism of our speech); and because literature is the center of value of both schools, neither can know much about anything except literature. Beat poetry is as academic as the Academic. Academic poetry, which has become noticeably gamy, is as gossipy (you might say "subversive") as the Beat. And both end up as a variety of social criticism, but of such a hieratic style that only the highly trained in poetry would even care to notice it. Both Beat and Academic, however, subscribe to the 19th-century hope, the hope of the *Oxford Book*, that in the end poetry will reinstate human virtue or national virtue or the virtue of oneself.

Modern poetry is a kind of lobby. It has something to

sell, it is not sure what, yet it knows it has a corporation of power behind it, either a thousand years of reputation or the idea of genius or sainthood. And it knows that this power is real, for Culture, with whole armies and navies behind it, has said so.

It is only with the greatest effort and charm that the Beat can convince us of his assertion of innocence; and only with the greatest diplomacy and wit that the Academic can convince us of his culpability.

Possibly poetry in America is obsolete or not yet born because it is literature-centered. This is precisely the thing that has always separated poetry from the other arts of writing. Even in this country one distinguishes between the poet and the writer—I am always pleased to be confronted with the question at those Nabokov-like places called Writers Conferences: Are you a writer or a poet? Poetry has always been the ultimate enemy of literature, and if poetry is good for anything, that is what it is good for.

And yet, how, in a nation where books are as plentiful as food, or more so, can the poet escape literature? How, where literature is also an industry, can poetry breathe? Here, where the latest literary movement is put on sale after the first manifesto is written, where every writer (and poet) hopes to be "controversial" in order to rise above the din of the linotype, how can the poet ever dream of such a thing as an audience when the audience is rejected both by the Beat (as bourgeois) and by the Academic (as bourgeois). For the Beat pretends to be the proletarian and the Academic pretends to be the aristocrat. And both—whatever bourgeois is supposed to mean at this late date—share in this bourgeois sensibility and morality. Both kinds of poetry are in a secret alliance to uphold Literature.

All I am saying is that, for me, American poetry has long since ceased to hold my attention, because it seems to me to aspire to a place in society. That is, the poet-in-residence in a university is no different from the poet-in-Skid Row. Both are on Culture Relief. Both are trying to prove to themselves that the fate of nations is bound up with their personal fates. Both, in the back of their minds, think in the way that Pound and Eliot and Yeats thought: *that poetry will tell people what to do.*

One can forgive poets for these hallucinations. It is harder to forgive governments for egging them on. I said earlier that I could never understand the marriage of wealth and culture. Even less can I understand the marriage of government and culture. I know I am standing at the moment somewhere on Capitol Hill, but I have always tried in a little way to keep State and Poetry separate. This is not in the Constitution. I hope the Constitution will never have occasion to think about such things as institutionalizing Poetry.

There was a fine young British poet killed on the battlefield in the First World War who wrote the famous line: "The Poetry is in the pity." He was referring to the pity of War. He was too late for the *Oxford Book* and a little premature for the 20th-century anthology. Wilfred Owen came into that no man's land between the end of the old poetry and the beginning of the new. He said that he was trying not to console but to warn; he went so far as to apologize for telling the truth about war. But the true poet must be truthful, he said.

The 20th-century poet is not so embattled except ideologically. He has somehow earned or inherited an intellectual leisure which has made him a parvenu of sensibility.

349

The 20th-century poet cannot locate the poetry, either in the pity or anywhere else. He locates it, or tries to, in vague and anxious dissatisfactions within himself or within what he thinks are the crimes and sins of society. He can't decide whether to be a peacock or a phoenix or an ostrich and takes turns trying to be each.

I mentioned Wilfred Owen to paraphrase him. With us the poetry is not in the pity, but the poetry is in the situation. As the *Oxford Book* failed the situation of war, for example—it would have ended with Rupert Brooke's "The Soldier" if it had had to face the trench war of 1914–18, and could not have ended with an antiwar poet without spoiling the whole illusion of the great tradition. Everyone at the turn of the century had the premonition that time had run out on the Tradition; it is extraordinary how many writers knew in their bones that what lay just ahead would be unlike anything that had ever been known before.

When Yeats later put together his *Oxford Book*—the *Oxford Book of Modern Verse, 1892–1935*, he enshrined the *Mona Lisa* on page one, taking a famous prose sentence from Pater, a bit of high mystification about her, and turning it into a piece of free verse. And there she remains, the patron saint of Academic poetry. And the Beat has failed to pry her off the wall.

American poetry is irrelevant. It does not pertain to our situation. It pertains only to language and literature and sensibility. It pertains only to form and to "philosophy" or to the personalized anguish of the socially angry. America is more than a campus, I am convinced, and more than a picturesque and disaffiliated slum. What it is is for the artist to reveal in every way he can. And, as I have said, all our artists have been busy revealing our world, with the

exception of the poets. The modern poet has closed his eyes
to life, as it has long since closed its eyes to nature. To the
modern poet, nature may sometimes provide a bestiary,
and, in fact, we have written the finest allegories about
moths and ants, praying mantises and flies. But all the ap-
ples are dead, except the Genesis apple. People in the modern anthology are dead or somnambulatory. The modern
anthology might just as well be copyrighted on the moon. I
forget the date of the death of the moon.

Perhaps I haven't progressed at all from the time I wrote
my verse critique in the tropics. I still wait for the poetry of
the situation. Our poetry has everything to do. It has to
escape from itself first of all. It has to liberate itself from
literature before it can do anything else. Most poets, I
think, have agreed that poetry is not an art of language and
not even an art. It is one of the techniques of revelation,
one of the powers through which we control relationships
and conciliate nature. The sculptor who drives to the junk-
yard, who makes beauty out of trash is performing this
function. Poetry has been making trash out of beauty for
the most part. This is tempting fate. Or if I am exaggerat-
ing, let us at least concede that it is the function of poetry
to propitiate, to quiet the anger of things. I am not talking
about affirmation and negation; that is a question of circumstance. I am talking about the poet in situ. If he is in
place, he is where he belongs. Whitman had a long recital
of things in their places, small things and cosmic things.
Williams took the least likely objects for poems—least
likely for the *Oxford Book*—a piece of brown wrapping
paper rolling in the street or a rotten apple. These poets
revealed things in their situation. There is something like
this in the Marquis de Sade, who says that in Tartary there

351

is a people which creates a new god for itself every day. This god has to be the first object encountered on waking in the morning. If by chance it happens to be an object of great revulsion, that thing is still the idol of the day.

Our poetry has been so industrious manufacturing values that it has practically forgotten how to do anything else. That is why it must empty its mind of its moral and ethical contents and of its esthetic contents as well. When it does so, it will be in a position to experience the world as our painters, our musicians, and our novelists have experienced it.

For myself, I have solved the problem of the racial wound, which drove me into the various retreats where I could assert myself and create myself. But it is too late for me ever to be assimilated into the Serious World. I can only play at responsibility. I am yet to be convinced that those who make the decisions by which we live are not play-acting. I hope that this sense—or perhaps gift—of amazement will never leave me.

The Poetry Wreck

THE TITLE of this chapter is not autobiographical, but I will say something about my background as a librarian. I studied to be a public librarian at the Enoch Pratt Library in Baltimore. It was an excellent course of study and I was within a few weeks of final examinations when I was drafted by the Army and not allowed to finish. I would probably be a professional librarian today had my name not been fished out of the goldfish bowl. Five years later, on being discharged from the Army, my first job was Consultant in Poetry at the Library of Congress. Subsequently I became editor of the Newberry Library journal of acquisitions and worked at that library for three years. I consider myself more or less of a professional in library affairs, more so at least than most professors and writers.

At the center of all human culture stands the library. At

the center of civilization stands the library. But now and then the apocalyptic question crosses our minds: Is the library still standing? If the university is moving toward a new Dark Age, if all public institutions are facing a new Dark Age, what of the library? If standards of value in every department of modern life are being threatened by barbarism and savagery, what of the books themselves and their keepers?

I am no Jeremiah and will leave the ranting to others. But as a teacher of reading and writing, as a reader and writer myself, as a literary critic and professor of literature for some twenty years, as a functionary of the teaching world, a proud member of the Establishment and what one poet calls a shameless patriot, I wish to report to you my version of the degeneration of the literary intelligence and its attendant confusions everywhere in our lives.

I call it the degeneration of the literary intelligence; others have other names. To book people this degeneration may seem to be local and, hopefully, of short duration; and to the "outside" world the degeneration may seem to be a signal for the arrival of the barbarians. When a professor at a venerable university has his life's work destroyed by student vandals, society may well begin to tremble. Who would have thought, at least since the defeat of Hitler, that American professors would begin to remove their notes and files from their offices and take them home; that they would begin to remove their best or their irreplaceable volumes; that libraries would begin the reduplication of indexes as a safety measure; that specially trained police and guards and firemen would replace the old innocuous campus cop. I apologize for evoking these commonplaces, and yet who, except Lewis Carroll perhaps, would have dreamed of students acquiring the power to fire faculties, presidents and chancellors, to determine curricula, and worst of all, to force personal political opinion and dogma upon the teaching community at large, and upon society itself. All under the name of Idealism, of course.

I would like to place an image in your minds. A professor at a famous west coast university told me that at the first meeting of the class, the students flicked through the assigned textbook, a newly published poetry anthology, flung it on the floor, and stalked out. They said that the textbook was not "relevant." Relevant to what is not known. The modern illiterate thinks that you will finish the sentence that he has forgotten how to formulate. I see this act of boorishness as a hair's breadth from book-burning. And everything that follows book-burning.

My experience as librarian-writer-professor is relatively unusual, and I believe I have a perspective upon the degenerative process in literature which should be shared. For example, I have been engaged in creative writing programs for twenty-odd years, virtually from the beginning of this kind of teaching. These programs have corroded steadily and today have reached the point of futility. Early writing programs, such as the one at the Johns Hopkins University, turned out novelists such as John Barth (at least Barth studied in their program). Students in similar programs today, according to my experience all over the United States, can no longer spell, can no longer construct a simple English sentence, much less a paragraph, and cannot speak. We have the most inarticulate generation of college students in our history, and this may well account for their mass outbreaks of violence. They have no more intelligent way to express themselves. But what is really distressing is that this generation cannot and does not read. I am speaking of university students in what are supposed to be our best universities. Their illiteracy is staggering. But of course they claim to read. They may slam the professor's anthology on the floor but they will go to the bookshop and buy the innumerable paperback bestsellers of Their Generation, which are almost always trashy rewrites of current sociological or philosophical fads. The kitsch-camp-op-pop-absurdist-revolutionary sweepings and swill with which they fill their wordless minds are what they bring to class. They do not want to read; they want to "experience." They do not want to learn; they want to "feel." They have become almost impossible to teach. By accident, I have discovered in recent years that the only students in poetry-writing classes who know how to write as simple and universal a thing as iambic pentameter have gone to Catholic schools. Iambic pentameter is not Catholic; it happens to be the metrical form in which almost all English poetry since Chaucer has been written and is still. Not only do the students not know what it is; *they do not want to know*, and say so.

I use *illiteracy* in the proper sense: the inability to read and write. As this condition becomes endemic in the American educational system the value and meaning of literature becomes obscured, literature falls into desuetude.

As far as I can tell, the high school has now reached the level of the grade school; the college is at high school level; the graduate school at college level; and whatever reading and writing is being done is being done by professors—the people who are taking their libraries home. Creative writing has hit the level of playschool, a kind of adult kindergarten.

One other note about the new university illiteracy. For at least a full generation the American educational system has been trying to abolish languages, not only Latin and Greek (which have practically disappeared) but all modern European languages, and it seems to me English itself. We are losing the battle to maintain even the most elementary language requirements, and every humanities professor will tell you in dismay in one manner or another that his graduate students are by and large linguistic cripples. The written dissertation has long been an academic joke, I maintain because of the bad writing. One can foresee the abolition of even this ultimate test of superior ability and knowledge.

It appears that the modern student enters the university with a contempt for the university, a contempt for society, a contempt for literature, and a contempt for himself. Where did he learn this? Not from his own school; not from the library. I don't think so. He learned it from what the new illiterates call the Media: TV, radio, newspaper, phonograph, rock festival, magazine and paperback bookstore. He learned it from what the new illiterates call their counter-culture; he learned it from his contemporaries and the exploiters of cults. For the first time in history the illiterates have a literature of their own: op-pop-camp-kitsch-existential-occult-nihilist sweepings and swill. Armed to the teeth with this quasi-literature it is little wonder that they slam the textbook on the floor and stomp out to their cars, barefooted.

I will now introduce the hero, or anti-hero, if you like. He is a real person and all the information I am going to give you is true and accurate, except for his name. I have changed his name not for any legalistic reason but because

I feel humiliated to have to bring up his name at all. Here then is Dylan MacGoon.

The good Welsh name Dylan has been appropriated and desecrated by pop singers since Thomas's death. It is unlikely that these show-biz and rebel Dylans have read or could understand Thomas's poetry, which is some of the finest and most obscure poetry of our time. The pseudo-Dylans, however, regard Thomas as a casualty of modern life (which he wasn't) and therefore a symbol of their own shabby and talentless selves. Thomas drank himself to death, as all the world knows and regrets, but he was the farthest thing from the pudgy Lenin or cherubic Castro his namesakes make him out to be. Anyhow, I call our latter-day hero Dylan because he is one of the many pseudo-Dylans who are passed off by the Media as today's poets.

I first heard of Dylan MacGoon as I was checking out of a hotel in Milwaukee. The girl behind the desk, who must have seen in the local paper that I was lecturing on poetry, asked me what I thought of the poetry of Dylan MacGoon. Who? I said. In the ensuing months the name began to come at me from all directions. In one university where I gave a poetry reading I was challenged by a student from the audience who wanted to know what I thought of MacGoon. I had seen some of his verses by then and answered that I didn't think anything of them; they were not even trash. The student then wanted to know what right I had to pass judgment on him. I mumbled something to the effect that I had earned the right, a divine right, so to speak.

MacGoon however would not go away. He followed me to every lecture I gave; he entered my classroom, via the mouths of my students; even when I turned on television he was there. Especially there. True, he was there as a balladeer-and-guitar-slinger, yet he was also designated as famous poet. One day I saw him interviewed by one of the top news commentators, the kind of reporter who is assigned only to prime ministers and field marshals. Mr. Mac-Goon, said the commentator in tones of authentic awe, you are the foremost best selling poet in the United States (I think he said world), and then proceeded to ask about his creative regimen—the sort of questions one would ask Michelangelo or Picasso perhaps. MacGoon tried to answer as best he could (language is not his strong point) and succeeded, between the awe of the commentator and his own honest dissimulations, in presenting the image of poet. His millions of readers and listeners—all under nineteen, I hope—must have been gladdened.

Millions of readers cannot be an exaggeration. An advertisement in a San Francisco paper a couple of weeks ago, an ad, by the way, for some *new* books of poems by Mac-Goon, said that he has already sold more than fifty million of his recordings.

I went to the little public library in the little town I live in, hoping against hope that there would be no MacGoon. There was. Still, I said to myself, the library is next door to a high school, and MacGoon is better for the kids than marijuana. Then again, maybe he isn't. In a desperate attempt to exorcise MacGoon I finally succumbed to the public prints and reviewed one of his three current best-sellers in a weekly New York book review. I called my remarks "The Rise of American Cockney" and they went more or less as follows:

Whoever visits an American bookstore in search of poetry can be sure of finding only one staple. Whether in San Francisco or Dubuque, Dallas, Boston or New York, and no matter what the size of the shop, he will find himself facing a row of cream-colored volumes by—Kahlil Gibran. If there is only one volume it will be Gibran's *The Prophet*, a quasi-mystical, quasi-poetic placebo which has trickled through the bloodstream of American adolescence for at least a generation. The book, in print for over forty years, must be rated as a minor sales miracle. It also throws a baleful sociological glare upon the poetics of the young.

Esthetic has become statistic. Wallace Stevens, whose *Harmonium* remains one of the finest achievements of modern literature, sold two hundred copies of the book over a period of a decade, very nearly driving an exquisite poet to suicide. But MacGoon is written up in mass magazines and newspapers as a *poet* and as a publishing phenomenon, which indeed he is. Yet it is irrelevant to speak of MacGoon as a poet; his writings are not even trash.

The cockneyizing of American poetry began with *Howl*, a highfalutin put-on which started up the seismographs of Berkeley and elsewhere. The name of the game was the inversion of values and it worked for everybody "under thirty" and everybody over who was bored, hysterical or narcissistic. Freak-out culture coincides with this poetical document. Poetic decomposition and *faisandage*, in America at least, date from this bored, hysterical and narcissistic drivel.

The downhill speed of American poetry in the last decade has been breathtaking, for those who watch the sport. Poetry plunged out of the classics, out of the modern masters, out of all standards, and plopped into the playpen. There we are entertained with the fecal-buccal carnival of the Naughties and the Uglies, who have their own magazines and publishing houses, and the love-lorn alienates, nihilists, disaffiliates who croon or "rock" their way into the legitimate publishing establishment. MacGoon falls into the latter category.

What hidden message have we here? Is the Beatleization of American poetry becoming a reality? Are the negative values on the rise in poetry also? Will the bilge work its way up to the library and the graduate school and to the art of writing itself? The answers to all these questions is a dismal groan.

Entertainment is a healthful and lifegiving diversion of the masses, and even the high-decibel howls of the pseudo-poets deserve a niche in the wall of time. But the deliberate obtrusion of the howler or the rocker-crooner upon the literate minority can serve no other purpose than to destroy the sensibilities of everyone concerned. Discrimination is a dirty word in the vocabulary of politics, but in literature it is one of the holiest of concepts. Without it all is offal.

Publishers, even those who formerly prided themselves on the quality of their publications, are now miring themselves in the dismal swamp of the adolescent revolution. They seem to drool at the sight of a rock festival, which attracts a quarter to a half million of the new humanoids. They cannot resist the temptation. They seek out—Mac-Goon—and pay their overhead.

The aftermath of my little critique was typical. There were letters and phone calls and a dressing-down from a reporter in Los Angeles who called to ask me to explain myself. He had been assigned to interview MacGoon. The crooner, it seems, had also read my diatribe. When asked what he thought of it he answered: who cares what *he* thinks?

And the weekly book review dropped me.

In one of the more literate sub-culture magazines I notice a serious *explication de texte* of a poem? song?, a very weak something-or-other written by a poet? named Buffy Sainte-Marie. Buffy's lines "Little wheel spin and spin/Big wheel turn around and around," which resemble the speech of the mental defective and are the norm of the new poetry, are explicated thus: "In Buffy's song the medieval and Elizabethan image of the microcosm mirroring the macrocosm becomes saturated with historical and political content." The article is on Herbert Marcuse.

We are experiencing a literary breakdown which is unlike anything I know of in the history of letters. It is something new and something to be reckoned with. We have reached the level of mindlessness at which students and the literate public can no longer distinguish between poetry and gibberish. Ten years ago nobody would have dreamed of comparing Robert W. Service or Edgar Guest (poor Edgar) or even Joyce Kilmer with Andrew Marvell or Robert Browning. But today I read in a California paper that a "serious critic . . . has likened the Beatles' lyrics to Shakespeare's work." I read that Bob Dylan is "the major poet of his generation." Arrogance and ignorance always go hand in hand, and now we are having both shoved at us from all sides: from publishers, from professional intellectual saboteurs, and from many dog-in-the-manger professors as well.

Some of you know, and I am proud to say, that I have been in the forefront of the fight against censorship all my life. Any schoolboy who buys his first copy of *Tropic of Cancer* will find my introduction in the front of it. It was my introduction which helped win the battle for that book in the Massachusetts courts and subsequently everywhere. I have defended and will continue to defend the principle

of absolute unqualified freedom to print and present anything and everything the human mind and sub-mind are
capable of advancing. I shudder to think of some of the
stuff I have given my sanction to.

But I believe equally in the principle of self-regulation
and the wielding of professional judgment and authority.
We have to assert endlessly and in every generation, and in
every way we can devise, standards of worth in literature.
Teaching has become cowardly and lax at every level, giving way to the pressures of special pleaders and mischief-
makers. The greed and cynicism of even the best publishers
appalls me; the wild exploitation of primitivism by the
Media has rendered us insensible and made us a prey to
every disease of esthetic decadence which the lower
reaches of the imagination can concoct. Every healthy ma-
ture culture needs folk art and popular art, entertainment,
show-biz, and amateur creativity. But where the elemental
forms of art become dominant and aggressive forms, the
culture dies of shock. We need only remind ourselves what
the arts were like under Hitler and Mussolini and what
they still are in Russia. When critics and university students can no longer tell the difference between rock lyrics
and songs of Shakespeare, teaching is no longer possible;
standards of good and inferior disappear; discrimination
dies; and the true artist goes into hiding. We are in the time
that Yeats predicted and when everyone is quoting his famous lines: "The best lack all conviction, while the worst/
Are full of passionate intensity."

One wonders whether it is too late to reverse the course
of the fashionable bourgeois revolutions, or college-kid revolutions, if you prefer. Personally, I am pessimistic and believe that cultural barbarism has already arrived. The

Media love it; the university is too demoralized and debilitated to exercise any real discipline against it; the public is buffeted back and forth by demonstrations of violence and Dadaist hijinks and finds itself shoved farther and farther to the right of reasonable center; the honest artist finds himself once again moving to the periphery of society; real poets are supplanted by guitar-slingers and high-decibel mocking-birds; the long and successful battles for freedom of speech and publication are filthied by entrepreneurs and commercial smuthounds; the textbook is thrown on the floor by the barefoot radical rich; and—to sum it up—chaos is come again. Yet, in its quiet majesty and unfathomable humility, sits the library, not yet overwhelmed by the tides that push the rotten stuff along the shore.

It is always possible, of course, that cultural illiteracy will reach the point at which nobody will sack the library because they won't know what it is.

At highbrow, "high-level" symposia of educators and social scientists, one of the main issues of debate is the definition of a university. One would think that professors would not need a *definition* or a justification of the university—this twentieth-century talk-show would not amuse Plato, for example. Yet it is symptomatic of our times that the leaders of culture question their own right to exist. These symposia, by the way, are conducted almost exclusively by humanists and social scientists. Real hard-core scientists already know that a university is a place where one trains the young in what one knows to be proven knowledge. The symposiasts, however, are not sure, and the main question that exercises them is whether the university is a place where the student seeks his identity or studies his lessons, the lessons of experts and professionals. There is no question in my mind that the identity crusaders are the villains of the cultural upheaval and can be held accountable for the dissolution of educational standards and values in this country. All of us are the victims of their guilts. In the Walpurgisnacht of campus upheavals, which are always led by faculty identity-seekers and could not exist without their leadership, all society becomes the victim, not merely the institutions which bind a civilization together.

The use of the university as an intellectual testing-ground of the personality is criminal. The university has one function only: to train the qualified student to the height of his capacity for learning, productivity in his skills, and imaginative research. Sensitivity training for twenty-year-olds is obscene. We have seen the results of the prolongation of adolescence into manhood and woman-hood and the sanction of childish behavior in maturity. Far from being attractive or interesting, many students of twenty are already driveling old men and women who even have the physical characteristics of the aged. Their only equipment seems to be a smoldering and murky indigna-tion against what they think is Society. Their sole emotion seems to be self-pity. They may be studying John Donne and Longinus but they are reading and quoting Dylan Mac-Goon.

About the Author

KARL SHAPIRO was born in Baltimore, Maryland, and attended the University of Virginia and Johns Hopkins University. In 1946 he was appointed Consultant in Poetry at the Library of Congress, and then, in 1947, he joined the faculty of Johns Hopkins University, where he taught writing courses. From 1950 to 1956 he was editor of *Poetry: A Magazine of Verse*. He was professor of English and editor of *The Prairie Schooner* at the University of Nebraska from 1956 to 1966 and professor of English at the Chicago Circle Campus of the University of Illinois from 1966 to 1968. He is now professor of English at the University of California at Davis. He is a member of the National Institute of Arts and Letters. His second volume of verse, *V-Letter and Other Poems*, was awarded the Pulitzer Prize in 1945. He was awarded the Bollingen Prize in Poetry in 1969.

95720